Ken Little

Alpha
Teach Yourself

Investing

in 24 hours

ALPHA

A Pearson Education Company

Alpha Teach Yourself Investing in 24 Hours

Copyright ©2000 by Ken Little

International Standard Book Number: 0-02-863898-0
Library of Congress Catalog Card Number: Available upon request.

Printed in the United States of America

First printing: 2000

05 04 03 02   5 4 3

Note: This publication contains the opinions and ideas of its author. It is intended to provide helpful and informative material on the subject matter covered. It is sold with the understanding that the author and publisher are not engaged in rendering professional services in the book. If the reader requires personal assistance or advice, a competent professional should be consulted.

Trademarks

For marketing and publicity, please call: 317-581-3722

The publisher offers discounts on this book when ordered in quantity for bulk purchases and special sales.

For sales within the United States, please contact: Corporate and Government Sales, 1-800-382-3419 or corpsales@pearsontechgroup.com

Outside the United States, please contact: International Sales, 317-581-3793 or international@pearsontechgroup.com

SENIOR ACQUISITIONS EDITOR
Renee Wilmeth

DEVELOPMENT EDITOR
Nancy D. Warner

PRODUCTION EDITOR
JoAnna Kremer

COPY EDITOR
Amy Borrelli

INDEXER
Angie Bess

PRODUCTION
Darin Crone
Terri Edwards
Donna Martin
Eric Miller

COVER DESIGNER
Alan Clements

BOOK DESIGNER
Gary Adair

MANAGING EDITOR
Cari Luna

PRODUCT MANAGER
Phil Kitchel

PUBLISHER
Marie Butler-Knight

This book is dedicated to my wife, Cyndy, who has never stopped believing in me, even when I have trouble believing in myself.

Overview

Appendixes

Contents

PART V Working Toward a Goal   287

HOUR 19 Asset Allocation   289

HOUR 20 Conservative/Low Cost Investing   303

Introduction

If your image of investing is a bunch of men in pinstriped suits smoking cigars and discussing index funds, have I got a surprise for you.

Today's investor is just as likely to be a woman who is too busy to sit around talking about much of anything. Men and women of all ages and backgrounds are today's investors.

The good news is that today's markets and products will accommodate just about any investment style—from the very passive investor who wants as much of his strategy as possible on automatic pilot, to the active investor who pores over all the news and research she can, genuinely enjoying a hands-on approach.

This book is addressed to those two and everyone in between. It is important for passive investors to understand what is happening even if they have turned most or all of their investments over to a mutual fund manager.

The more active investors will appreciate the nuts-and-bolts approach that gives them the foundation information and encourages continued study and research.

The book begins with the basics, including investing terminology and instruments, and builds on this foundation. Every Hour adds to the previous ones, either introducing new concepts or expanding on previously covered topics.

Each Hour is designed to be a self-contained unit that builds on previous material and is sprinkled with tips, warnings, and additional information in the form of short sidebars.

Short quizzes and workshops help reinforce the material and provide a span from unit to unit.

All of the terms introduced here—and a few that aren't directly addressed—are in a glossary at the end of this book. You will also find a resource appendix, which will direct you to further readings or Web sites.

I believe this book will give beginning investors a solid foundation to begin investment programs on their own. It will also serve as a springboard to other study and research for those wanting a more detailed look as some of the concepts.

I won't close this introduction with a polite "good luck," because you will not need luck to be a successful investor after absorbing the principles of this book.

WHAT YOU'LL FIND IN THIS BOOK

Part I, "Getting Started," will lay the groundwork for your investing program. Clearing the deck of the things that might get in the way of your success is your first step. We will also go over some basic investment terms and instruments so that everybody is on the same page.

Part II, "Doing the Research," will give you the tools you need to wade through your existing retirement benefits at your job. There are some key numbers you will need to understand as you begin analyzing investments, and we will also go over stock and mutual fund tables like those in the newspaper. Research and news reports will keep you on top of important investing facts and trends. And, finally, we will go over the different types of brokers, looking at their strengths and weaknesses.

Part III, "Mutual Funds, Stocks, and Bonds," will focus on the three major investment vehicles available to most investors. We will look at the large variety of mutual funds, stocks, and bonds. When you finish this section you will have a firm grasp of the basic varieties and features of these investment instruments.

Part IV, "Making Choices," will look at investment strategies, risk tolerance, and reward in the context of building your personal investment program. How you pick a mutual fund and/or stock is part of a system that includes investment objectives and tolerance to risk.

Part V, "Working Toward a Goal," will cover the important process of asset allocation along with a detailed look at three different models of investing: conservative/low cost, active, and aggressive. Retirement planning is examined in detail. Finally, we will wrap it all up and send you on your way to investing.

EXTRAS

At the end of each hour you'll find a short quiz to help you support what you've learned (the answers are in Appendix D, "Answers to Quiz Questions," at the end of the book). This is where you can pat yourself on the back for a job well done and know that you're ready for the next building block.

Take the quiz again the next time you sit down to read an Hour. It will act as a refresher to help you remember what you've learned and to get your mind in gear for the next round of personal finance. You can also use the glossary in Appendix C, "Glossary," as a quick reference guide for investing terms that you're not completely comfortable with yet.

Each Hour also has a list of five things you can do today. These items may be suggestions for further study or action. Please note that in some Hours you will be requested to gather material for future Hours.

The Hour also concludes with a "workshop" that contains exercises for some hands-on experience. A few of these exercises, such as setting goals, will be used several times throughout the book.

We know you don't have a lot of extra time. You're a hard-working individual whose life is probably spent taking care of others, whether it's your boss or your family, and you want to do something for yourself. We've created this book for you, to make investing fun and profitable.

Last, but not least, this book contains a lot of miscellaneous cross-references, tips, shortcuts, and warnings as sidebars from the regular text. These odds and ends are given particular names, and here's how they stack up:

GO TO ▶
This sidebar cross-references another point in the book to learn more about a particular topic. For example, see Hour 14, "Bonds," to find out more about types of bonds.

JUST A MINUTE

This sidebar offers advice or teaches an easier way to do something.

TIME SAVER

This sidebar offers a faster way to do something.

PROCEED WITH CAUTION

This sidebar is a warning. It advises you about potential problems and helps you steer clear of trouble. Generally, a Time Out has some ramifications/repercussions. If you don't heed the advice in this sidebar, you could lose money or waste time.

About the Author

KEN LITTLE is an editor and writer specializing in business and investing subjects. He is the editor of a Web site for beginning investors at www.beginnersinvest.about.com, which is a part of About.com.

He has been the business editor of a major daily newspaper, the senior marketing officer for a major financial services organization, and the publisher of several magazines.

Little has also served as a technical editor on financial subjects. He is the communications coordinator for a national family ministry group.

"Investing is not the complicated, almost mystical experience many people have been led to believe. It is a matter of applying common sense and the appropriate information," according to Little.

"This book will arm you with the information, tools, and resources you need to be successful," he said.

Little lives with his wife, daughter, and two stepsons in Wisconsin.

Acknowledgments

I wish to thank the special people who have made this book possible:

Renee Wilmeth, Senior Acquisitions Editor

Nancy D. Warner, Development Editor

And a special thanks to my agent, Lisa Swayne of The Swayne Agency, who made this book possible.

PART I
Getting Started

HOUR 1
Why Invest?

LESSON PLAN:

In this Hour you will learn about ...

- How investing can change your life.
- Investing myths exploded.
- Models for success.
- Setting investment goals.
- Retirement investing—introduction.
- Traditional investing—debt and equity instruments.
- Nontraditional investing.

If I could show you a way to become a millionaire, you would probably be interested, wouldn't you? What if I told you this system would only cost $19.95? You would probably want to invest $19.95 in your future, wouldn't you? (If you have already purchased this book, never mind.) Of course, you would want this book if it could make you millionaire, wouldn't you? Well, it can't. (It might make me a millionaire if you and 999,999 of your friends buy six copies each.)

You are smart enough to know that no book, computer, or software, in and of itself, will make you wealthy. What this book *will* do is give you the tools you need to become a successful investor. If that success leads you to a million dollars ... good for you.

Most of us have more modest goals: college for the kids, a nice house, and a financially secure retirement. None of these goals will mean much if you work yourself to death trying to achieve them.

This is where investing can make a difference. An active investing program makes your money work for you by multiplying your efforts.

INVESTING VERSUS SAVING

Investing is *not* the same as saving. *Saving* is a passive use of your money. That is, your money is parked somewhere, most likely in a bank certificate of deposit (CD) or savings account. It is earning interest, but not enough to really grow.

GO TO ▶
See Hour 4, "Investing Instruments," for more information on CDs and other cash accounts.

For example, you invest $100 in your bank and it earns 5 percent interest. At the end of a year, you will have $105 (your principle $100 plus the earnings $5). Unfortunately, it is not that simple. Inflation, also known as the cost of living, eats part of your investment, say 2 percent. Then federal, state, and local taxes take a big bite of your earnings, say 30 percent. Now do the math:

$105 × 2% =	$2.10
$5 × 30% =	$1.50
Total:	$3.60
Principle+Interest =	$105.00
Total Deductions =	$3.60
Actual return	$101.40 (or 1.4%)

The financial term for this level of return is … pitiful.

Many of us grew up with the notion that saving for the future meant opening a savings account and making regular deposits. That strategy may have worked years ago, but in today's fast moving economy it just won't get the job done. You need your money to work as hard as you do. Saving accounts are the financial equivalent of treading water. Investing is the way you move from standing still to "getting ahead."

INVESTING MYTHS

Investing is the process of being proactive about where your money works and how much it earns. You want your money to earn enough so that inflation and taxes don't eat it up with nothing left for you. Investing allows you to direct your financial future with a great deal more control than you may have guessed.

TIME SAVER

Begin an investing notebook or file to keep track of investment goals, worksheets, and other papers you generate as you work through this book. Keep it handy because some of the chapters will challenge you to complete projects. It will also get you in the habit of organizing your papers, which will come in handy as your investments grow.

MYTH #1: INVESTING IS RISKY

Investing is only as risky as you make it. The more risk you are comfortable taking, the greater your return is likely to be. I will look at risk in much more depth as we work through the book, but it is important that you be honest with yourself.

There are many lower risk opportunities you can choose that will get you to your goals without keeping you awake at night worrying about your investments. Peace of mind is an important investment also. (Remember the story of the race between the tortoise and the hare. It was the slow but steady tortoise who won. I will show you just such a strategy—among others.)

Keep in mind that often the risk of *not* doing anything is as great or greater than being proactive.

Myth #2: Investing is Hard

Anyone who can program a VCR can be successful in investing. (Okay, bad example.) Seriously, it is not that hard to put together a solid investment plan and make adjustments as they are needed.

I will walk you through the process Hour by Hour. When we are through with this book, you will have a solid foundation to begin your investing program. You will have all the tools you need (or know where to find them) to make intelligent investment decisions.

Myth #3: You Must Be an Economics Major

Don't worry about economics. The media gives great attention to key indicators from "the dismal science," and rightly so. Key economic indicators are important bits of information and may give clues to future movement of the economy and stock market.

But fortunately, you have at your disposal for free—or at very little cost—the best minds in the world to digest and interpret these figures for you.

A bigger reality is that these same experts have predicted what those key numbers are likely to be and the market has absorbed them before they are announced. If the actual numbers differ dramatically from the consensus opinion, the market may react abruptly—sometimes up and sometimes down.

This book will tell you who to listen to and what it all means to your investment plans.

Myth #4: You Need to Be a Computer Nerd

Nope. All the information you need to make successful investment decisions is available the old-fashioned way. However, a basic knowledge of the Internet will dramatically improve your ability to access information rapidly and with greater efficiency.

Keep in mind that you don't need to buy a computer to access the Internet. Most public libraries have computers with Internet access that you can use for free. Some even offer classes in getting started.

GO TO ▶
See Appendix B, "Resources," for a description of an affordable personal computer system.

My personal recommendation is to buy a computer and sign up for Internet service. You will find investing is much easier and more efficient this way. A computer adequately outfitted to access the Internet for investing information should not cost more than $1,200–$1,500.

Unlimited Internet access will not usually cost more than $20 per month. Included in the service will be e-mail capabilities, which will allow you to subscribe to free investing newsletters, and so on.

INVESTMENT GOALS

You may have specific financial goals to achieve, or they may be as general as I mentioned above: college for the kids, a nice home, a financially secure retirement.

As we work through this book, we will be talking about a variety of goals expressed by the time frame necessary to achieve them. There will be short-range (2 to 5 years); mid-range (5 to 15 years); and long-range goals (15 years +); and corresponding investment strategies.

TIME SAVER

Investment goals should be stated in 20 words or less. Make your goals simple with declarative sentences. For example, "I want to retire by age 65 with an annual income of $50,000." Save the details for your actual plan. It is easier to focus on simply stated goals.

GO TO ▶
See Hour 3, "Investing Basics," to walk through the miracle of compounding in detail and how to harness the greatest wealth builder in the world.

Your present age plays a large role in determining your goals and whether they are short-, mid-, or long-term.

For right now, it is important to understand that time is your best tool for meeting your investment goals. This leads us to Little's Golden Rule of Investing:

The best time to start investing was yesterday. The second best time is today. Tomorrow is better than nothing.

This rule applies whether the market is up or down or sideways. It applies whether you are 25 or 65. Procrastination is your worst enemy, and make no mistake, it is a powerful one.

Many people find it more comfortable to avoid committing to an investment program. This book will move you out of that comfort zone and into a new one where you can make investments with confidence.

I expect each and every one of you to make an investment by the time you finish this book. If you already have some investments, I expect you to reconsider those in the light of what you learn and make a commitment to keep moving.

Don't worry that you might not have more than a couple of hundred dollars right now. I'll show you how to get started with a small amount. (I'll also show you where to find more money to invest without having to get a paper route for extra income.)

Don't worry if your 50th birthday party is just a memory. I'll show how you can get ready for retirement, even if you don't have a penny in a retirement program.

RETIREMENT INVESTING

Most of us will have investing for retirement as one of our major financial goals. I will cover investing for retirement in much more detail later, but let's take a look at the magic of compounding and time for different ages to see what can happen.

GO TO ▶
See Hour 23, "Retirement Planning," for more information on 401(k)s, 403(b)s, regular IRAs, Roth IRAs, and calculating your retirement needs.

The great thing about investing for retirement is that you can do it within a *tax-deferred* environment, meaning taxes are not paid on gains in your account. There are some exceptions to this rule, but it's your decision how to handle taxes.

The following examples ignore the effect of inflation because I want to impress you with my math later, when we'll look at a more realistic picture.

THE EARLY BIRD GETS THE COMPOUNDING

Our first intrepid investor is Sally. At age 25, she has a promising career in accounting. She sets up a retirement account earning 10 percent and deposits $50 a month for the next 40 years. At age 65, she gets a gold watch and a check for $316,204. Not too shabby.

But Sally is smarter than that, thanks to her bean-counting skills. She knows how compounding and time can work for her. So she sets up the same retirement account earning 10 percent and deposits $50 the first month. Then, every month she increases her deposit by $1. So the second month she deposits $51 and the next month she deposits $52, etc.

Now at age 65, she gets a gold watch and a check for $1,011,276! That's over 319 percent more, and all she did was add $1 a month. Her retirement fund grew by over $695,000 and she did it by adding $1 each month.

Besides the magic of time and compounding, this example raises another good point. Some of you who are clever in math figured out that Sally was depositing over $500 a month toward the end of her career.

That may seem like a lot, but consider Sally's strategy. By forcing herself to increase each month, even if by only a dollar, she established a disciplined approach to her investing. This conditioned her to not miss that additional dollar each month (or the payment, either). Besides, when you figure a modest 3% annual inflation over 40 years, $500 will be the equivalent of about $150 of today's dollars.

TIME SAVER

Get to know the *Rule of 72*. To determine how long it will take for an investor to double his or her money, divide the fixed rate of compound interest into 72. For example, at 10 percent interest, it will take 7.2 years to double. To you this means that $10,000 today, invested wisely at 10 percent, will be $20,000 in *7.2 years*. It also means that $10,000 today, invested poorly at 2 percent, will be $20,000 in *36 years*. Big difference!

BETTER LATE THAN NEVER

Our next hero is Bob, age 50 and overweight—oops, that's me. Anyway, Bob always wanted to set up a retirement account, but somehow just never got around to it. As a moderately successful kumquat salesman, Bob has a modestly growing income thanks to residuals. (Residuals are commissions on sales paid out over time.)

After reading this book, Bob boldly commits to establishing a retirement account, which he opens with $1,000 from his annual bonus. Each month he deposits $250 into the account, which is earning 10 percent. Each year he adds another $1,000 from his bonus and ups his monthly contribution by $25.

While Bob won't become a millionaire this way, he will build a nest egg of almost $194,000. Not bad, considering he started with nothing.

Comparing Sally and Bob further reveals the power of compounding and the magic of time. Sally's total investment in her retirement is $138,431 and it yields over a million dollars. Bob's investment is $91,500 with a yield of almost $194,000.

Sally gets a return of over seven-fold on her investment, while Bob just doubles his money—not bad, but think where he would be if he had started earlier. More importantly, Bob has less time for maneuvering. Because Bob started late, he can't afford to try different strategies and take a chance that he will get caught in a down market just when he needs to start living off his investments.

With 15 years to work with, Bob can up his nest egg by increasing his monthly contribution by $25. So every year, he ups his monthly contribution by $50 over the previous year. This is probably going to pinch his lifestyle.

It does manage to get his total up over $247,000 with an investment of $123,000, but you will notice his yield is still just barely double.

More about retirement investing, compounding, and so on in later chapters, but I hope I have convinced you that there is some urgency for you to get started with your own investment program.

TRADITIONAL INVESTING

This book will focus primarily on the traditional investment arenas of stocks and bonds. However, we will also take a look at some less traditional investments. The idea is that your situation is unique, and you are the best person to decide what works for you and what does not.

Within the traditional framework, we will cover common stocks, mutual funds, bonds, and cash instruments. You are probably familiar with most of these terms, or at least you think you are.

One of the problems in a society that is overly saturated with information is that words and phrases are used on a regular basis with the assumption that everyone knows what they mean. In this book we will define all of these terms in ways that make sense. Traditional investments can be broken down into two major categories: debt and equity instruments. We will cover these types of traditional investments in the sections to follow.

DEBT INSTRUMENTS

GO TO ▶
See Hour 4, "Investing Instruments," for a complete discussion of bank CDs.

Many years ago when banks were paying 12 percent and more on certificates of deposit (CDs), I shared with a relative how depressed I was that there was no money for commercial loans at less than 15 percent. He was appalled. How could banks be such robbers, he wondered. How did banks expect businesses to survive if they had to pay that much interest?

He did not connect the fact that banks were paying him handsomely for his deposits, and then lending the money out at a higher rate. The only way commercial (and residential) loan rates were going to drop was for deposit rates to drop first. *Commercial loans* are loans made to businesses, usually by banks, for purposes of expansion or financing inventory. *Residential loans* are mortgages for the purchase or renovation of a house and are made by savings and loans, banks, and credit unions.

Debt instruments are bank savings accounts and bonds. When you deposit money in a bank or purchase a bank CD, you are lending the bank money. CDs carry a fixed amount of time the money must stay in the account—take it out earlier and you will pay a substantial penalty. The bank then must lend the money out at a higher rate to make a profit (simply put).

GO TO ▶
See Hour 14, "Bonds," for more information on government, municipal, corporate, and junk bonds.

Bonds are debts to government entities and corporations. When you buy a bond, you are lending a governmental agency or corporation money to run its affairs. Bonds carry a fixed maturity date when they can be redeemed for their face value. You can buy and sell bonds at any time before the maturity date, but since bonds are sensitive to interest rates you may have to sell at a discount.

EQUITY INSTRUMENTS

Common and preferred stock are equity instruments. A share of stock represents an ownership interest in a company. Buy 100 shares of Microsoft and you and Bill Gates will have something in common, other than the fact that you both have computers that crash. Just joking.

When you buy 100 shares of a publicly traded company, the money normally does not go to the company. It goes to some other investor who wanted to sell 100 shares. The two of you are matched on the stock exchanges, for a small fee.

Sometimes companies issue new stock or issue stock for the first time. In these cases, the money goes to the company to raise capital for expansion, acquisitions, or other legitimate business of the company.

The very first issue of stock to the public is called an *initial public offering* (IPO). We will look at IPOs in greater detail later. For now, understand that this is how small companies raise large sums of money to grow their businesses to the next level.

GO TO ▶
See Hour 13, "Stocks—Part II Size," for more information on initial public offerings, the hype surrounding them, and whether they are a good investment.

I call mutual funds equity instruments, even though some are, in fact, made up of bonds and other money instruments. A *mutual fund* is created when a large group of people pool their money and entrust it to a professional manager.

The fund has specific objectives, and those objectives drive which stocks are purchased and sold by the fund. For example, an Internet stock mutual fund would only invest in Internet companies.

The advantages of mutual funds are professional management and diversification, which means your investment is spread over a number of different companies. Diversification reduces your risk.

GO TO ▶
See Hours 9 through 11 for more information on mutual fund classifications, the types of funds, and investment objectives.

Later, we'll dig deeper into mutual funds and learn about the many varieties and how to identify those just right for your investment program. Some financial advisers recommend that investors stick with mutual funds and avoid owning individual stocks. By the end of this book, you will be able to make that decision for yourself.

NONTRADITIONAL INVESTING

Nontraditional investments are included in this book because you will hear about them (or already have) and you need the proper information to help you decide if any of these are for you.

HARD ASSETS

Hard assets are further divided into two subcategories: real estate and precious metals.

Yes, I know many people consider real estate an essential investment and will probably be offended at it being classified as nontraditional. They will certainly be offended to find it in the same category as gold and silver.

Here's my reasoning. Hard assets such as real estate and gold have been considered good inflation hedges. History shows that in periods of high inflation money is driven to assets that have intrinsic value (like gold and real estate). When confidence in the money weakens (during inflation), investors have looked to convert paper money into hard assets (like precious metals and gold coins).

JUST A MINUTE

Inflation is when too much money is chasing too few goods. It is characterized by sharply rising prices with no apparent increase in product value. The result is that money is devalued, or worth less. For example, if you were planning to live on $2,000 a month income in retirement, inflation might make that $2,000 buy only $1,700 worth of goods. Your standard of living would drop $300 per month.

While there are no guarantees that high inflation will not return, it seems unlikely. The Federal Reserve Bank, which controls the money supply, has shown it is willing to apply the brakes to the economy if it seems to be heading for an inflationary period.

If you take the inflation out of the economy, hard assets like real estate and gold don't appreciate very rapidly as a rule. Let's look at real estate.

REAL ESTATE

We all probably know someone who bought the right piece of property at the right time for the right price and made a killing. The average real estate investor is more likely to own residential properties that are rented out.

GO TO ▶
See Hour 4, "Investing Instruments," where I'll discuss real estate in more detail, but I must tell you my concerns against owning real estate upfront. It is hard work. There is an easier way I'll show you later in the book.

I know several people who have been doing this for years and have been very successful. People always need a place to live and the cost of home ownership is going to be out of reach for a number of potential renters. There are plenty of tax advantages as well.

PRECIOUS METALS

As for gold and precious metals, I don't have much positive to say. If you believe the global economy is going to collapse any minute, then you may want to own gold. On the other hand, if our society falls apart at the seams, you'll want to get out of town fast. Any quantity of gold is going to slow you down.

If you feel you need precious metals in your portfolio, I suggest you purchase a mutual fund that invests in mining company stocks.

LIFESTYLE INVESTING

The other category of nontraditional investments I called lifestyle investing. This group includes art and other collectibles. I don't want to even consider this investing, but Americans seem to have this need to find things that give us pleasure, and then turn them into a business.

If you love art, love it for its beauty and the pleasure it brings you. Keep your baseball cards to share with your kids. We have managed to ruin just about every hobby you can think of by putting a price tag on it.

PROCEED WITH CAUTION

Collecting dolls as an investment is using a hobby for a purpose other than that for which it was intended. Stick with stocks, bonds, and mutual funds for your true investment needs.

Arabian horses are beautiful animals. Not many years ago people were going crazy over them. Investors who wouldn't know a stallion from a mare were bidding up prices through the roof. What really makes this nuts is that Arabian horses have no utilitarian value. They aren't like racehorses that can win money and breed champions.

Beanie Babies, Pokémon whatevers—you name it and Americans (and others) will collect them and drive up prices. If you want to collect or raise or trade your hobby, do so and enjoy it, but don't plan on retiring off your beer bottle collection or that black velvet painting of Elvis in *Viva Las Vegas*.

WHAT CAN YOU DO?

The following is a list of five things you can do today:

1. Fill out the worksheet at the end of this chapter on investment goals.
2. Ask friends and family which brokers they use and begin compiling a list.
3. If you have access to one of the business cable channels, listen to 30 minutes of financial news to get a feel for the language.
4. Begin thinking about ways to accumulate a sum, however small, of money you can invest every month.

5. Congratulate yourself for taking a strong, positive step towards securing a sound financial future.

WORKSHOP

Use the following worksheet to begin putting your goals in writing. Don't worry about being too specific at this point. Start off simply and concisely. For example, a long-term goal might be:

"I/We want to retire by age XX with no major debt." Try to get at least one goal under each heading:

Short-term goals (2–5 years)

Mid-term goals (5–15 years)

Long-term goals (15 years+)

HOUR'S UP!

Investing is the process of taking charge of your financial future rather than being blown around by the winds of fate and not knowing how you got there. This short quiz will help focus your thinking.

1. Investing makes your money …
   A. Work for you.
   B. Earn interest upon interest.
   C. An active part of your life.
   D. All of the above.

2. Successful investing requires …
   A. Years of training.
   B. A commitment to a better future.
   C. Lots of money.

3. Investment goals are most effective when …
   A. They are inflexible.
   B. You put them in writing.
   C. They are long and detailed.

4. Retirement investing …

   A. Is something you can worry about later.

   B. Requires sophisticated planning skills.

   C. Should start young.

5. Traditional investing includes …

   A. Stocks and bonds.

   B. Mutual funds.

   C. Cash instruments.

   D. All of the above.

6. A debt instrument is …

   A. Often heard in a band.

   B. A common stock.

   C. A loan to another person or institution.

7. An equity instrument represents …

   A. Ownership in a corporation.

   B. The balance of a mortgage.

   C. Fairness in business.

8. Companies raise money by …

   A. Raising prices.

   B. Selling shares of stock.

   C. Asking for donations.

9. A mutual fund benefits its shareholders by …

   A. Pooling their money for investment.

   B. Hiring professional investment managers.

   C. Having specific investment objectives.

   D. All of the above.

10. Common and preferred stock represent …

   A. Different classes of investors.

   B. Debt owed to the owner of the stock.

   C. An ownership interest in a corporation.

Quiz

HOUR 2
Getting Ready

CHAPTER SUMMARY

LESSON PLAN:

In this Hour you will learn about ...

- Cleaning up your credit card debt.
- Finding money to pay off credit cards.
- Emergency reserves of cash.
- Life insurance.

My wife and I live in an old house (almost 100 years old) that requires a lot of painting. The previous owners had a fondness for blue, yellow, pink, green, and fuchsia woodwork. Our tastes don't run in those directions.

We are not great painters, although my wife is getting there, but we have learned that before you begin painting you have to prepare the surface correctly. If you don't, your hard work will not last long.

The same is true for investing. You've already begun your preparation by reading this book, but there are several other steps you need to take before you begin your investment program. These steps will help you make the most efficient use of your investment dollars and avoid the mistake of having the right hand work against the left hand.

We are going to look at your debt, your safety net, how to budget money for investing, and setting realistic goals. Once we have these components taken care of, you will find your confidence and optimism increasing.

CLEANING UP DEBT

Let's face it. We are addicted to credit cards. We whip out the plastic without even thinking about how or when we are going to pay off the balance. In addition, the credit card companies keep sending them or upping our credit limits.

Without thinking about it, we are up to our wazoo in credit card debt. But when the bills do come, we notice that all they expect is this small minimum monthly payment. We can handle that.

What we may not notice is that we are paying 18 percent (or more) in interest and, if you look closely at your bill, you may find that the friendly minimum balance they want you to pay is LESS than the finance charges.

PROCEED WITH CAUTION

 Be careful of the "transfer your balance" ads from credit card companies. After a short period at the advertised low rate, the interest charge will shoot back up.

This means that if you only pay the minimum balance, you will never pay off the debt because all you are paying is interest. Your principal is never reduced.

Gather all of your credit card statements and any other high-interest debt you have and compare the interest rates. Make a list from highest interest to lowest and begin paying off from the top down. The first investment you are going to make is in yourself. You are going to stick those high-interest credit cards in your desk drawer and not use them again until you have paid off or substantially paid down what you owe.

The reason is obvious. If you are paying a credit card 18 percent on a $5,000 balance and earning 12 percent on a $5,000 investment, you are taking two steps forward and three back. It's actually worse than that.

You cannot make an investment that isn't overwrought with risk that will pay you enough to offset the money gushing out of your checking account. It may not be as much fun as buying stocks, but there is nothing you can do that makes more financial sense than getting rid of high-interest debt. More importantly, the object of investing is not to break even, but to get ahead.

Is 90 Days Really "Same as Cash"?

Time for a reality check. Do you honestly think businesses are primarily concerned with your well being? Of course not. Businesses are primarily concerned with making a profit. There is nothing wrong with making a profit—it's how they will stay in business. The conflict arises when businesses offer you great deals—just because they love you so much. These "great" deals often take the form of buy now and pay much later. A good example is the furniture business.

How many times have you seen a furniture store advertise "buy now and no payments or interest for one year"? Are you really getting an interest-free loan for a year? Of course not. You will pay interest, and quite a lot in many cases.

There are at least two ways you will pay for that year with no payments and no interest. First, when you do begin making payments, the interest rate can exceed 18 percent in some cases. The second way you will pay is through an inflated purchase price, which has interest charges built into it.

Here's how it might work:

The store offers a sofa and chair for $1,000 retail. The storeowner paid $500 for the items. They are offered for sale at $1,000 with no payment or interest for the first year, then 18 percent for the next three years. The owner sells you the sofa and chair on the above terms. Once you sign the contract (essentially a loan), she sells the note to a third party for $750. She pays off the wholesaler and has a gross profit of $250.

The third party holds your note and receives your payments. At the end of four years, you have paid over $1,600 for the $1,000 furniture and the third party has made an $850 profit. In addition, should you miss a payment or two, you may be liable for repaying the first year that was interest-free.

Can you make these situations work to your advantage? The first alternative is somewhat unconventional, but certainly doable. If you have the money in hand to buy the furniture, offer the store $750 cash right now. You would be surprised at how many merchants will negotiate prices, especially for cash.

The second alternative is to agree to the stated terms, but save up enough over the year to pay the $1,000 in full. This saves you the high interest charges. However, be very careful the contract doesn't have a prepayment penalty. (A prepayment penalty is a fee for paying off a debt early.)

CASH ADVANCES

There are times when only cash will do—not credit cards, not checks. One of the great things about credit cards is you can convert credit into cash, usually quite easily.

Most credit cards allow you to take up to 50 percent of your available credit in cash. Most banks will be glad to do this for you. However, you will pay dearly for this luxury.

Many cards charge a higher interest rate on cash advances and begin computing the interest from the moment you get the cash. In addition, your friendly banker will likely take a fee for providing the cash, sometimes up to $25 or more.

Unless you need the cash to bribe a foreign jailer to let your spouse off death row, find another way to pay for your fun or do without until you can save enough.

If you are in the habit of taking regular cash advances, gather your credit card statements for the past year and add up what it has cost you. (Have a friend standing by to call 911 when you see the total.)

As bad as cash advances from credit cards are, they pale in comparison to the "check holding" services.

These bandits will take your personal check and hold it for up to 14 days, presumably until you get another paycheck. By the time you pay their fee plus interest, the charges can exceed 1,000 percent on an annual basis. Several states are looking into regulating these businesses or shutting them down.

If you are continually running out of cash between pay periods and taking cash advances, something is amiss with your personal spending habits. Consider getting professional debt counseling to stop this destructive habit.

GETTING RID OF THE DEBT

It was certainly easier to build up the debt than it will be to get rid of it. But that is your task. How you go about it will vary from person to person, but here are some strategies.

First, I would encourage you to consider paying off this debt your highest financial priority after providing the basic necessities of food, shelter, and so on.

You need to take a hard look at your monthly income and expenses. How much are you spending on necessities and how much on luxuries? Until you get the credit card paid off, consider anything beyond food and shelter a luxury and subject to cuts or elimination.

TIME SAVER

 Be honest with yourself about your debt. If you have a problem, seek professional help. The Consumer Credit Counseling service is a nonprofit organization that will help you put together a plan to get you out of debt. You can usually find them in the yellow pages. You can also find a whole Web site dedicated to helping you with debt problems at credit.about.com/finance/credit/mbody.htm.

A personal income/expense statement follows. Fill it out honestly and begin thinking about where you could cut. This is a painful process to most people, but let's look at what this pain is going to buy you.

This table is a monthly summary of your income and expenses. I always use a monthly table because that is how most of our bills arrive. If you are paid on a weekly basis, take your annual income and divide by 12. Likewise, if you are paid every two weeks, figure your annual income and divide by 12.

If you have bills that are quarterly or semiannual, convert them to a monthly figure and add to the chart.

Income/Expense Statement

Income

Salary 1:

Salary 2:

Bonus:

Other:

Total Income:

Expenses

Rent/Mortgage:

Utilities:

Food:

Auto 1 Payment:

Auto 2 Payment:

Auto Gas:

Insurance:

Telephone:

Medical:

Haircuts:

Charity:

Movies:

Eat Out:

Cable TV:

Recreation:

Travel:

Other:

Total Expenses:

Difference (Total Income – Expenses)

If you eliminate the $900 per year interest you are paying the credit card, you will have an extra $75 per month to invest. If you invest that money at 10 percent for 10 years it will build to over $5,500 in your investment account. It will be money that is yours and not going out the door to the credit card company.

Do the Math

If you have a credit card with a $5,000 balance at 18 percent interest, you'll pay $900 in interest per year.

If instead you have $5,000 invested at 12 percent interest, this calculates out to be $600 in earnings per year. Here is the difference:

Minus 2 percent inflation (off the $5,000)   = ($100)

Minus 30 percent taxes (off the $600 in interest)   = ($180)

Total: $320 profit

To offset the interest paid on the credit card, you would need to invest over $14,000! Alternatively, you would need to invest your $5,000 where it would have to earn almost 29 percent to offset the credit card interest.

$900 interest payment to credit card

Amount needed to earn $900 in interest: $14,000

$14,000 at 12 percent interest = $1,680

Minus 2 percent inflation (off the $14,000) = $280

Minus 30 percent taxes (off $1,680 in interest) = $504

Total: $784

$1,680 minus $784 = $896

or

$900 interest payment to credit card

Interest on $5,000 needed to earn $900 = 29%

$5,000 at 29% interest = $1,450

Minus 2 percent inflation (off the $5,000) = $100

Minus 30 percent taxes (off $1,450 in interest) = $435

Total: $535

$1,450 minus $535 = $915

PAY IT OFF

Here are some other ways to pay off the debt:

- Got a bonus coming? Why not dedicate all of it to paying off the credit card debt?
- How about a tax refund? Why not use it to pay off the debt?
- Get any cash for Christmas? Why not use it to pay for any holiday expenses you would have put on your credit card?
- Plan on having a garage sale? Why not put it toward paying off your credit cards instead of buying something new with the money from the old stuff?

You get the picture. Be creative and relentless. The sooner you pay off this debt, the sooner you are going to reverse your downward financial spiral and begin the road to wealth.

JUST A MINUTE

Finding money to pay off credit card debts is a challenge, but most people can squeeze extra money out of their daily lives. Start keeping track of all those extra sodas, cigarettes, and candy—notice that the little things aren't good for you and they add up fast.

FINDING $200 A MONTH EXTRA

I promise you that virtually any middle- or higher-income family or single person has at least $200 going out the door every month that would not be radically missed if it were redirected toward your debt repayment.

Here are some places to look:

- Eating out. How many times a week or month do you eat out? Do you go out for lunch at work? Consider cutting your restaurant trips in half. Take a lunch to work. Some families will get the whole $200 right here.
- Movies. Where I live, it costs about $20 for two adults to see a movie with popcorn and soda. Rent a movie instead. One or two fewer movies a month will add up. How about that extra money you spend on cable movie channels? Do you really watch $15 worth of good movies? It can end up saving you another $180 a year, which makes a nice start for a monthly investment account.

- Recreational shopping. Do you "crawl the mall" and end up buying stuff you like—but don't really need?
- Because I work at home and we live in a small town, we get by with only one car. When we need a second car, we rent one. It is a whole lot cheaper than paying for and maintaining a second car. We figure that's worth a couple hundred bucks a month right there.

Well, you get the idea. You will be surprised at how little you miss these things, especially when you consider what they are buying you: a debt-free life. If you apply this extra $200 to your credit card payment, you'll have it down to nothing at all in no time.

The other great thing about being more intentional with your money is that once the credit card is paid off, you have a source of investment money already a part of your budget.

Want to know what that $200 per month is worth over 10 years at 10 percent? How about $41,000?

If you did not pay off that credit card and continued paying just the minimum, in 10 years you will have paid the credit card company over $9,000 and still owe them $5,000.

Which sounds better to you: $9,000 in interest paid and $5,000 in debt, or $41,000 in the bank and no debt? Can you imagine how great that second scenario will feel? It will make the small sacrifices you make now seem like a miniscule price to pay.

EXTREME MEASURES

Paying off credit card debt is so important to your success that it deserves radical solutions if more conventional ones don't work.

I am normally not a big fan of borrowing to pay off debt, but if you can reduce your interest rate by half, it will be a lot easier to pay off.

Consider the following:

- Savings. If you have money in a savings account or a CD about to mature, use that to pay off your debt. I know, you were saving that money for a rainy day, but in financial terms your credit card debt is a monsoon. I'll show you a way to cover emergency cash shortly.

- Life insurance. Cash value in a life insurance policy can be "borrowed" to pay off the debt. In this case you are borrowing from yourself and you can pay it back when and if you want. You may pay a small processing fee, but nothing too bad.

- Pension plan. Some company pension plans will let you borrow money from your account. Check with the plan administrator for the policy and any tax implications.

- Home equity loan. If you own a home with substantial equity, you may be able to borrow enough to pay off your credit cards. As a bonus, the interest payments to the home equity loan may be tax-deductible. Check with a tax professional.

You will still have a debt to pay back, but the terms will be much more favorable than those from the credit card company.

EMERGENCY RESERVES

You have probably heard that you need an emergency reserve of cash to cover three to six months of expenses in case you and/or your partner lose your jobs or some other emergency cuts off your income.

GO TO ▶
See Hour 9, "Mutual Funds—Part I Classifications," for a detailed discussion of mutual funds.

I think this is a great idea, but you need to think about it carefully or you will have too much cash tied up in unproductive assets. This rule was first postulated when the average person put his or her money in the bank for safekeeping. Very few average folks invested in stocks or mutual funds.

The reason for having money in the bank is so you can access it quickly. The financial world has changed dramatically since people began thinking about these rules.

In this day and age, if you need money out of a mutual fund, it shouldn't take more than a couple of business days; in some cases you can have it wired to your bank account sooner. Some mutual funds will give you check-writing privileges. Even individual stocks can be sold in a hurry and the proceeds received as quickly.

JUST A MINUTE

Get in the habit of paying cash for almost everything. If you need to make a big purchase on your credit card, have a plan to pay it off in four months or less.

The point is, your investments can also double as part of your emergency reserve if need be. They can be tapped in real emergencies, but you don't want to do that unless you have to.

I hope that the kinds of emergencies you will face are the "refrigerator goes into cardiac arrest on Friday night" variety. You don't want to cash in your mutual funds for something like that. But on the other hand, you may not want $1,000 sitting around, either.

What's the answer? Credit cards, of course. Yes, the same credit cards I spent a considerable amount of space urging you to get out from under.

PROCEED WITH CAUTION

Using credit cards responsibly—meaning you make your payments on time and pay more than the minimum due—will help maintain a credit limit that can be used for emergencies.

I have nothing against credit cards. They are wonderfully convenient, especially for dead refrigerator emergencies and for pleasant things like buying cheap airline tickets over the Internet.

When you want to use a credit card for a big-ticket purchase, have a repayment plan in place that will get your balance down to zero in a hurry. For emergencies, you may need to figure it out after the fact, but don't let it slide from month to month if you can help it.

Using credit cards responsibly is also a way to build and maintain your credit. If you are considering buying your first house in the future, it will be important to show a history of responsible credit use. Responsible is the operative word here. Let a few payments be missed or late and your credit report will not inspire confidence in a lender.

It is not a bad idea to keep a couple of credit cards and use them occasionally just to keep your credit current. If you have a good credit history and a reasonable income, it is not impossible for you to have $10,000–$15,000 of credit available between two cards. This amount of credit, plus your investments, should give you plenty of protection against most of life's ordinary emergencies.

The worksheet mentioned earlier will give you an idea of how much you need to "keep the doors open" in an emergency. Between your credit cards and investments, you should plan to cover three months if you are single and five months if you have a family.

The reasoning behind this is that a single person has more options in terms of moving to a new job than a family person with roots.

LIFE INSURANCE

I am not a big fan of life insurance policies that combine a death benefit and investment component (universal life, for example). These policies are sold as a way for undisciplined folks to invest their money while providing a death benefit.

However, I acknowledge the need for life insurance protection. If you have a family that relies on your income, it is important that the income stream be protected against loss. Working couples should be sure both income streams are protected.

If your income is $35,000 per year, you probably need $350,000 in life insurance. Upon your death, that sum could be invested and return about the equivalent of your income annually.

WHAT CAN YOU DO?

The following is a list of five things you can do today:

1. Get out your credit card statements and read the fine print. Are you paying interest from the date of the charge or is there a "grace period" before interest is applied? Consider changing credit cards to one that lets you pay off the balance without an interest charge.

2. Make a list of any *extra* money you anticipate, such as a bonus, tax refund, gifts, and so on. Write on your calendar when you anticipate receiving the money and note that it is committed to debt repayment.

3. If your credit card use is out of control, seek help through a credit counseling service. Look for nonprofit agencies that are not going to charge you an outrageous fee to repair your credit.

4. If you have access to the Internet, go to www.bankrate.com. You'll find information on where to get the best credit card rates.

5. Mark on your calendar when you make payments against your debt. Project when it will be paid off. Treat yourself to a nice dinner that night (pay cash).

WORKSHOP

We all know life is going to throw us some curves now and then, so you should prepare a Contingency Plan. Hopefully, these curves will be of the "dead refrigerator" variety.

Consider some of the minor, but annoying, emergencies you might face in the future and create a plan of attack.

The following is an example of what this might look like. Adjust the emergencies to your particular lifestyle. For example, someone with an executive position might find replacing a $1,000 refrigerator troublesome, but definitely not an emergency. However, for the intern just getting started, a new refrigerator, even a more modest one, might be a financial crisis.

Potential Emergencies	Solution
New refrigerator ($500 – $1,000)	
New air conditioner/heater ($750 – $1,500)	
Brakes for the car ($250 – $450)	
(Add your own)	

HOUR'S UP!

Investing, like anything important you do, requires some preparation, including cleaning up debt, preparing a budget, and setting goals. Are you ready? Take this short quiz and you'll know.

1. Credit cards are great conveniences and they …
    - **A.** Can sabotage your investing plan.
    - **B.** Are a cheap way to pay for a quick, large purchase.
    - **C.** Are better than checks.

2. You should always pay more than the minimum on your credit card because …
    - **A.** You will eventually pay off the balance.
    - **B.** High interest charges will defeat your investing plans.
    - **C.** Extra amounts go to the principal of the loan.
    - **D.** All of the above.

3. Eliminating high-interest payments will …

    A. Reduce your income tax.

    B. Free money for investing.

    C. Free up credit.

4. You can find money for investing …

    A. Under the sofa cushions.

    B. By raiding the kid's piggybank.

    C. By cutting down on expensive luxuries.

5. A good source of emergency reserve cash is …

    A. A credit card.

    B. Your bookie.

    C. Your kid's piggybank.

6. A home equity loan can be used …

    A. To pay off high credit card debt.

    B. To play the lottery.

    C. For paying off your mortgage.

7. When you make a big purchase on a credit card, you …

    A. Will get a nice note from the credit card company.

    B. Should have a plan in place to pay it off.

    C. Will look like a big spender.

8. A good use for a tax refund is …

    A. To buy a new stereo.

    B. To pay off credit card debt.

    C. To put it under your mattress.

9. Redirecting money to pay off debt will also …

    A. Begin a habit of savings that can be used for investments.

    B. Help you lose weight.

    C. Make your life miserable.

10. Life insurance is …

    A. Only good if you are the beneficiary.

    B. A way to protect income.

    C. A good way to get rich.

Quiz

HOUR 3
Investing Basics

CHAPTER SUMMARY

LESSON PLAN:

In this Hour you will learn about ...

- The miracle of compounding.
- How to make compounding work for you.
- Common investment terms.
- The stock exchanges.
- Market indicators.

I'll be the first to admit I am mathematically challenged. I can remember years ago spending hours on an important proposal. At the heart of the proposal was a large block of calculations.

These calculations involved computing the percent change between two numbers for a series of scenarios. The answers were then converted to graphs.

As I sat outside the room, waiting to make my presentation, I looked through the package one more time. To my horror, I realized that I had done the math wrong.

This traumatic incident almost made me change my career to something that would never, ever require me to do math again. However, I stuck with it and found ways to work around my problems with numbers.

The point is that you do not have to be a math whiz to learn investing.

I did most of the math in this book using calculators I got off the Internet or problems I set up on a spreadsheet.

Hopefully your mind is at ease about facing math as we go forward in the book, so let's get down to the real important mathematical concepts you need to grasp.

THE MIRACLE OF COMPOUNDING

You were already introduced to compounding in the first Hour, but I want to build on it a little more. It is important that you understand the *power* of compounding.

JUST A MINUTE

Compounding is like the rapids on a river. Canoeing with the rapids is investing. Canoeing against the rapids is borrowing.

Compounding is the single most powerful tool in an investor's arsenal. Without it, investing becomes the equivalent of putting your money under your mattress.

Here is a radical example of the power of compounding:

On Day 1 you give me a penny. On Day 2 you double it to two cents. On Day 3 you double it again to four cents. And so on for 30 days. On the 30th day you will pay me almost $5.4 million!

This is compounding. In just 30 steps, a penny grows to almost $5.4 million.

Of course, you aren't going to get 100 percent interest unless you lend money in dark alleys and break people's kneecaps when they don't pay.

Nevertheless, compounding is the basic mechanism for creating wealth. It is what will help you achieve your goals.

How to Make Compounding Work for You

The example I used involves an initial deposit (one penny) and interest only. What would happen if you added a penny each day in addition to the interest?

If you are clever in math, you might have figured this one out. Here's the problem restated:

On Day 1 you give me a penny. On Day 2 you give me two cents (your original penny plus 100 percent interest) and another penny for a total of three cents. On Day 3 you give me six cents (three cents plus 100 percent interest) and another penny for a total of seven cents. And so on for 30 days. On the 30th day you pay me over $10.7 million dollars (double the total in the original problem.) The only difference is you gave me an additional 29 cents over the 30-day period.

This illustrates an important point: compounding can be made to work harder by periodically adding to the balance. Let's use some real world examples.

Say you open an investment account with $50 earning 10 percent and every month you deposit another $50. In 10 years your account will be worth almost $10,400 (ignoring taxes and inflation.)

If you could manage to make an additional $5 deposit each month bringing your total to $55, in 10 years your account would be worth $11,396—over $1,000 more. Your investment increased by $600 ($5 per month × 120 months), but you earned $1,000.

One way to look at this is that the extra $600 you invested over 10 years earned you a 66 percent return ($600 × 66 percent = $396).

This process also works on loans. If you make an additional $50 per month payment on your mortgage, it will be paid off much sooner. Why? Because that extra $50 goes to the principal of the loan, and thus there is a smaller amount used to compute interest charges.

THE MIRACLE OF TIME

Part of the magic of compounding comes from how long the process is allowed to work. The more time you have to compound, the more money you'll make.

JUST A MINUTE

Time is one component of the investment formula. The other two components are amount invested and interest earned.

In the example above, you opened an investment account for 10 years. What would happen if you could let it work for 15 years or 20 years?

Here's the scenario: $50 invested at 10 percent interest and another $50 added monthly.

For 10 years the total is: $10,372

For 15 years the total is: $20,938

For 20 years the total is: $38,314

This is why Little's Golden Rule of Investing is so important:

The best time to start investing was yesterday. The second best time is today. Tomorrow is better than nothing.

A chart showing the effect of compounding.

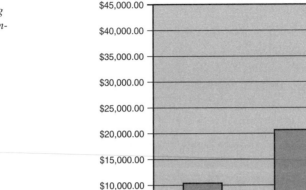

In summary, compounding is the best thing since sliced bread. It will work for you with your investments or it will work against you when you borrow. Either way, it is *the* force of the financial world.

INVESTING TERMS

The language of investing has its own jargon and buzzwords. To paraphrase an old golf quote, "I may not invest like a professional, but I can talk like one."

GO TO ▶
See Appendix C, "Glossary," in the back of the book for even more investing terms.

I want you to do both. To that end, I'm going to review some of the basic investing terms you will encounter on a daily basis.

You may know many of these, but I encourage you to read this section carefully. Some of the terms may be new to you and others may have unfamiliar nuances. All of these terms will be explored in much more detail as we work through the book.

COMMON STOCK

Common stock is the primary unit of ownership in a company. A share of common stock grants you voting rights on major issues concerning the company. In some cases, it earns you a proportional piece of the profits of the company. However, your liability in the event the company collapses financially or is found guilty of some offense is limited by the number of your shares. When you read about stocks or hear a newscast referring to stocks closing up or down, you are hearing about common stock. Most news reports leave off the "common" unless there is a reason to distinguish them from another class of stock.

JUST A MINUTE

The term *blue chip* refers to poker chips—blue ones are the most expensive. Thus, a blue chip stock would be the top of the line.

PREFERRED STOCK

Preferred stock is a different class of common stock. As the name suggests, holders of preferred stock receive certain benefits ahead of common-stock holders, including first rights to dividends. In some cases, preferred stock shares receive a fixed dividend whether other stockholders receive dividends or not.

Preferred stock is identified in *The Wall Street Journal* stock tables by the letters "pf" following the stock's name. You will often see another letter after the "pf," such as "pfA." This indicates there may be more than one series of preferred stock.

BONDS

Bonds represent a debt to the holder. Bonds do not convey any ownership rights or responsibilities. They are obligations of the issuing entity. Governmental units including the U.S. Treasury and various federal agencies, state governments, municipal governments, and various special-purpose governmental units may issue bonds.

Corporations may also issue bonds as an alternative to issuing more stock or borrowing from commercial lenders. Bonds represent a debt to be repaid. If the corporation issues more stock without a corresponding increase in assets, current stockholders will get angry because their holdings are worth less.

For example, if corporation ABC has 10,000,000 shares of stock outstanding and $100,000,000 in assets, then each share of stock represents $10 in assets:

$100,000,000 / 10,000,000 = $10

If the company issues 2,000,000 new shares of stock, then each share of stock now represents $8.33 in assets:

$100,000,000 / 12,000,000 = $8.33

GO TO ▶
See Hour 14, "Bonds," for a complete discussion of the types of bonds and their uses.

This is an oversimplified example, but it illustrates why corporations do not like to issue additional stock without some corresponding increase in value for the stockholders. An acquisition done with stock is an example of issuing new stock with a corresponding increase in value for the stockholders.

Likewise, corporations often prefer bonds over commercial loans because they can often get more favorable interest rates and a longer payback period than a commercial lender might give them. Companies often use junk bonds for acquisitions since junk or zero coupon bonds don't require periodic interest payments. Hour 14 explains junk bonds in detail.

CASH EQUIVALENTS

Cash equivalents are financial instruments that represent a deposit of cash. They include CDs, savings accounts, money market accounts, and a variety of lesser-used instruments. They all represent a holding of cash and, for the most part, can be quickly converted into cash if needed. You may hear different investments described as either being "liquid" or "illiquid." Liquidity refers to how quickly and easily an asset can be converted to cash.

Cash equivalents are all liquid, although to greater or lesser degrees. For example, savings or checking accounts are highly liquid, since they are quickly and easily converted to cash. On the other hand, CDs are not quite as liquid since you have to go to the bank and close the account. If you close it before the CD matures you will have to pay a penalty.

MUTUAL FUNDS

Mutual funds are investment instruments that are characterized by a pool of money that is invested by professional managers to achieve specific objectives. The money is raised when the public invests in the mutual fund because it meets similar personal investment objectives.

Mutual funds invest in stocks, bonds, cash equivalents, and other types of investments. The fund may be a pure stock fund (meaning 100 percent of the investments in the mutual fund are in stocks) or bond fund (meaning 100 percent of the investments are in bonds), or a combination of both stocks and bonds (for example, 50 percent stocks and 50 percent bonds). Mutual funds have specific objectives that drive their buying and selling strategies. Refer to Hours 9 through 11 for more information on mutual funds.

JUST A MINUTE

There are mutual funds that can be bought for just a few hundred dollars' initial investment—not a high barrier to investing. You can find a list of mutual funds that will let you open an account with initial investments as low as $25 at www.mfea.com.

WARRANTS

Warrants give the holder the right, but not the obligation, to purchase a certain number of shares of stock at a certain price. Warrants are often coupled with a new issue of stock as an incentive.

For example, a company might offer a new stock issue with these terms: For every five shares of stock you purchase, you are issued a warrant to purchase two shares of the stock at a specific price at some date in the future.

If the stock were currently selling for $20 per share and you buy 1,000 shares, your warrants might give you the opportunity to purchase 400 shares at $25 per share in six months.

1,000 shares / 5 = 200

$200 \times 2 = 400$ shares

OPTIONS

Options give the holder the right—but not the obligation—to buy or sell a certain number of shares at a certain price before a certain date. They differ from warrants in that the company does not issue them. They are facilitated by the stock exchanges (NYSE, NASDAQ, and so on) where they can be bought and sold.

FUTURES

Futures are contracts to deliver a specific commodity or certain financial instruments at a certain date. Most people may be more familiar with the agricultural commodities of the futures market, such as cotton, hog bellies (or pork bellies), orange juice, or soybeans. Futures are also sold on such things as heating oil, unleaded gasoline, or lumber. Increasingly, futures on financial instruments and market indicators are also being traded.

Financial instruments include U.S Treasury Bonds, Bills, and Notes along with 30-day federal funds. All of these instruments are interest-rate sensitive

GO TO ▶
See Hour 22, "Aggressive Investing," for more information on options and futures.

and are used by institutions to protect themselves from adverse swings in interest rates.

Futures on market indicators such as the S&P 500 index, the Dow Jones Industrial Average, and others have become very popular in recent years. These futures are used by institutions to protect themselves from abrupt changes in market direction. They are also used by speculators who try to predict the direction of the market in advance and profit by being invested in futures.

MARKET ACTIVITY TERMS

There are a number of terms used to describe market activity. Some are familiar and obvious, while others may be new to you.

TRADE

Trade, for our purposes, means the buying and selling of financial instruments (stocks, bonds, and so on). "Trading was active … " is a common phrase used to describe the whole of market activity or the activity of an individual stock. In a strict sense, no trading actually occurs.

JUST A MINUTE

The context of a term such as "trade" will tell you whether it refers to individual activity or the market as a whole.

No one says, "I'll trade you 100 shares of IBM for 100 shares of ATT." To trade includes the buying and selling of investments, whether by an individual or the whole market.

TRADING VOLUME

Trading volume is the number of shares of stock that move through the exchanges. Thanks to the high-tech nature of stock exchanges today, it is routinely reported that trading volume in a single day is in the hundreds of millions and many days exceeds 1 billion shares traded on both the New York Stock Exchange and the Nasdaq.

Trading volume is an indicator of market interest. Sometimes before a key piece of economic news is released, the market will trade at a much slower pace, only to be followed by a frantic day when the information is made public.

Buy and Sell

These are familiar terms and are true to their common definitions. The twist from an investment point of view is that it is possible to buy an instrument that gives you the right to sell or sell an instrument that gives you the right to buy.

The most common usage remains the basic one: I bought 100 shares of ABC at $43 per share. This will become clearer as we go along.

Long and Short

These are somewhat the equivalent of "buy" and "sell." If you tell your broker you want to "go long 100 shares of IBM," she will know you want to buy IBM. Likewise, to "short IBM" is to sell IBM.

However, long and short are more commonly used to describe your position in an investment. Your statement from a broker might show "Long Positions." Under this heading would be the stocks that you own. Likewise your statement might show "Short Positions," the stocks you have sold or shorted (see next definition).

Short Selling

The stock market is the only place I know where you can legally sell something you don't own. It is called "shorting" a stock and is used when an investor believes a stock is going to fall in price.

Your broker will "borrow" the stock from a client. You sell the stock. If the stock does indeed fall, you buy the stock at the lower price to replace the borrowed shares and pocket the difference. Should the stock rise, however, you will have to buy it back at a higher price and suffer a loss. Here's how it works.

You believe ABC stock is about to drop significantly. You alert your broker that you want to short ABC. Your broker finds shares of ABC held in trust by the brokerage firm and "loans" them to you. You sell them on the market and pocket the money, less commissions. Sure enough, ABC goes into the dumpster. You now buy ABC (called covering your short) at a lower price on the open market and return the borrowed shares. Your profit is the difference between what you sold them for and what you paid. Here are the numbers (ignoring commissions):

ABC stock is currently selling for $20 per share.

You short 100 shares of the stock and pocket $2,000.

The price drops to $15 dollars per share.

You cover your short by buying 100 shares for $1,500.

Your profit is $500.

The shares are returned to the brokerage account. The broker is able to do this because most stock held by the broker for clients is registered in the street name. This means when you want to sell the stock there is no need for you to come in and sign the certificates. Think of it as a "power of attorney" you give the brokerage house.

JUST A MINUTE

Selling short and buying stock on margin are not for beginners, but once you get your feet on the ground, they may present some good opportunities if you are comfortable with risk.

MARGIN

Margin is a way to finance part of your stock purchases. If you buy a stock "on margin," your broker will lend you up to 50 percent of the purchase price, depending on your credit worthiness and market conditions. This will allow you to buy twice as much stock.

Your broker will charge you interest for the loan and require you to maintain the account at a certain equity level. This means as long as the stock is rising, everything is okay, but should the stock start to fall, your broker will require you to close out the position or add money to your account to protect the broker's loan. This is known as a *margin call*. Here's how these numbers (excluding commissions) work:

ABC stock is selling for $50 per share.

You have $5,000 to buy 100 shares.

You borrow another $5,000 to buy another 100 shares.

You now own 200 shares of ABC worth $10,000 and have a brokerage loan of $5,000 at 7 percent interest.

ABC stock climbs to $60 per share and you sell for $12,000.

You repay the $5,000 brokerage loan plus $30 interest (this assumes you had the loan for one month).

$12,000 gross

Minus $5,030 loan and interest

Minus your $5,000

Total profit = $1,970 or a return of almost 40 percent

If you had not margined the stock and only bought 100 shares, your profit would have been $1,000, or 20 percent.

POSITION

Position describes your current holdings in a particular investment. It is often used with the terms "long" and "short" to describe how you stand at a particular moment.

If you own 100 shares of IBM, you are said to be "long IBM." Likewise, if you have shorted IBM, you are said to be "short IBM."

THE MARKETS

The stock market is a catchall phrase that actually describes several different markets or exchanges. Together these *markets* facilitate the business of buying and selling financial instruments.

Their role in the process is to match buyers and sellers. How they do that varies in the details from market to market. The markets also set standards that companies have to meet and maintain before they can be "listed" or traded on a particular exchange.

THE NEW YORK STOCK EXCHANGE

The New York Stock Exchange or NYSE is the granddaddy of all exchanges. Its history goes back over 100 years. It is still considered the most prestigious of the exchanges by many professionals.

This is where you will find the nation's blue chip companies listed. *Blue chip* refers to those companies that have proven to be steady investments over many years. Blue chip stocks include General Electric, IBM, American Express, AT&T, and Coca-Cola. All of these stocks are part of the Dow Jones Industrial Average. You can find a complete list of the Dow stocks in Appendix B.

The NYSE and the American Exchange are *listed exchanges*, which means brokerage firms provide specialists in each of the listed stocks. Brokers purchase "seats" on the exchanges.

JUST A MINUTE

An auction market is where the buyer and seller compete for the best prices. In a transaction, the stock is sold to the highest bidder and bought from the lowest offer.

Each specialist is responsible for matching buyers and sellers of that particular stock. Often called the *auction market*, here is how it works:

You want to buy 100 shares of XYZ company and place your buy order. The specialist in the stock finds someone willing to sell at that price and the deal is done. You will pay the asking price, plus a small fee that goes to the brokers.

This fee can range from 12.5 cents per share to a flat $6. The fee is determined by the price of the stock. The buyer pays the fee. Note: this is not the same fee or commission you pay your broker—that fee is paid whether you are buying or selling.

Online quotes during the trading day indicate the price at which you may buy or sell a particular stock (excluding fees).

THE NASDAQ

The NASDAQ Stock Exchange is a different breed from the NYSE, although they both do the same thing. The NASDAQ is the new kid on the block and home to many of today's high-tech stocks stars. For example, Amazon.com (AMZN) and Microsoft (MSFT) are NASDAQ stocks. Some of the others that Morningstar.com calls Technical Titans include: Cisco Systems (CSCO), Dell Computer (DELL), Veritas Software (VRTS), and Check Point Software Technologies.

Companies listed on this market tend to be younger companies in fast-moving industries. The volume of activity has risen dramatically in the last few years and approaches the NYSE in daily sales volume.

The NASDAQ is known as an "over-the-counter" market and it handles trades a little differently than the NYSE. In this market, brokers handle only one side of the trade; one broker represents the seller and one represents the buyer. Here's how it works:

You want to buy 100 shares of XYZ company and place a buy order. The specialist handling the selling side of the trade contacts a broker representing buyers and a match is made.

PROCEED WITH CAUTION

There are thousands of small companies that seldom trade, but are listed on the over-the-counter market (that is, on the NASDAQ).

In the NASDAQ, two different prices are quoted. One price is the *bid price* and that is the amount that goes to the seller. The other price is the *ask*, and that is the amount that the buyer pays.

XYZ is quoted at "bid $100" and "ask at $100.50." The difference is known as the *spread* and is split between the two brokers. The buyer pays the fee since their price ("ask") is the higher.

When you look up a quote on a NASDAQ stock, you will see these two prices.

The spread is not the commission you pay your broker. That is a separate fee.

PROCEED WITH CAUTION

You will also hear a lot about "penny stocks." These stocks, for the most part, don't meet the regular listing requirement and are sold on the promise of quick riches. Unfortunately, many of these deals are frauds and con games. Stay away from these scams.

THE ELECTRONIC MARKET

Whether you are using an online broker or a regular broker, there are several vast electronic networks that make this all work. They keep track of who sold what stock and who bought what stock and what brokers were involved. It finds buyers and sellers.

Perhaps their greatest contribution has been to increase the liquidity of the market, making it possible for incredible numbers of trades to occur each day. Tens of thousands of trades and hundreds of millions of shares pass through the market each day.

MARKET INDICATORS

Market indicators are benchmarks used for measuring the relative movement of the market, either up or down. They are all *indexes*; that is, they represent movement away or toward an arbitrary beginning. They are important barometers of the market's health.

DOW JONES INDUSTRIAL AVERAGE

GO TO ▶
See Appendix B, "Resources," for a list of the 30 stocks that make up the Dow.

You are probably familiar with the Dow Jones Industrial Average, also know as the Dow. This is the oldest and most widely known indicator and the one you most often hear quoted on the news.

For all its popularity, it is a rather narrow measure of market health. The Dow covers just 30 individual stocks. These 30 stocks which change fairly infrequently are considered the leaders in their particular industry sectors by the originators of the Dow, the Dow Jones Company, publisher of *The Wall Street Journal* and other financial publications.

The Dow may be a better "mood ring" of the market than a purely analytical tool. (For those younger readers, mood rings were sold years ago. Supposedly, the color of the stone would change depending on your emotional state. I still have mine somewhere.)

S&P 500

The S&P 500 is an index developed by the Standard and Poor Company. Standard and Poor is a well-respected leader in financial research and analysis in addition to generating other products and services.

The S&P 500 consists of 500 of the largest corporations and is the most widely used benchmark of market performance in the world. Investment managers compare their results against the S&P 500 and can boast that their investments "beat the market" if they did better than the S&P 500 over time.

JUST A MINUTE

Market indicators like the Dow and the S&P 500 are helpful in watching movement in the market, but they do not reflect overall trends. For example, the Dow can be *up*, yet there may be more losing stocks than gaining stocks.

Because it covers a larger number of stocks than the Dow, many consider it a more accurate reflection of the health of large corporations.

The NASDAQ Composite Index

The NASDAQ Composite Index covers the NASDAQ market and the 5,000+ stocks traded there. The companies traded on the NASDAQ are young, growing, and often high-tech companies.

This makes this index important. By measuring the entire market, this index gives a good picture of the relative health of smaller companies. Because there is a wide disparity in the size and age of NASDAQ stocks, the index is not as widely regarded.

Yet, this market has passed the New York Stock Exchange in terms of daily volume and cannot be dismissed lightly. The exchange began electronic trading in 1971 and has not stopped growing since. It is truly a virtual market, because there is no physical exchange where brokers meet to trade. Everything is done over their vast computer network.

Although lacking the starched white shirt image of the New York Stock Exchange, the NASDAQ fits very nicely in today's high tech, "casual dress all week" economy.

Russell 2000 Index

Developed by the Frank Russell Company, now a part of Northwestern Mutual, this index measures the fortunes of 2,000 smaller companies.

Small companies are considered the source of real economic and employment growth, so this is an important index to watch.

Many investors find investing in small companies an aggressive but potentially profitable strategy.

The Russell Company produces 18 various indexes covering U.S. securities and a variety of market segments. Some of them follow.

- The Russell 3000 Index measures 3,000 of the largest corporations based on market capitalization, which represents approximately 98 percent of the investable U.S. stock markets.

- The Russell 1000 Index measures the performance of the 1,000 largest companies in the Russell 3000 Index, which represents approximately 92 percent of the total market capitalization of the Russell 3000 Index.

- The Russell Top 200 Index, which measures 200 of the largest companies of the Russell 1000 Index.

- The Russell Midcap Index measures the performance of the 800 small-est companies in the Russell 1000 Index, which represents approximately 26 percent of the total market capitalization of the Russell 1000 Index.

The other Russell indexes monitor growth and value stocks. You can find more information about the Russell Indexes at Russell.com.

THE NEW YORK STOCK EXCHANGE COMPOSITE INDEX

The New York Stock Exchange Index covers all the stocks traded on the exchange. Its broad coverage makes it a good indicator of how larger companies are doing.

The index reflects changes in the average trading price for all securities listed on the New York Stock Exchange. The index was created in 1966 and set at 50.00, which was close to the average price of all common stocks at the beginning of that year.

The index is created by a complicated formula that considers the market value of all listed stocks on the NYSE and tracks changes based on sales activity.

There are four subgroup indexes: industrial, transportation, utility, and finance.

FOLLOWING THE STOCKS

Here's an exercise to get you used to working with stock numbers and tables.

Using *The Wall Street Journal*, your local newspaper, or the Internet, pick out five stocks you would like to follow. If there are some companies you are interested in, you can choose those. Choose some from the New York Stock Exchange and a couple from the NASDAQ market, then fill in the chart below.

Portfolio Tracker

Stock	Closing Price	52-Week High	52-Week Low	Volume
_____	_____	_____	_____	_____
_____	_____	_____	_____	_____
_____	_____	_____	_____	_____
_____	_____	_____	_____	_____
_____	_____	_____	_____	_____

It will be fun to come back after you've finished reading this book and see how your picks did.

WHAT CAN YOU DO?

The following is a list of five things you can do today:

1. Get out your copy of *The Wall Street Journal* I asked you to buy and look through the stock tables. I'll explain them to you in a future hour, but for right now, just get a feel for the many different markets represented.

2. Order a prospectus from a mutual fund. There will almost certainly be several advertised in *The Wall Street Journal*. If you have access to the Internet, you can go to any of the finance sites and find funds that you can order a prospectus for online. We will need this later. It doesn't matter what kind of fund, but if you can identify one as a stock fund, choose it.

3. Find all the indexes mentioned in this Hour in the tables of *The Wall Street Journal*. Write down the name, the points up or down, and the percent up or down. Based on what I told you about the indexes, do you see any similarity in movement between the two indexes? How would you account for that?

4. Find the Dow Jones Industrial Average chart in *The Wall Street Journal*. You should find a listing of all 30 companies that may up the Dow. Do these names surprise you? Are there companies listed that you have never heard of?

5. If you own your home, look at what an extra $50 or more per month would do to your total interest payments. More importantly, if you can see retirement down the road, you may want to figure out what you would have to do to pay off the mortgage before you retire. Many personal finance software packages will do this. If not, contact your mortgage holder.

WORKSHOP

You find your dream home and finance it with a $100,000 mortgage at 8 percent for 30 years. Your monthly loan payment is $734. Here's what your mortgage looks like at the end of 30 years:

# of Years	Monthly	Borrowed Amount	Interest Paid	Total Paid
30	$734	$100,000	$164,160	$264,160

Ouch! I thought that was a $100,000 note! How come it cost $264,160? The answer is compounding.

Now let's put compounding to work for us. Say we can afford to add $50 to our $734 monthly payment. Here's what that looks like compared to our original deal.

# of Years	Monthly Payment	Borrowed Amount	Interest Paid	Total Paid
30	$734	$100,000	$164,160	$264,160
23 yrs 11 mo	$784	$100,000	$124,249	$224,249

Notice that it takes six years and one month less than the original 30 years to pay off the originally borrowed $100,000. In addition, you pay $39,911 less in overall interest payments. The reason is that the extra $50 each month goes towards the principal, meaning that there is less to pay interest on for the remaining payments. This same principle works on your credit card or virtually any other debt.

When choosing a loan, make sure you are allowed to make additional payments to the principal. Some loans, though they aren't as common, charge you a fee to do so. In addition, you might check with your lender to see if they can reassess your mortgage for free (or a nominal fee) during the life of your loan, in case you have made so much additional payment toward the principal that you want to reap the benefits of a lower monthly payment. Then, if you keep making the $784 payment, you would pay off the loan even faster.

Now what if you can't count on having extra money for both investing and paying down the mortgage, how do you know which you should do?

This is not an easy question to answer without a lot more information, but here is a general rule of thumb: interest paid on a primary residence mortgage is usually tax deductible. Investing outside a retirement account could generate current income and/or capital gains. On a tax basis, it would seem that it makes more sense to invest and not pay down your note. However, if you are nearing retirement, it might make perfect sense to pay off your mortgage.

HOUR'S UP!

Investing has a vocabulary of its own, but I bet you are familiar with many of the terms and descriptions. Here is a short quiz to check your progress.

1. Compounding is …
    A. The mathematical engine of investing.
    B. A certain wealth builder.
    C. How your money can work for you.
    D. All of the above.

2. Investing over a long term …
    A. Is very risky.
    B. Can help you achieve your financial goals.
    C. Is not necessary.

3. Common and preferred stock …
    A. Represent shares of ownership in a corporation.
    B. Are forms of debt.
    C. Are used in farming.

4. Mutual funds are characterized by …
    A. Professional management.
    B. Diversified holdings.
    C. An investment policy.
    D. All of the above.

5. To trade means …
    A. To give one share of stock in exchange for another.
    B. To rat on your friends.
    C. To buy and sell stocks, mutual funds, and other investment products.

6. The terms long and short …
    A. Refer to different size warrants.
    B. Mean the same as buy and sell.
    C. Indicate the relative position of your bills and your cash.

7. The New York Stock Exchange …
    A. Is actually in New Jersey.
    B. Is too expensive for the average investor.
    C. Is the oldest and most prestigious of all stock exchanges.

Quiz

8. The NASDAQ Exchange …

   A. Is primarily an electronic market.

   B. Is only for very small companies.

   C. Uses only one price for buying and selling.

9. The Dow Jones Industrial Average is …

   A. A product of Dow Chemical Company.

   B. A measure of how large the average company is.

   C. An indicator of how market-leading companies did during any day of trading.

10. The S&P 500 Index is …

    A. A well-known company.

    B. The most widely used indicator of market activity.

    C. One half the size of the S&P 1000.

Hour 4
Investing Instruments

Chapter Summary

LESSON PLAN:

In this Hour you will learn about ...

- Common stock.
- Stock pricing.
- Preferred stocks.
- Mutual funds.
- Bonds.
- Cash equivalents.
- Other investment opportunities.

"The hunting bear follows many trails," according to ancient American Indian wisdom.

Actually, I made that up because I couldn't think of a way to start this section without using a tired cliché.

In this section, I want us to focus on the variety of investment instruments available to us. Most of us will only use a few of these tools, but it is important to have an overview of what is out there. This will be a broad overview to give you a flavor for what is coming in future hours.

We will spend more time on the more common instruments and less time on some of the more exotic and risky ones. All of these tools have an appropriate use, but not all of us will have an appropriate need for them.

Common Stock

We learned in the previous Hour that common stock represents an ownership interest in a corporation. This ownership interest is also known as an *equity interest*.

This equity interest gives the owner certain rights concerning the activities of the corporation:

- A vote at annual meetings
- Periodic financial updates from the corporation
- A say in the election of the company's board of directors

Some major decisions about the life of the corporation, such as mergers and so on, are decided by stockholder votes. The board of directors that represents the stockholders' interests handles all other major decisions.

It is not quite that pure. Stockholder rights groups accuse many corporations of loading the board of directors with members whose loyalty may lie with management rather than the stockholders. A good example of what can happen in these situations occurred during the merger mania of the 1970s and 80s. Corporate leaders were given "golden parachutes" so that if the company was taken over by outside interests the executives would walk away with huge severance settlements.

A board of directors that was more sympathetic to management than shareholders might fight a merger that was good for the stockholders, but bad for management.

JUST A MINUTE

Most voting at annual meetings is done by mail, although as a stockholder of even one share you are entitled to attend the annual meeting in person.

Some corporations, with the approval of the board of directors, pay *dividends*. Dividends represent a share of the company's profit returned to the stockholders (owners). Other companies choose to invest profits back into the organization to finance growth.

Even though you own part of a corporation, you have no liability for the company's actions beyond the value of your stock.

PROCEED WITH CAUTION

Your liability is limited to the value of the stock; however, officers of the corporation may be held personally liable in some situations where they took actions that were illegal or knew of illegal activity within the company, but failed to do anything about it.

For example, if you own some stock in XYZ Corporation and read in the newspaper that they have been found guilty of hurting small puppies, your only potential loss is the value of your stock, which may drop to next to nothing; however, you are not going to be sued personally by puppy lovers.

This "liability shield" is the cornerstone of investor confidence in the stock market.

Why Invest in Common Stock?

The only reason to own stock in an individual company is to participate in anticipated growth of that company. The participation can come in the form of dividends or increased stock value, or both. Hopefully, this translates to more dollars for you and the other stockholders.

Over time, an investment in stocks has proven the best choice for financial success. Notice the *time* caveat. The economy and the stock market move through natural, but unpredictable cycles of growth and recession. Although both are subject to cycles, the stock market may cycle for different reasons and different times than the economy. The stock market's cycles are called "bull" and "bear." Bull markets are marked by periods of growth and expansion, while bear markets are noted for retreats and decline in stock prices and market indexes.

JUST A MINUTE

An investment in the stock of a quality company has proven the consistently superior choice. However, if you buy a dog of a company and hold it for a long time you will probably just own an old dog.

There are plenty of investments with limited windows of opportunity that have made the lucky few rich. Oil, gold, silver, and real estate, to name a few, have all had their huge run ups and equally spectacular crashes.

For those who knew when to get in and when to get out, fortunes were made. Of course, if a frog had wings it wouldn't bump its rump every time it hopped. "If" is a mighty powerful word.

Buying quality stocks at reasonable prices and holding them for long periods is a formula for success, but it is not a guarantee for success. Almost all companies go through periods of ups and downs for a variety of reasons: market cycles, economic cycles, competitive cycles, etc.

How Stocks Are Priced

An individual stock is priced according to many considerations. The company's history, its market position, its future prospects, and financial structure are all analyzed and a "fair market" price emerges.

How the price actually emerges is a bit simpler than that. A stock, any stock, is worth what someone is willing to pay for it. If you think the stock is worth $50 and I think it is worth $52, you will probably sell it to me at the stock's price of $52. Reverse the numbers and the price drops.

PROCEED WITH CAUTION

The stock market is said to be "efficient" in that everyone knows the same thing at the same time. It's not quite that simple, but it also doesn't take into account how you react to the information. If two investors have the same information at the same time, the difference between a successful investor and the other who is not is the ability to see not only the short-term implications of the information, but the long-term consequences too.

The market sets the price each time a stock is traded. Newspapers report the stock's price at the market close. That does not mean the stock will open at that price the next day. Investors are constantly reassessing the value of a stock and setting the price they want to buy or sell at.

Obviously, news can change those assessments rapidly. Often bad news, whether it is about the company or the economy, is reported after the market closes. Armed with new information, an investor who wanted to buy at $50 the evening before may now feel the stock is only worth $45 per share. If enough investors feel this way, the stock will open markedly lower from the afternoon before.

GO TO ▶
See Hour 20, "Conservative/Low Cost Investing," for information on how you can buy stock in small amounts using DIPs and DRIPs. DIPs, or direct investment programs, and DRIPs, or dividend reinvestment programs, are programs to buy stock without using a broker.

Stocks are normally bought in *round lots* of 100 shares. You can buy stock in quantities not divisible by 100, but you may pay a premium in commissions and not get the price you hoped to get.

What Are Preferred Stocks?

Preferred stock is a special class of stock that has additional rights attached to it. These special rights are usually related to dividends and who gets paid first.

If you are counting on dividends to cover living expenses in your retirement, you may want to consider preferred stocks.

There are other classes of stock, and you will see these noted in the stock tables in your newspaper. Most of these classes were created to accommodate a merger or acquisition where stock was used in the transaction.

With a very few exceptions, common stock is probably your best bet.

MUTUAL FUNDS

A mutual fund is characterized as a pool of money managed by professionals with specific investment goals and objectives. These goals and objectives drive the investment decisions of the professional managers.

Everything you want to know about the fund is found in a document called a *prospectus*. Reading a prospectus is about as much fun as clipping your toenails—necessary, but not likely to stir your soul.

INVESTMENT GOALS AND OBJECTIVES

Every mutual fund has a well-defined set of goals and objectives. These allow investors to choose the type of fund that fits their particular investment strategy. Fund managers cannot deviate from these stated objectives.

JUST A MINUTE

Mutual funds often are named with an eye to marketing rather than being an accurate description of the fund. For example, ACME Mutual Funds might offer a fund called "American Stock Growth Fund." However, when you read the prospectus you discover that 40 percent of the fund is in bonds. Investing in bonds is not a growth strategy.

There are many varieties and flavors of mutual funds. In later chapters we will examine them more closely, but for now, let's broadly classify them:

- Stock funds—mainly invest in common stocks
- Bond funds—mainly invest in bonds
- Combination funds—may invest in both stocks and bonds
- Money market funds—mainly invest in cash instruments

These funds can be further broken down as taxable and tax-free funds, and again by whether the fund is actively managed or an index fund.

If you are getting a mental image of a massive grid filled in with many different combinations of funds, you are right on target. However, it is not as confusing as it may seem at this point.

Right now, we are stepping back and looking at the big picture. In later chapters, we will focus on the main types of mutual funds and this will all seem much clearer.

PERFORMANCE HISTORY

The prospectus will also provide a section with some history on the fund and how it has performed in the past. How big and prominent this section is will depend on how proud the managers are of past performance.

In this section you will also find a disclaimer that says something to the effect that "past performance is no guarantee of future success." While this is true, looking at past performance can be helpful.

PROCEED WITH CAUTION

 Past performance may not point to future winners, but it will tag future losers. A poor performance history does not inspire future confidence.

Frequently, the fund will show its performance relative to the S&P 500 index. If they exceed the S&P 500, they are said to have "beat the market." Funds that fall below this mark will try desperately to put some kind of positive spin on their history.

When we discuss picking a mutual fund, we will go into detail about how to use this information in making your decision.

MANAGEMENT

Many analysts believe that the management of a mutual fund is the single most important consideration when picking a fund. The fund manager is responsible for making the buy and sell decisions for the fund.

JUST A MINUTE

Avoid looking at short-term performance. Anyone can get lucky once. Look for consistent performance over a long period.

Their ability to do this with consistent success means they are well known in the business and handsomely rewarded. One of the markers analysts look for is how long the current management has been in place and what past success or failure occurred on their watch. A recent change in management may signal a performance change.

INVESTMENT STRATEGIES

Mutual funds follow two basic investment strategies: active management and indexing.

This is an important part of the prospectus because it tells you what to expect in the way of portfolio turnover and potential tax liabilities.

ACTIVE MANAGEMENT

An active management strategy means the manager will buy and sell stocks and/or bonds in a proactive attempt to stay ahead of the market (i.e., the S&P 500). This strategy can result in spectacular gains or losses depending on the skill and luck of the manager. It can also generate extraordinary tax liabilities when profits are made.

INDEXING

An index fund, on the other hand, seeks to match the market's performance by mimicking the index. For example, an index fund focused on the S&P 500 will hold a portfolio of stocks that the manager believes is a proxy for the underlying stocks of the index. The fund will then, theoretically, move in tandem with the index. There are index funds for many different indexes and they number in the hundreds.

GO TO ▶
See Hour 9, "Mutual Funds—Part I Classifications," for a more complete explanation of index funds.

Index funds tend to have lower costs and tax liabilities because there is less *churning* (buying and selling) of the portfolio.

SALES FEES

The fund is charged a fee to cover administrative costs (salaries, record keeping, etc.) and marketing by the management company. Funds are divided into two groups according to their fee structure: load and no-load.

LOADED FUNDS

Loaded funds have a sales fee or commission that is paid to the person who sold you the fund. Unless you owe your brother-in-law, the broker, a lot of money, there are not many good reasons to buy a loaded fund.

No-load

No-load funds have no sales fee or commission, but they are not free, either. You still have to pay for administrative and marketing expenses, but these should run about 1.5 percent or less of your assets.

Pricing a Mutual Fund

Mutual funds are priced differently than individual stocks. Stocks have a price, which you multiply times 100 (or some other round lot) and that is your investment, excluding commissions and fees.

Mutual funds are sold based on a number called the *net asset value* (N.A.V.). The net asset value is calculated at the market close every day. This number roughly relates to a "share" price with the exception that you can own fractions of shares and there is no round lot constraint.

For example, a mutual fund has a N.A.V. of $39.75. If you open an account with $2,000, you have bought 50.31 "shares." The next week the fund's N.A.V. is $41.25. Your stake in the fund is now worth $2,075.29. Here is a table for those of you who like charts:

# Shares	N.A.V.	$ Worth
50.31	$39.75	$2,000.00
50.31	$41.25	$2,075.29

Thus, you have "earned" $75.29 in a week. If you sell, this isn't a bad return (actually, 196 percent on an annual basis).

Mutual funds have a minimum opening deposit that can range from several thousand dollars to a couple of hundred. Many mutual funds can be opened as an IRA account for less than the stated minimum. Most will let you set up a direct debit from your checking account to the fund every month. The money market funds usually offer check-writing privileges (see the section "Money Market Accounts" later in this Hour for more information).

Getting your money out of a mutual fund is usually an easy and quick matter involving the redemption of all or part of your investment. You can often do this by telephone and expect a check within a few working days. Mutual funds are often part of a "family of funds" which allows you to switch from one fund to another member of the family.

This liquidity makes mutual funds very attractive, since you can cash out quickly in an emergency. *Liquidity* refers to how fast or slow an investment can be converted into cash.

When you sell an individual stock, it is to another investor. When you redeem part or all of your mutual fund investment, it is bought back by the fund.

BONDS AND CASH EQUIVALENTS

Bonds. James Bonds.

Sorry, I couldn't resist. Bonds are boring, in my opinion. I have a hard time finding a good use for them other than parking money for short (less than five years) periods. Nevertheless, they are an important investment tool worthy of our consideration. We will look at them in more depth in later chapters and show you ways to use them effectively.

Bonds are a loan to a governmental unit or corporation. They normally do not have any ownership rights. Bonds are used to finance a variety of projects for the government and corporations.

U.S. TREASURY BONDS

The U.S. government borrows money through bonds it auctions off or issues. U.S. government bonds are the safest investment you can make. Bonds are backed by the "full faith and credit" of the U.S. government and are free of state income tax.

If the only consideration is safety, these bonds are your best investment. However, as we will learn in a later chapter, this safety comes with a price. The yields are at the bottom of the stack.

U.S. Treasury Bonds are sold in a variety of denominations starting at $1,000, and are actually called three different names depending on the length of maturity:

- Treasury bills mature within one year
- Treasury notes mature between one and ten years
- Treasury bonds mature in more than ten years

U.S. Bonds play an important role in our economy for several reasons. First, the federal government uses bonds to finance the difference between what it collects in taxes and its expenses. Secondly, many Americans are more intimately touched by the market for U.S. Treasury Bonds. Many commercial loans and residential mortgages are tied to the U.S. Treasury Bond rate. When that rate goes up, so does the interest consumers pay on a variety of loans.

OTHER GOVERNMENTAL BONDS

A number of other governmental agencies issue bonds for a variety of reasons, including financing mortgages and student loans. State and municipal governments issue bonds to finance highway construction, dams, and other large projects. These bonds are usually free from federal income tax and state income tax in the state where they are issued.

CORPORATE BONDS

GO TO ▶
See Hour 14, "Bonds," for a complete discussion of the risks associated with different types of bonds.

Companies issue bonds to finance operations and to make large acquisitions. The interest paid by corporate bonds is fully taxable by local, state, and U.S. governments.

They are priced in part on the creditworthiness of the company. Junk bonds offer very high yields, but have a corresponding high risk of default.

Some corporate bonds can be *called*, which means the company can buy them back before maturity. This can play havoc with your plans if you are not careful. For example, you often buy a bond to meet a known upcoming expense (college tuition). If the bond is called before its maturity, you will have to buy another bond to replace it. If the bond market has exploded since you bought the original bond, you may find yourself short of money to buy a replacement.

Other corporate bonds are *convertible bonds*, meaning under certain circumstances they can be converted into stock in the company.

CASH EQUIVALENTS

Cash equivalents are those instruments that serve as short-term parking places for cash. They are discussed in the following sections.

MONEY MARKET ACCOUNTS

I have included money market accounts here, even though they are also mutual funds because they are designed as short-term holding strategies for excess cash. They differ from regular mutual funds in that they only invest in other cash instruments.

Money market accounts typically pay more interest than regular savings accounts, although not enough to warrant leaving large sums of money in them for extended periods. If you keep an emergency cash reserve, a money market account would be a good choice.

They offer check-writing privileges, although most have some restrictions. One way people use them is to keep only enough money in their regular checking account to cover their monthly expenses. They will often deposit all their income into the money market account and then write themselves one check to cover all the bills.

JUST A MINUTE

Money market funds usually offer a better rate of return than savings accounts and have check-writing privileges.

Many stock brokerages will offer access to a money market account as a place to park uninvested cash temporarily. For example, if you sell a stock and intend to invest the money in another stock, but are waiting for your price, you might park your cash in a money market account.

CASH MANAGEMENT ACCOUNTS

Cash management accounts are similar in function to money market accounts, but they are not mutual funds. Brokers typically offer them as a service to high-end investors.

The accounts have check-writing privileges and a debit card to access ATM networks for cash. They sometimes utilize a "sweep" feature that will automatically move uninvested cash into an interest-bearing account and back into the checking account when needed.

BANK CERTIFICATES OF DEPOSIT (CDs)

Certificates of deposit are accounts offered by banks that pay a higher interest rate than regular savings accounts in exchange for the depositor locking up his or her money for a period of time.

They are insured (up to $100,000) by the Federal Deposit Insurance Corporation (FDIC), which is part of the federal government. You have probably seen the "Insured by FDIC" signs in your local bank. About the only reason to use CDs is if this insurance is important to you. They also might be of limited value if you knew you needed a certain sum of money on a certain date in the future.

If your child needs a college tuition payment in September, it might make sense to park that money short term (one year or less) in a CD that would mature on or before the date tuition is due.

As a long-term (one year or more) strategy, they don't make much sense except in very rare cases. For instance, back in the 70s when inflation was high and the interest rates on CDs were in the double digits, keeping your money in a CD was common.

REGULAR SAVINGS ACCOUNTS

I haven't even mentioned regular savings accounts. There are too many other places to put your money that would be more profitable. However, I would urge parents to consider opening a savings account for each of your young children as a learning tool.

JUST A MINUTE

Open a savings account for your children and let them deposit a portion of their allowance, chore money, gifts, and so on in the account every month. This will get them into the habit of saving money and even help with planning for purchases. It is amazing to see the wheels of decision grinding in your children's heads when they realize that to buy a CD player, for example, they have to take money out of their *own* account—not Mom and Dad's.

Make a point of taking them to the bank on a regular basis and depositing some of their allowance, chore money, or gifts. You can't start too early getting them in the savings habit.

OTHER INVESTMENT INSTRUMENTS

There are a number of other investment instruments besides stocks, bonds, mutual funds, and cash equivalents. They range from the obscure to the dangerously risky. We will touch on some of them briefly here and expand on the more common ones in coming chapters.

ANNUITIES

Annuities are contracts with life insurance companies guaranteeing a certain payout at or over a certain period of time. These contracts contain a death benefit that ensures your beneficiary will be paid a certain amount.

Annuities have a benefit of accumulating tax deferred. This may make them attractive to a person in a high income tax bracket who has maxed out on the amount of money that can be sheltered in a retirement account. However, contributions are not tax deductible. If you are in this situation, you should consider contacting a financial planning professional (fee-based only) for help with more sophisticated tax strategies than I can discuss here. Tax-free bonds and mutual funds can provide some tax-free income, but no deduction.

JUST A MINUTE

Annuities can be used to provide regular income for a relative with special health needs. They are frequently used in estates to provide for the relative's care.

The fees to cover the death benefit make the annuity an expensive investment for short-term consideration. Annuities have some specialized uses that make sense, but as a pure investment there are better alternatives.

REAL ESTATE LIMITED PARTNERSHIPS

Real estate–limited partnerships are investment organizations of investors that pool money to invest in income-producing real estate such as office buildings and shopping centers. If they are open to the public, they must be registered with the Securities and Exchange Commission and follow rigid offering requirements. Private partnerships are offered to a very few well-heeled individuals and normally don't have to be registered.

Public real estate partnerships have not been as popular recently as in the past. The ones sold through brokers are usually loaded with heavy commissions. While offering some significant returns and potential tax advantages, limited partnerships suffer from two problems:

- There are better, safer investments available.
- They are very *illiquid*, meaning that if you need to get out of one, it might be difficult at best.

If you want to invest in real estate, consider the next investment instrument, Real Estate Investment Trusts.

REAL ESTATE INVESTMENT TRUSTS (REITS)

Real Estate Investment Trusts are something like mutual funds for real estate. They are pools of money managed by professionals who invest in commercial real estate projects.

REITs differ significantly from limited partnerships, most noticeably in their liquidity. They are sold as securities on major stock exchanges and therefore have corresponding liquidity. They can be included in a qualified retirement account and let you participate in the real estate market without the dangers and hassles of limited partnerships or direct ownership.

JUST A MINUTE

Real estate and precious metals funds have been in the dumpster for several years. There are too many other good investments, like stocks, bonds, and mutual funds that are attracting investment dollars.

It is also possible to buy a mutual fund that invests in REITs, making it even easier to participate in real estate.

PRECIOUS METALS

People have had a fascination with gold for centuries. Even today, when the winds of inflation start to blow, people turn to gold for security. There are several ways you can invest in gold and precious metals:

- Direct ownership through bullion or coins, but you have to pay someone to store it for you.

- Mining company stocks have been attractive one day and in the toilet the next as the price of the metal they're mining rises or falls.

- Mutual funds that invest in mining stocks and other related industries are probably the safest way to invest in precious metals, but their performance has been spotty at best.

Not many years ago, most financial professionals recommended a small percentage of every investor's portfolio be dedicated to gold or precious metals. Now almost nobody is recommending gold.

BULLS AND BEARS

No one is sure where the terms "bulls" and "bears" came from, but they are among the most commonly understood terms by the general public.

People may not know much about the stock market, but they do know that a bull market is good and a bear market is bad. However, savvy investors would not share that assessment.

Investors who look beyond the obvious will find ways to profit, no matter which way the market is moving. In the first place, there are many stocks that will drop in a bull market and many stocks that will rise in a bear market. The terms describe a general direction of the market, not the fate of every listed stock.

Investors in the know will look at bear markets as bargain shopping opportunities and bull markets as time to let the profits run. The important lesson about the bulls and the bears is that for the individual investor they are basically meaningless.

WHAT CAN YOU DO?

The following is a list of five things you can do today:

1. Make a schedule of how much time you are willing to spend on your investments. One hour a day? Three hours a week? This will be helpful later on as we look at ways to manage your investments. This number may change as you gain knowledge about the financial world.

2. Review your most recent income tax return. Determine your tax bracket. (There is a guide to this in Appendix B, "Resources.") Do you need to shelter more of your income? Are you itemizing or taking the standard deduction? Write a "tax profile" of yourself.

3. If you have a 401(k) plan with your employer, dig out the information about the account and what investment options you have within the plan. You should also be getting periodic statements, which will show how your contributions are being allocated. Hold onto this; we will need it later.

4. If you have an IRA, get a copy of the most recent statement and add it to the list of documents for later review.

5. If you are eligible for an IRA but don't currently have one, see what a $2,000 deduction to your gross income would have meant on your last tax return.

WORKSHOP

In preparation for work in future hours, begin constructing your personal balance sheet. A balance sheet lists assets and liabilities and is helpful in determining where you stand financially. Here is the information you need to collect:

Assets

Fair market value of your home:

Current value of retirement account:

Current value of other investments:

Cash value of life insurance:

Cash in savings, checking, etc.

Liabilities

Mortgage on house:

Credit card debts:

Automobile loans:

Other loans:

Net worth (Assets–Liabilities):

This is a very simplistic balance sheet that doesn't adequately cover all assets and liabilities, but our purpose is to get down on paper the major categories. In the resource section of the book, there are more complete examples.

HOUR'S UP!

You have been introduced to a large number of investment instruments this hour. Let's see how well you remember some of the more important ones.

1. Common stock is best suited for …

   A. Short-term goals.

   B. Retired schoolteachers.

   C. Long-term investors.

2. A share of stock is worth …

   A. More than you paid for it.

   B. What the market says.

   C. Less than you paid for it.

3. A mutual fund prospectus contains all of these except …

   A. Performance history.

   B. Fees.

   C. Investment strategies.

   D. The investment manager's home phone number.

4. Bond funds may be …

  A. Tax-free from federal income tax.

  B. Tax-free from state and local tax.

  C. Tax-free in specific states.

  D. All of the above.

5. Mutual fund shares are different from stock shares …

  A. Because they can be sold in fractions.

  B. They are priced every time they are bought or sold.

  C. They always go up.

6. A loaded mutual fund is …

  A. A fund with a sales fee.

  B. A fund with heavy investments.

  C. A fund with no sales fee.

7. Corporate bonds are used to …

  A. Avoid issuing more stock.

  B. Avoid high commercial lending costs.

  C. Finance expansion and acquisitions.

  D. All of the above.

8. Money market accounts …

  A. Pay a higher interest than regular savings.

  B. Can be used to invest long term.

  C. Are the best place to put cash you don't need right away.

9. An annuity …

  A. Is an investment with a death benefit attached.

  B. Is well-suited for investors with limited cash.

  C. Is taxed every step of the way.

10. Real estate is often a good investment …

  A. For busy people.

  B. If you may need to get your money out in a hurry.

  C. During times of rising inflation.

Quiz

PART II

Doing the Research

HOUR 5

Existing Benefits Review

CHAPTER SUMMARY

LESSON PLAN:

In this Hour you will learn about ...

- Stock options.
- Direct investment plans.
- Qualified retirement plans.
- Defined contribution plans.
- 401(k) plans.
- IRAs and Roth IRAs.
- SEP-IRAs.
- The importance of beginning early.

Before we spend a lot of time gazing over the fence at a greener pasture, let's be sure we are taking advantage of every tool we already have or can easily acquire.

Most of the financial benefits offered by employers are related to retirement. There are a couple that are not necessarily tied to a retirement plan that, if available, you should consider.

STOCK OPTIONS

The term "stock options" has an almost mystical quality about it. Not too many years ago, stock options were reserved for senior management and were seen as an incentive to spur performance and to retain key managers.

Now the Internet economy has given new meaning to the term. Many Internet startups rewarded employees in the very early days with stock options in lieu of big salaries. Consequently, if you worked for a company like Microsoft or America Online, you made millions (or billions) in stock profits.

We have all heard those stories. However, what we don't hear about are about employees who labor in a startup for years collecting stock options only to have the company go belly up and the options prove worthless.

So, should you take advantage of stock options if they are offered? That depends. If you have a choice between stock options and some other benefit, you will have to weigh the relative merits of each.

The bottom line is that stock options are only as valuable as the underlying stock. At any rate, don't tie up all of your investment assets in one company, even the one you work for.

DIRECT INVESTMENT PLANS (DIPs)

GO TO ▶
See Hour 20, "Conservative/Low Cost Investing," for an expanded discussion of DIPs and their cousins, DRIPs (Dividend Reinvestment Plans).

Direct investment plans allow you to buy stock directly from the company in small monthly deposits. These programs are also available to the public.

This is a great way to buy stock without paying broker fees. Like stock options above, don't plan on spending all your investment dollars with one company.

RETIREMENT PLANS

A financially secure retirement is the most common reason people invest. Medical advances are allowing us to live longer and be more active. This means we need to plan for an extended retirement, something that was not a problem several generations ago.

If you are about 25 years old and don't have any high-risk hobbies or habits, you can probably plan on needing about 20 years' worth of retirement savings. Even in today's dollars, that is a fairly big chunk of change.

We'll look at retirement planning in more depth later, but for right now I want to inventory some of the tools you can use.

QUALIFIED RETIREMENT PLANS

Qualified retirement plans are authorized by the Internal Revenue Service and must adhere to certain rules and regulations. These rules aren't especially onerous, but break them and you could face a big tax bill and stiff penalties. The plans can be offered through an employer or you can start one on your own.

PROCEED WITH CAUTION

 Pretax dollar contributions reduce your current tax liability, but if you violate the rules the IRS will want its tax—and then some.

There are several benefits to qualified retirement plans that make them attractive for employers and employees.

EMPLOYEES

Employees may contribute to the plans in pretax dollars. This means your contribution comes out of your paycheck before taxes are applied.

EXAMPLE 1

If your paycheck is $1,500 you are hit with Social Security, Medicare, and federal and state withholding taxes before you get you arrive at your take-home pay. To keep the math simple, assume that figure comes to 25 percent of your gross pay of $1,500. Here's the math:

$1,500   gross pay

($375)   taxes—25 percent

$1,125   take-home pay

EXAMPLE 2

Now suppose you invested 10 percent of your pay in a qualified retirement plan. Here's the math:

$1,500   gross pay

($150)   retirement contribution—10 percent

$1,350   adjusted gross

($337.50)   taxes—25 percent

$1,012.50   take-home pay

Now let's see where we stand:

	Taxes	Take-Home Pay	Retirement Account
Example 1	$375.00	$1,125.00	$0.00
Example 2	$337.50	$1,012.50	$150.00
Difference	($37.50)	($112.50)	$150.00

How did we do? Your tax bill has been reduced by $37.50 and your retirement account has increased by $150, giving you a benefit of $187.50 per check. Your cost was only $112.50 (the lower take-home pay amount).

And the goodies don't stop there. The $150 you put into the qualified retirement account grows tax deferred, meaning neither it nor the interest it earns is taxed until it is withdrawn after you are 59½ years of age. Withdraw it before then and you will face stiff penalties in most circumstances.

If you have a qualified retirement account with an employer and leave for another job, the money and earnings in the account can often be "rolled over" into another qualified account, again deferring taxes. There are severe penalties for taking money out of a retirement account, such as tax on all of your earnings, plus a 10 percent penalty. When you move from one company to another or want to move your retirement account to a different broker, you are not penalized if you reinvest the money before 60 days have passed in another qualified retirement account. This is called "rolling over" your account.

See Example 3 in the 401(k) section later in this Hour for an example of a company that matches your IRA contributions.

EMPLOYERS

Employers can deduct the amount, if any, they contribute to an employee's plan. Sponsoring a retirement plan also encourages workers to stay with a company.

NONQUALIFIED RETIREMENT PLANS

As the name states, the IRS doesn't qualify *nonqualified retirement plans*. Most of these plans are used to reward top management and generally lack any of the tax benefits. You should seek professional tax advice before becoming involved in one of these plans.

TYPES OF QUALIFIED RETIREMENT PLANS

There are several types of retirement plans that meet the IRS requirements for qualified plans. These plans differ in how they are set up and administered as well as how contributions are handled, but all still qualify for the benefits listed above (although withdrawals may be handled differently).

We will examine these plans in detail later in the book. Right now, I want to give you an overview of what is available to employees—and self-employed folks, also. These plans are divided into two groups: defined contribution plans and defined benefit plans.

DEFINED CONTRIBUTION PLANS

Defined contribution plans are plans where the contribution is specified, but the ultimate benefit is not. Who contributes and how much is contributed to the plan characterize these plans.

Unlike their counterpart, the ultimate benefit paid by a defined contribution plan at retirement depends on a number of factors, including the amount and timing of contributions and appreciation over the life of the plan.

Most of the responsibility for the ultimate benefit is assumed by the employee, who may have the responsibility for picking the investment vehicles used in the plan from a limited selection offered by the employer. This is a radical departure from the traditional defined benefit plans discussed below.

Plans Offered by Employers

The following sections cover some of the more popular defined contribution plans offered by employers.

401(k) Plans

The term *401(k)* refers to the section of the IRS code that authorized the plans. Count on the IRS to come up with those snappy marketing names. These plans have grown rapidly from their authorization in 1978.

TIME SAVER

Employee-sponsored retirement plans have the added benefit of making your contributions painless by deducting them from your paycheck before you ever receive the money.

Employers like 401(k)s because a third party can administer them and employees bear a large share of the responsibility. They are attractive benefits, and some employers even match part of the employee's contribution.

Why would employers match part of their employees' contribution? It could be because they are genuinely concerned with their employees' welfare. It could be because it is a way to help retain valuable employees. The truth, for many employers, is a little more self-serving than that.

GO TO ▶
See Hour 23, "Retirement Planning," for more information on qualified retirement plans.

The IRS monitors retirement plans closely looking for ones that benefit the higher paid executives over rank and file employees. One of the tests that is used involves what percentage of the employees participate in the program.

If the IRS found a retirement program where 100 percent of the executives participated and only 10 percent of the other employees participated, they could conclude the plan was discriminatory.

Matching part of their employees' contributions helps increase the participation and avoids nasty notes from the IRS.

Employees like them because they have some control in deciding how their money is invested. Employees also like the fact that if they change jobs, the plan's assets can come with them if they are rolled over into another qualified retirement plan.

This type of plan is one of the best investment vehicles for your retirement and, if your employer contributes to your plan, there is none better. If you are not participating in a company-sponsored 401(k) plan or if you are not participating to the maximum, run, don't walk, to your employer and sign up for the maximum.

EXAMPLE 3

If for every $1 you put into your 401(k), your company will put a certain percent, it is like making free money—so do it! If your company offers this type of program and matches at 50 percent, this translates to the following (when compared with the examples given earlier in this Hour):

	Taxes	Take-Home Pay	Retirement Account
Example 1	$375.00	$1,125.00	$0.00
Example 2	$337.50	$1,012.50	$150.00
Example 3	$337.50	$1,012.50	$150.00 + $75.00
Difference	($37.50)	($112.50)	$225.00

So, along with the $150 you added to your retirement account, your employer matched 50 percent of your dollars, equaling an additional $75, for a total of $225.

You can't beat free money. This money doesn't come out of your paycheck and isn't taxed. If your company offers a matching amount, be sure you at least fund your account with the minimum to qualify for all the free money.

There is one little fly in the ointment, however. You don't qualify for the free money from day one. Remember, I said earlier that employers like to use these plans to retain valuable employees? One of the ways they do this is to require you to work a certain amount of time before you receive the full benefit of their matching dollars. This is called *vesting* and it usually involves setting a schedule before you receive full benefit.

Companies vary in how they implement vesting; some take three years, while others may stretch it out over five years.

Others might vest you full all at once after three years. Check with your human resources office for details. One important item you need to know: No matter how long you work at a company, all the money you put in is yours.

403(B) PLANS

Like their cousin the 401(k), *403(b)* plans are tax-sheltered or tax-deferred annuity plans; they are offered to nonprofit religious, educational, and charitable organizations as defined by the IRS code.

They differ from 401(k) plans in that they cannot invest in stocks, but only mutual funds and annuities. Under certain conditions, participants can contribute more annually than they could in a 401(k) plan.

PROCEED WITH CAUTION

Profit-sharing plans are very attractive, but the employer is under no obligation to fund them even if the company makes a profit.

PROFIT-SHARING PLANS

Profit-sharing plans are used to allow employees to participate in the profits of the company by passing a percentage along to the employee's retirement account.

They are popular with employees because the employer makes all the contributions. These plans are sometimes used with other plans such as 401(k) plans to allow the employee to make pretax contributions.

Employers are generally not required to make a contribution in any year, regardless of profitability.

EMPLOYEE STOCK OWNERSHIP PLANS

Employee stock ownership plans (ESOPs) use company stock to fund a retirement account for employees based on the employee's compensation.

A defined contribution plan, ESOPs may also be combined with a 401(k) plan. The ESOP benefit is determined by the price of the stock, which can be taken with a departing employee or cashed in.

PLANS FOR INDIVIDUALS

The following sections cover some of the more popular defined contribution plans offered for individuals.

INDIVIDUAL RETIREMENT ACCOUNTS

GO TO ▶
See Hour 23, "Retirement Planning," for a complete discussion of IRAs and how you can use them.

Individual retirement accounts (IRAs) are defined contribution plans for individuals who receive taxable income and are not covered by an employer-sponsored plan.

In most cases, contributions to an IRA are deductible up to $2,000 per year. Earnings in the account are tax deferred until withdrawn after age $59^1/_2$. Like other qualified plans, an early withdrawal may cause the distribution to be taxed as ordinary income, plus incur a hefty penalty payment from the IRS.

If you are covered by an employer-sponsored qualified plan, you may not deduct your IRA contribution; however, if your spouse is covered and you are not, you may take an IRA deduction. There are exceptions for people who are covered by an employer-sponsored plan and have adjusted gross incomes (AGI) under certain limits. Here are those AGI limits for 2000:

Filing Status	Deduction reduced	Deduction eliminated
Single or head of household	$32,000 to $42,000	$42,000 or more
Married—joint return or qualifying widow	$52,000 to $62,000	$62,000 or more
Married—separate return	$0 to $10,000	$10,000 or more

ROTH IRA

The Roth IRA is the new kid on the block and causing quite a stir. Contributions and distributions to the *Roth IRA* are handled differently from its cousins. The annual contribution is not tax deductible, meaning there is no immediate tax benefit. The real kicker is that the account and its earnings are free of taxes not only as it is growing, but when you begin taking distributions.

There are some income limits. Single filers must have an AGI of $95,000 or less to make the full $2,000 contribution and $150,000 or less for joint filers.

The Roth IRA is not for everybody, but it does offer some attractive benefits. Later in the book we'll go over the details so you can decide if this particular retirement account makes sense for you.

KEOGH PLANS

Keogh plans are designed for self-employed people, partnerships, or owners of unincorporated businesses. A Keogh may be a defined benefit plan or a defined contribution plan.

Contribution limits are the lesser of 25 percent of taxable income or $30,000, and the lesser of 20 percent of taxable income or $30,000 for employee-owners. Distributions generally follow the usual rules against early withdrawal and may be rolled over into an IRA. Loans are not permitted.

SIMPLIFIED EMPLOYEE PENSIONS

Simplified employee pensions (SEP) are qualified retirement plans designed for the self-employed, partnerships, and unincorporated businesses. Basically, these plans establish and fund IRAs for each employee, and thus are also known as SEP-IRAs.

Even though SEP-IRAs are targeted at the groups mentioned above, any business can establish one. Under these plans, the employee owns the IRA and controls it completely. The employer may or may not make contributions, but all employees must be treated equally.

Employers like SEP-IRA plans because they are easy to set up and administer, and employer contributions are not mandated. All the regular IRA rules regarding funding limits and distributions apply.

DEFINED BENEFIT PLAN

A *defined benefit plan* differs from the defined contribution plans listed previously in that it is the benefit that is targeted rather than the contribution. These are better known as traditional pension plans.

The retirement benefit is based on some formula which considers compensation, years of employment, and so on. The employer funds the plan and is responsible for it.

These plans are not as popular now that there are other alternatives. In addition, there have been some horror stories about pension funds being raided by the corporation, businesses folding, and leaving their employees with nothing, and so on.

Some forms of distributions from the plans may be rolled into an IRA and others may not. If you are approaching retirement and are covered by a defined benefit plan, seek professional tax advice about how to handle distributions.

THE IMPORTANCE OF STARTING EARLY

I cannot overstate the importance of starting early on your retirement plan. For most of us, this will be the single most important investing decision we will make. The longer you put off doing something about it, the harder it will be to reach your goal.

Later in the book, we will look at all the options above and go over specific investment choices and strategies. For right now, I want to highlight the consequences of putting off this decision. With any luck, I'll convince you that this is a deal you can't afford to pass up.

THE EARLY BIRD DOES GET THE WORM

Let's review the benefits of the qualified, defined contribution plans listed above:

- Immediate tax savings (in most cases) by reducing current taxable income
- Earnings grow in a tax-deferred environment
- Distributions (in most cases) taxed upon withdrawal at a presumably lower tax rate
- Under some plans your employer may make contributions to your account

What are the drawbacks of funding your retirement plan?

- Slightly lower take-home pay

This should be a no-brainer, right? Well, don't be too hard on yourself. The lure of immediate gratification is more than most of us can bear. However, I hope the following examples will help you make up your mind to get started now.

Suppose you are 25 years old and have just landed your first big job. What would happen if you signed up for a qualified plan and put $2,000 a year in until you retire at age 65? Assuming a 10 percent rate of return, the numbers would look like this:

Annual Contribution	Rate of Return	Years Invested	Retirement Value
$2,000	10 percent	40	$973,704

Now suppose you decide to buy a hot new sports car instead and a few other expenses come along; before you know it, you are 35 when you start investing. Look what happens to the numbers:

Annual Contribution	Rate of Return	Years Invested	Retirement Value
$2,000	10 percent	30	$361,886

Ouch! I hope the sports car was worth it. Delaying your investment decision 10 years cost you over $600,000. It gets worse. You're now 45 with a family and responsibilities, but you want a comfortable retirement. Sticking with our scenario, here's your account at age 45:

Annual Contribution	Rate of Return	Years Invested	Retirement Value
$2,000	10 percent	20	$126,000

JUST A MINUTE

The longer you wait to begin investing, the more you will have to invest to make up for the time you have lost.

You've gone from being a virtual millionaire at retirement to flipping burgers to supplement your retirement income. Not a pretty picture.

Of course, this is a simple example of the power of time and tax-deferred earnings to make you rich.

How can our 35-year-old match the 25-year-old's results? The number of years to invest is fixed and the rate of return will stay the same. The only other variable is the annual contribution. What would our 35-year-old have to invest on an annual basis to match the 25-year-old?

Annual Contribution	Interest Rate	Years Invested	Retirement Value
$5,380	10 percent	30	$973,700

Increasing the contribution to $5,380 will get our 35-year-old close to the target. In this case, succumbing to immediate gratification when you are 25 will cost you almost $300 per month for the next 30 years when you are 35. ($5,380–$2,000/12 = $282 per month.) To add insult to injury, our hero may not be able to put that much money away each year without overrunning his contribution limits on retirement plans. Then you're looking at annuities and other tax-advantaged investments with reduced earnings and no reduction of current taxes.

I'll admit that it is unlikely I'm going to convince many 25-year-olds that funding a retirement 40 years away is important. My long-range plan when I was 25 usually involved picking out a movie to see over the weekend.

Yet, I am pleasantly surprised by mail I receive from young people who are a lot more serious about their financial future than I was. Good for them.

Now, if you really want to get your socks blown off, look at this example.

Remember earlier when we discussed that some plans allow employers to make contributions to your account? Let's revisit our 25-year-old and see what happens when the employer kicks in 10 percent of the employee's contribution, or $200.

Annual Contribution	Interest Rate	Years Invested	Retirement Value
$2,200	10 percent	40	$1.07 million

The retirement value increases by 10 percent, or $111,200. Not a bad return, considering that our heroine didn't put any more of her money into the deal and the employer only put $8,000 over the life of the investment.

Could you use an extra $96,296 without lifting a finger?

These are very simplistic scenarios. I would hope that our 25-year-old friend would increase her participation every time she got a raise. This would dramatically improve all the preceding examples.

JUST A MINUTE

Always fund your IRA as soon as you can—January 1 in most cases. The longer your money earns interest, the more it will grow.

Even if she could only afford a 10 percent increase in her contribution every 5 years, that would earn her $165,000 extra for retirement.

Now let's look at a straight IRA example. We'll compare the fortunes of two 35-year-olds who open IRAs. One deposits the $2,000 annual contribution on January 1 for that year. The other deposits the $2,000 annual contribution on January 1 for the previous year. Under present law you can deposit your IRA contribution by April 15th of the next year and still claim the deduction.

Deposit Timing	Annual Contribution	Interest Rate	Years Invested	Retirement Value
	$2,000	10 percent	30	
Beginning				$361,900
End				$329,000
Difference				$32,900

They say that timing is everything. In this case, it may not be everything, but it is $32,900 and that's not bad.

WHAT CAN YOU DO?

The following is a list of five things you can do today:

1. If your employer is a publicly traded company, contact the appropriate department and see if the company offers a direct investment plan. If they do, request information about the details.

2. Find out if your employer offers a qualified retirement plan and what the requirements and limitations are if you are not already signed up.

3. If you are covered by a 403(b) plan, find out what options you have for your investments. You may have to request the information from the plan administrator.

4. If you are self-employed or the owner of a small, unincorporated business, consider establishing a SEP-IRA. Information sources are listed in the resource section in Appendix B, "Resources."

5. Check with the Human Relations Department at your company to see if there are other options for funding your retirement account. Ask about the possibility of putting any bonus directly into your retirement account, so you don't have to pay taxes on it. If you are already at or near the maximum contribution, this may not be possible.

WORKSHOP

Make a list of your existing benefits and assign a dollar value to them, either what you have invested through your retirement plan or what it would cost you to "buy" the benefit on the open market.

HOUR'S UP!

It is important that we not overlook existing tools that will help up achieve our investment goals. See if you captured the important messages this hour.

1. Stock options are …

   A. A great way to finance your entire retirement.

   B. The route to certain riches.

   C. Only as good as the underlying stock.

2. Qualified retirement plans allow …

   A. Your contributions and interest to grow free from current income taxes.

   B. You to quit work anytime you want.

   C. You to withdraw money anytime you want with no penalty.

3. Defined contribution plans …

   A. Specify what amount you are to receive upon retirement.

   B. Specify how much is to be contributed.

   C. Specify who is responsible if there is not enough money in the plan at retirement.

4. 401(k) plans are …

    A. Employer-sponsored, qualified retirement plans.

    B. Retirement plans for IRS agents.

    C. Usually not that good a deal.

5. IRAs are …

    A. Retirement plans for the Irish Republican Army.

    B. Available in numerous varieties.

    C. Allow you to contribute up to $5,000 per year.

6. You should begin funding your retirement plan …

    A. When you don't have anything else to buy.

    B. As soon as you start earning an income.

    C. No later than age 40.

7. Retirement plans in which the employer contributes to your plan are …

    A. A source of free money.

    B. In somebody's dreams.

    C. Of questionable value.

8. Profit-sharing plans are popular with employees because …

    A. The employer makes all the contributions.

    B. It's better than stealing office supplies.

    C. You always get something every year.

9. Roth IRAs are …

    A. Only for people named Roth.

    B. More complicated than regular IRAs.

    C. Compound at a higher rate.

10. You may begin taking withdrawals from an IRA without a penalty …

    A. When you need bifocals.

    B. At any age over 45.

    C. Not before age $59\frac{1}{2}$.

Quiz

HOUR 6

Understanding the Numbers

CHAPTER SUMMARY

LESSON PLAN:

In this Hour you will learn about ...

- Important investing numbers.
- Reading stock tables in the newspaper.
- Online stock/mutual fund information.
- Reading mutual fund tables in the newspaper.

Don't panic. Remain calm. Take deep breaths.

Yes, this hour is about math. But don't worry—it is not nearly as bad as you might fear. For the most part, the actual math has already been done for you. We'll zero in on what the numbers mean and how they can help you make better investment decisions.

So relax and have some fun with this hour of math and numbers. There will be a test at the end—but don't stress!

THE NUMBERS

There are a few basic mathematical expressions you need to get comfortable with to navigate the investment waters. These may not be 100 percent accurate mathematical definitions, but for us lay people who don't know a logarithm from a prime number, they will do.

RATIO

A *ratio* is simply a relationship between two related items. The price to earnings ratio (P/E), which we will discuss later this Hour, is a way to compare to companies in the same industry.

For example, when a company makes $5 in sales for every $1 spent on marketing, you could say they have a marketing/sales ratio of 5 (5/1 = 5). Another company may spend $1 in marketing, but only achieve $3 in sales.

Their marketing/sales ratio would be 3 (3/1 = 3). Now you have a way to compare the two companies in marketing efficiency.

INDEX

An *index* is another way to measure activity. We have already talked about some of the major indexes (Dow, S&P 500, and so on) and how they work. An index is always tied to a beginning point. This point may be arbitrary.

For example, I could start the Little Stocks Nobody Ever Heard of Index (LSNEHI—kind of rolls off your tongue, doesn't it?). On January 1, 2000, I set the index at 100. Then every day I measure the increase or decrease in the value of the stocks in this index and adjust the index accordingly. If the next day the LSNEHI stocks gained an average of $3.25 per share, I would report the index at 103.25.

JUST A MINUTE

Calculating an investment's yield is a way to compare two dissimilar products. This puts the companies on an even basis, since it is the yield you will ultimately receive.

YIELD

Yield is another way of saying return, and is usually expressed as a percentage. Although there are some more specific definitions when talking about bonds, yield for stocks means the percent returned to stockholders in dividends. The dividend yield is calculated by taking the company's dividend per share and dividing it by the current price per share.

For example, if a company's dividend is currently $1.50 per share and the stock price is $28 per share, the dividend yield is 5.35%:

$1.50 / $28 = 0.0535

WHERE TO LOOK FOR NUMBERS

There are a number of sources for obtaining financial and market information about a company.

NEWSPAPER STOCK TABLES

The stock tables in your daily newspaper contain a wealth of information about companies and their relative financial health. Unfortunately, these numbers are meaningless to most people without some deciphering.

1	2	3			6	7	8	9	10	11
52 Week		Stock			PE	Volume	High	Low	Close	Net
		Sym	iv	ld						
High	Low				Ratio					Change
7	3	BadDeal			9	16	6	6	6	+1
8.50	8.25	BAD		.11		367	4.25	3.00	4.25	.25

A typical listing you might find in The Wall Street Journal; *some newspapers do not include all of the columns.*

COLUMNS 1 & 2—52 WEEK HIGH & LOW

These columns give you a moving picture of the past 52 weeks of highs and lows for this stock. If there is a new high or low, there will be a corresponding arrow in the left margin. These columns tell you a couple of things. First, they give you an indication of whether the stock is trading near a recent high or low. Secondly, the spread between the high and the low indicate a degree of volatility. In this case, the company is relatively volatile, meaning there is a chance for you to make or lose a significant amount in a short period of time.

COLUMN 3—STOCK SYM

This column gives you the name of the company, often abbreviated. *The Wall Street Journal* also lists the symbol the company trades under. The New York Stock Exchange and American Stock Exchange use one to three letter symbols, while the NASDAQ uses four or five letters.

COLUMN 4—DIVIDEND

This column reports dividends. If a company pays no dividend, this column will be blank. In this case, the company will pay an estimated annual dividend of $2 per share. This means that for each share of stock you own, you will receive $2. Dividends are usually paid quarterly. If you owned 100 shares of this stock, you would receive a quarterly check for $50. Companies pay dividends as a way of returning some of their profits to the owners/shareholders.

COLUMN 5—PERCENT YIELD

GO TO ▶
See Hour 7, "Market News/Research," for sources of key numbers.

Percent yield is a way of measuring your return from this investment. If the company pays no dividend, this column will be blank. You compute the yield by dividing the dividend by the closing price. For example, $2/64.25 = 0.0311$ or 3.11 percent. This measure also gives you a way to compare a company's earnings with other investments.

COLUMN 6—P/E RATIO

P/E ratio stands for price/earnings ratio and is a way of measuring the relative value of a company's stock. The P/E is calculated by dividing the current price by the last year's earnings per share. The earnings per share number is not a part of the table reported in the newspaper. If a company reported negative earnings, the symbol "dd" will appear in this slot.

The number is helpful in evaluating companies in the same industry. If company A has a P/E of 12 and company B has a P/E of 35, an investor might conclude that company A was a better buy since it is trading close to its relative value. Company B is considered overpriced, since its earnings are much lower relative to its stock price.

P/E is a good number to understand, but it does not give a complete picture. First, the number reflects a historical value, not a forward estimate.

Secondly, there may be good reasons for a high P/E. Young, growing companies often report very poor earnings, but may have a bright future. Companies that don't have positive earnings may be poised on the brink of tremendous growth, or headed for the toilet.

COLUMN 7—VOLUME

Volume of shares traded is reported in hundreds. On this day, BadDeal had a volume of 1,636,700 shares. If the symbol "z" appears before the number, it means that the number reported is actual and not in the hundreds. *The Wall Street Journal* notes significant activity in a stock by underlining it.

COLUMN 8 & 9 & 10—HIGH, LOW, & CLOSE

These columns report the highest and lowest price paid for the stock, plus the closing price. You normally will not see a big spread between the high and low unless the market is reacting to some news that affects the company.

COLUMN 11—NET CHANGE

The *net change* is the difference between the closing price and the previous closing price. In our case, the stock was up $1.25.

NEWSPAPER MUTUAL FUND TABLES

Like stocks, mutual fund information is often reported in major daily newspapers. Although there seems to be a growing trend to print less information and not more, newspapers are still important sources for this information.

I will use a composite chart that includes the way *The Wall Street Journal* and other publications print mutual fund information.

1	2	3	4	5	6	7	8	9
	Inv.		Offer	NAV		- Total Return -		YTD
	Obj.	NAV	Price	Chg.	YTD	39 wks	5 yrs	percentret
BumDeal								
Gldsod	SEC	6.07	NL	-	+5.2	+13.2	+7.6	+22.6
p				-0.05				
Inpest	GRO	10.23	10.75	+0.1	+12.3	+22.1	+4.2	+18.3
r								

Not all publications will publish tables this complete—The Wall Street Journal entries are shaded.

COLUMN 1—NAMES AND FEES

The first column contains three pieces of information. The first is the mutual fund company's name, which appears in bold type. Next come the names of various funds managed by this company. I have listed only two in this example, but some companies manage numerous funds.

The third piece of information relates to the "p" following the name "Gldsod" and the "r" following the name "Inpest." These codes tell you about various fees charged by the funds. The "p" refers to what is known as *12b-1 fees*. These are fees the fund charges for marketing and distribution costs.

The "r" lets you know that the fund charges a fee for redeeming shares for cash. This is known as a *backend load*.

If there is a "t" after the name, you know that the fund charges both of the above fees.

GO TO ▶
See Hour 9, "Mutual Funds—Part I Classifications," for a complete discussion of various fees charged by mutual funds.

Column 2—Investment Objective

This three-letter code stands for the investment objectives of the fund. In this case, SEC stands for sector fund and GRO stands for growth fund. A legend explaining the codes is usually printed among the mutual fund listings.

Column 3—Net Asset Value (NAV)

The net asset value is the mutual fund equivalent of a "share" of common stock. It is the price the fund pays you when you sell. (When you cash out of a mutual fund, the fund buys back the shares; they aren't sold to another investor as with stocks.)

Mutual funds are also different from stocks in that you can buy fractions. For example, if you invested $2,000 in Gldsod with a NAV of $6.07 you would effectively own 329.49 "shares" ($2,000/$6.07 = 329.49). If the NAV goes up to $6.27, your investment would be worth $2,065.90 ($6.27 × 329.49 = $2,065.90).

To compute the NAV, take the fund's holdings and divide by the number of shares.

Column 4—Offer Price

You have probably heard of no-load mutual funds. These funds charge no sales commission. Funds that fall into this category will have a NL in this column.

PROCEED WITH CAUTION

The offer price is what you will pay when you buy a loaded mutual fund.

Other funds do charge a sales fee. When there is a number in this column, you can figure the load or sales commission by subtracting the offer price from the NAV.

In this example, Inpest has an offer price of $10.75 and an NAV of $10.23, giving you a load or sales fee of $0.52. Some listings may show an NAV and offer price the same. This may indicate there are backend fees.

COLUMN 5—NAV CHANGE

As the title suggests, this number represents the change in the NAV from the previous day. Unlike stocks, mutual funds are valued at the market close for that day since the value depends on the value of the underlying holdings and additions or losses of shares.

COLUMNS 6, 7, & 8—PERFORMANCE AND FEES

These columns change, reflecting a different set of numbers regarding performance and fees. Below are the explanations.

1	2
Max Initil Chrg	Total Exp Ratio
0.52	1.400

Columns 6, 7, and 8 (labled 1 and 2 here) reflect the performance and fees.

Column 6—Maximum Initial Charge—The *maximum initial charge* is the load or sales charge the buyer pays. In our example, the load or fee, which we computed in the explanation of column 4, is $0.52.

Column 7—Total Expense Ratio—The *total expense ratio* captures all the fees for the fund. These fees are found in the fund's prospectus.

When these two measures are reported, there is usually no Column 8; however, when the fund's performance is reported in three time frames like Figure 4, there is a Column 8.

6	7	8
- Total Return -		
YTD	4 wks	1 yr
+5.2	+0.6	+10.2
+12.3	+0.3	+5.6

These numbers look at a short-term measurement of fund performance. They look back just four weeks and one year.

These numbers may be helpful in comparing the fund's performance to financial benchmarks like the S&P 500 Index. You can also look at similar funds to see how this one is holding up. If it is down for the year and most other similar funds are up, you may want to know why before investing.

These numbers look at 13 weeks or one quarter and an annualized three-year return.

6	7	8
- Total Return -		
YTD	13 wks	3 yrs

An annualized return smoothes out the peaks and valleys by taking a longer period and dividing it by three, rather than looking back exactly three years ago and reporting that single number.

These numbers stretch out far enough, 26 weeks, that a comparison with the year-to-date figure begins to have some meaning.

6	7	8
- Total Return -		
YTD	26 wks	4 yrs

If the 26-week (one half year) number is greater than the year-to-date, that tells you something about the first half of the year. Looking back four years gives you a perspective of the consistency of the fund's performance.

The last set of numbers (the ones in our very first example) give analysts the best look at a fund's staying power.

6	7	8
- Total Return -		
YTD	39 wks	5 yrs

Do not be surprised to see plenty of NS codes in this column. NS signifies the fund was not in existence five years ago.

COLUMN 9—YEAR-TO-DATE PERCENTAGE RETURN

This floating number keeps track of the fund's performance on a current-year basis. This number is helpful in looking at short-term movement, but not particularly meaningful because of the short time frame.

ONLINE INFORMATION

The Internet has opened up a whole new world of information resources for the investor. If you have resisted learning how to use the Internet up until now, I hope this section and others in the book will convince you that you are missing a valuable tool. Like I said earlier, you don't have to invest in a computer to access the Internet. Visit your local public library. Many have Internet enabled computers you can use for free.

What type of financial information can you find on the Internet? Just about anything you want and, probably a whole lot more than you need. Your biggest problem will be sorting through the details to find those elements that are truly important. Not surprisingly, there are sites that will even do that for you.

Contrary to what you may have heard, not everything on the Internet is free. Financial information comes in three basic forms:

- Free
- Moderately priced
- Expensive

FREE INFORMATION

There are thousands of financial Web sites on the Internet, and the majority of them offer free access. They are supported by the advertisements placed on each Web page with the information. In that sense, they are very similar to conventional media—newspapers, magazines, and television—that draw all or most of their support from advertisers.

Don't equate free access with low quality. Some of these sites offer the best information available on the Internet. In addition to basic information, some of the sites offer a wide variety of extra services including charting, historical trends, detailed fundamental analysis (more about this later), and other sevices.

One particular service that is quite common allows you to track a personal portfolio of stocks and/or mutual funds. You enter the companies you want to follow (they don't care whether you actually own the stocks or not) and every day the service will update your holdings with the latest prices, plus alert you to news about any of the companies or funds.

Access these sites while the market is open and you can see quotes and information about market activity in a particular stock. These quotes are usually delayed by 15 minutes by the exchange. This delay is built in to give brokers on the floor time to react to violent market swings.

Many of these sites have analysts writing columns about various stocks, mutual funds, or industry trends. Most are good, but take care in following recommendations from any source. They may have a financial interest in seeing a stock rise or fall.

TIME SAVER

 Almost all of the sites that require a modest subscription for access to all the contents will give you a one-time, 30-day, free trial. Sign up and try several before you spend any money.

MODERATELY PRICED

These sites differ from the free sites in that part of the site is reserved for subscribers, while the rest is free. These sites offer pretty much the same level of service as the free sites, but save the best information and advice for paying customers.

Often their top recommendations come with the "premium" service, which means a subscription fee of anywhere from $10 to $25 per month, with some even higher.

These sites often offer deeper quotes with more information about sales and movement trends than the free sites. Some will even offer buy and sell tips on specific stocks.

Are they worth the extra money? Some are and others are not. Most of the legitimate sites offer a free trial period where you can try out their premium services and evaluate them for yourselves.

Unless you are going to be an active trader or just love to read everything you can about investing, these premium sites are probably more than you want or need.

Expensive

The expensive sites on the Internet are usually linked to either to a broker offering more direct access to the market or a high-powered investment professional.

Access to these sites can easily run several hundred dollars a month or more. They are not appropriate for a beginning investor. Be wary of high-pressure offers to use these services; not all of them are legitimate.

Annual Reports and Prospectus

All publicly traded companies and mutual funds must, by law, publish an annual report detailing significant financial and market-related information. Many of the numbers from above will also be found in the annual report.

We will look at the annual report numbers in more detail later, but armed with the information above, you will be well on your way to understanding what the company or mutual fund is trying to tell you—or what they hope you don't notice.

You cannot buy a mutual fund without first receiving a prospectus. A prospectus is a legal document about as interesting as your car's warranty, yet it contains significant information that you should be aware of before you invest.

The mutual fund company must disclose its intentions for the fund (objectives), define a business plan for achieving those objectives, and disclose all fees. The mutual fund company also has to disclose information about the top management and their credentials to operate the fund.

If you invest in a mutual fund without going over the prospectus, you do so at your own risk. Later we'll walk you through the prospectus and point out the things to watch for.

What Can You Do?

The following is a list of five things you can do today:

1. If you have Internet access, go to www.morningstar.com. There you will see navigation buttons to look at stocks and mutual funds. Go to the "stocks" area and look up some of the stocks you are interested in. Compare the quotes to the ones you find in your copy of *The Wall Street Journal*. Notice the online site offers a wealth of information not found in the newspaper.

2. Do the same thing with the "funds" navigation button at www. morningstar.com. Look at the wealth of information available. All of this is on the free portion of the site.

3. If you have an annual report of a mutual fund, look for the key numbers mentioned in this Hour. If you don't have an annual report, see if a friend or coworker might loan you one or call the fund directly.

4. Look in the yellow pages for local mutual fund companies. Call one and see if they would let you have a copy of their annual report. It will be helpful to have one for later sections.

5. Look at the volume leaders and "Gainers and Losers" section of *The Wall Street Journal*. Do you notice any thing they have in common? Sometimes, although not all the time, big moves in a stock's price are accompanied by big trading volumes. There will be an article on the stock market activity that will offer explanations for these numbers. Does their explanation make sense to you? By the time you finish this book, most of what you read will at least sound familiar and much of it you will know.

WORKSHOP

Time for a reality check. If you are going to be intentional about your finances and investments, you need a system to keep track of your income and expenses that is a little more sophisticated than a checkbook.

There are several popular personal finance software packages on the market, if you are comfortable with a computer. At the end of this book are some software recommendations (see Appendix B, "Resources").

If you are more comfortable with paper and pencil, invest in an accounting pad or whatever you are comfortable with. Keep a monthly list of income and expenses. When you began investing, you may want to track those on a daily basis.

The goal with either system is to be clear about what and how much you are spending. Money is a particularly loaded subject in marriages. Find a common ground that feels comfortable to both partners.

HOUR'S UP!

Investing information is awash in numbers, indexes, and ratios. Sorting them out can be a challenge. This short quiz will see if you can make it all add up.

1. Yield is important because …

    A. It captures the true essence of the business.

    B. It lets you compare two different investments.

    C. You can never have too much.

2. A good source of numbers on stocks is …

    A. *The Wall Street Journal.*

    B. Online information providers.

    C. Annual reports.

    D. All of the above.

3. Dividends are paid …

    A. At the annual meeting.

    B. Only to the company's officers.

    C. Quarterly to all stockholders.

4. A stock's volume as reported in the newspaper stock tables is usually expressed …

    A. In 1,000s.

    B. In Arabic.

    C. In 100s, unless noted otherwise.

5. Financial information on the Internet is …

    A. Free or moderately priced.

    B. Not worth the electrons it is displayed on.

    C. Not reliable.

6. Mutual fund tables in the newspaper …

    A. Will tell you almost nothing.

    B. Are very up-to-date.

    C. Are impossible to read.

7. Expensive information on the Internet …

    A. Must be good or they wouldn't charge that much.

    B. May not be worth the price.

    C. Is the only kind available.

Quiz

8. Online stock quotes …

   A. Are not reliable because you don't know where they came from.

   B. Are available only at the expensive sites.

   C. May be delayed by 15 minutes.

9. Mutual fund performance is most significant …

   A. When it follows two consecutive months of gains.

   B. When it shows week-to-week gains.

   C. When viewed over a long time to see how the fund did in good times and bad.

10. Annual reports are …

   A. Expensive documents produced to hide the facts.

   B. Audited by national accounting firms.

   C. A way for management to pat themselves on the back.

Hour 7

Market News/Research

Chapter Summary

LESSON PLAN:
In this Hour you will learn about ...

- Information overload.
- History of research business.
- Sorting through information.
- Avoiding "fortune-tellers".
- Confusing advertising and information.
- Finding good information.

Finding information on companies or mutual funds is not hard. Sorting through the information and making any sense of it is the real task.

This is one area where access to the Internet will pay for itself in no time. There is a tremendous amount of information available online and many services that will help you sort through it.

Don't get nervous. You don't have to be CPA to get and analyze the information you need to make intelligent investment decisions. In this Hour, we will go over the basic information you need and where you can find it. Later in the book, I'll walk you through the analytical steps. You don't have to do much math, because most of the computations have already been done, but you will need to know what they mean.

Sorting It All Out

Years ago I was business editor of a major daily newspaper. On my first day (a Monday) on the job, the mail clerk dropped about 500 pieces of mail on my desk. I felt it must be important so I looked through it all.

That was pretty much all I did Monday. Tuesday, the mail clerk dropped another couple of hundred pieces of mail. The same thing happened on Wednesday. I began to wonder how my predecessor got anything done.

Late Wednesday afternoon I noticed that my large trash can was overflowing. I realized that 98 percent of the mail I received was meaningless to my readers. I soon developed a system for sorting the mail; that same 98 percent went into the trash unopened.

This is the hurdle you face in looking for information. Not only was the 98 percent of the mail that went in the trash meaningless to my readers, but most of it was also self-serving puff pieces.

JUST A MINUTE

Information is not wisdom. Wisdom is making sense of information.

And that is the other problem you will face—sorting out the facts from the hype and downright fraud that tries to pass itself off as information.

So in the interest of full disclosure, I want you to know that you will not find any recommendations for individual stocks, mutual funds, or any other investment in this book. I will encourage you to invest, but what you pick is up to you.

Now, let's also be clear about my intention. My intention and hope is that you will buy this book and that you will find it helpful (if you are reading this at the store, please go pay for it—my family needs the money). You will then buy other books that I write and little Johnny can have that operation.

WHERE DID ALL THIS INFORMATION COME FROM?

Before we can pin that down, we need to do a very quick history lesson. Not too many years ago, access to the stock market for the average person was controlled by a handful of large, national brokerages.

There were plenty of smaller local and regional brokerages, but the big national companies controlled the business. If you are old enough, you probably remember television ads with bulls and people whispering and other nonsense that somehow was supposed to convince us to use this national company or that national company.

Then in 1975, commissions paid to brokers were deregulated and all of a sudden, discount brokers began popping up all over the place. These folks offered commissions on trades at a fraction of what the full-service brokers charged.

The one thing the big national brokerages held on to was their research. Smart folks saw an opportunity and jumped in with books, magazines, newsletters, radio, television, and now Web sites on the Internet.

Nature abhors a vacuum, and entrepreneurs like to solve problems. In no time, there was more information available than anyone could possibly use.

While all this upheaval was shaping up the retail brokerage market, interest in mutual funds and other investments begin a long, steady climb. More customers meant more products.

Add into this mix globalization and an explosion in information technology.

Retirement plans like 401(k)s and IRAs put increasing emphasis on the individual investor and removed some or all of those decisions from the corporate retirement office.

This snowballing of consumer demand and need, increasing investment options, and information technology has been fueled by one of the greatest economic expansions in history.

Given the tremendous interest in money and investing wisely, it is not surprising that a whole industry has grown up hoping to fill your head with their particular brand of baloney.

JUST A MINUTE

Publicly traded companies are under heavy scrutiny by regulatory agencies to make sure the information they report is accurate and not misleading. This is to establish credibility and instill confidence in the stock market. Unregulated markets, like penny stocks, are riddled with fraud, thus reducing investor confidence.

Every bit of information you need to make an informed investment decision is available for free or at a very nominal cost. The Securities and Exchange Commission (SEC) and the other agencies that regulate publicly traded companies mandate that this information be made available in a timely manner and be audited by an outside firm.

I will tell you right now that you do not have to attend a $5,000 seminar to be a successful investor. You don't even have to subscribe to a dozen newspapers, magazines, or newsletters to be successful.

How to Sort Through the Mess

One of the ways to sort through the information mess is to use a series of filters to screen out the obviously outrageous and self-serving, then the advertising designed as "news" or insight, then the biased information.

TIME SAVER

Don't bother chasing "miracle investing systems," "millionaire reveals secrets" articles, "secret trading formulas," or any of the other goofy ideas that claim certain riches await you.

Your First Cut—The Obviously Outrageous

This is where you really need to rely on your common sense. If it appears too good to be true, most likely it's not true. Here are some things to keep in mind:

- **There are no systems for making you wealthy**. I am amazed at the number of infomercials that run on late night television promoting schemes from real estate to direct mail that you can operate 30 minutes a day and get rich.

- **There are no systems that will consistently make profitable trades**. I get a lot of junk "snail mail" (via the U.S. Postal Service) and e-mail because of my work on the Internet. You would be shocked at the number of "secret" systems for making money I have been pitched. Everything from bizarre options trading to futures to complicated market-timing systems have made me rich (or would have had I bought the book, seminar, newsletter, whatever).

- **Be wary of marketing catchphrases**. If you see the words or phrases "secrets," "secrets revealed," "pro tips," "hot products," "millionaire reveals secrets," or anything like that, wrap fish in it or line your bird's cage with it, but don't believe it.

I am constantly surprised at the schemes people will fall for with the hope of making a "killing" in the market. Not long ago, I received an e-mail from a man who had invested $20,000 to get in on a "hot" IPO that was almost ready to be sold to the public.

When the man became concerned, he called the representative that sold him the investment—a man he had never met in person. The phone number was disconnected. He called information and got a number of the company the representative worked for in New York. That number was dead as well.

I did a quick Internet search and could find no trace of the man or the company. I also searched for this supposed IPO but could find no information on it. I advised the man to call the Better Business Bureau in New York, the

New York Attorney General's office, and his personal attorney. I'm afraid, though, the $20,000 was gone for good.

ASK YOURSELF "WHY?"

If someone contacts you that you don't know and they offer to let you in on a "hot deal," ask yourself why. Why would a complete stranger offer you such an opportunity? In addition, even if they use the name of someone you know, never invest in a hot deal.

Most of the scams out there are not nearly as blatant as this one. The perpetrators wrap themselves in respectability by providing all sorts of testimonials from satisfied customers. It is hard to listen to these pitches and not believe there must be some truth to them.

Many of these scams want to convince you that investing is complicated and confusing, but they have discovered a "secret formula" or "system" that makes it easy. Anyone can do it.

JUST A MINUTE

Scams and other frauds will do anything to appear legitimate, including advertising in reputable publications and on television.

These scams appear in newspaper and magazine ads, newsletters, television, radio, and the Internet. When you see them in prestigious publications, it is natural that you will transfer some of the credibility from the publication to the ad. That is exactly what they want you to do.

CRITICAL THINKING

When I was growing up, no teacher ever taught me critical thinking skills. Critical thinking is the process by which you do not accept things at face value, but look at the underlying arguments for soundness.

Fortunately, I learned these skills in journalism school. There are millions of people who will believe anything they read in a publication, see on television, hear on the radio, or find on the Internet. They have never been taught to examine claims for truth.

You have just had your first lesson in critical thinking. Before you accept something as the truth, ask yourself the following questions:

- Does this make any sense?
- What does the author stand to gain?
- Am I being manipulated?

I am always surprised to hear people say, "It must be true or they wouldn't let them (print it, put it on television, and so on)." Nothing could be farther from the truth. If you doubt this, look at the magazine rack next to the checkout at the grocery store.

"Aliens Bring Cure for Cancer"

"Two-Headed Man Debates with Himself"

"Elvis Works at K-Mart"

Give me a break. Another waste of time is listening to market gurus who claim they can predict when the market will go up or down. Despite what you read in their ads, no one can successfully and consistently call the market.

PROGNOSTICATORS

Another group of these bandits pass themselves off as being able to call market turns. Simply stated, they claim if you follow their advice, you will realize tremendous gains by buying low and selling high.

Their claims often start off like this: "If you had invested $10,000 with us 10 years ago, that investment would be worth $6,000,000 today." You could achieve those returns if you had bought cocaine futures, but nothing legal will achieve such returns.

So, how do they get by with those claims? If they are not outright lies, which is not uncommon, they probably achieved those results by constructing their systems on historical returns.

If you know what has happened with stock prices it is easy to build a model that will hit all the highs and avoid all the lows. Can these models actually look forward with any degree of accuracy? In a word, no.

Past performance claims mean nothing unless they reflect actual performance and not "this is what you would have earned if in fact we had even been in business then, which we weren't, and had actually invested money then, which we didn't."

Past performance also means nothing unless an independent national accounting firm audits it.

No one can predict the future. The only thing these scam artists can predict with any accuracy is that if you subscribe to their newsletter, buy their book, and so on, you will have less money than before you became their customer.

Is There Any Place to Get Good Information?

A good place to start looking for reliable information is the public library. Most libraries subscribe to major financial newspapers and magazines. Look through the following:

- *The Wall Street Journal*
- *Investors Business Daily*
- *Forbes*
- *Money Magazine*

I will share more Web sites and other information sources in Appendix B, "Resources."

You will be surprised how quickly you can begin picking out the baloney from the good information.

It is not my intention to turn you into cynics. I am aware I have spent most of this hour telling you what to avoid. I trust your common sense to spot the obvious scams. I am more concerned about advertisements passing as news.

The magazines and Web sites I have listed are, for the most part, trying to present a fair view of the investment business.

There are others equally as competent, and after awhile you will discover those for yourself. Just remember your critical thinking skills.

Regulators

The stock markets are highly regulated businesses that are accountable to state and federal regulators. The stock exchanges also have an important self regulatory role.

Stock brokers and the firms they work for must be licensed by the National Association of Securities Dealers (NASD), an industry group, and the Securities and Exchange Commission (SEC), an agency of the federal government.

Stock brokers must pass a series of tests and meet strict ethical standards. The firms they work for must keep detailed records and are subject to fines and closure for not dealing fairly with the public.

The SEC also approves stock offerings and has oversight for much of the securities business.

The NASD licenses stock brokers and the companies where they work.

The securities industry is one of the most highly-regulated businesses in America. All of this oversight is to make sure everyone is treated fairly and that there are no "under the table" dealings that will destroy confidence in the market.

WHAT CAN YOU DO?

The following is a list of five things you can do today:

1. Go to the library and check out the publications listed in this Hour. They will all probably offer more than you are interested in reading on a regular basis, but if you do find them helpful, consider subscribing. Buy a copy and look for a trial subscription offer.

2. Look through your local newspaper and see if any of the news stories sound more like advertisements than news.

3. Check out the recommended Web sites. Several offer free trials for the paid portion of the site. Several have personal portfolio areas where you can record your investments (I would not recommend entering actual investments for security reasons). This is a good way to get comfortable with investing sites and software.

4. Find a get-rich-quick scheme, either on television or on the Internet, and look at it closely. Are the holes obvious? Remember, it is not unheard of for these crooks to outright lie about their claims.

5. On the other hand, just because the news about a stock is positive doesn't mean it is not the truth. Look through *The Wall Street Journal* for a positive story. How is the news supported; that is, what facts do they cite as proof?

WORKSHOP

Spend some time thinking seriously about how much of your personal time you are willing and able to spend on your investments. This is a critical decision, because as we move further into the book you will see there are high-maintenance investments requiring more of your time than low-maintenance investments.

One way to get an accurate picture of your tolerance for this is to set a schedule for a couple of weeks, where you drop everything to work on your investments.

See what kind of schedule you can realistically maintain. As you become more familiar with investing, you may find that your tolerance for study grows. Above all, be honest with yourself and you will establish an investing program you can maintain.

HOUR'S UP!

It is a confusing world of financial information out there, but with some common sense and a few tips you learned this hour, you should be in good shape to separate fact and fiction. You can, can't you?

1. Investment information is …
    A. Hard to come by.
    B. In short supply.
    C. In abundant quantity.

2. Information became an important commodity when …
    A. Bill Gates claimed he owned it all.
    B. When CNN was started.
    C. When commissions on securities transactions were deregulated.

3. More and more people are …
    A. Responsible for managing their investments through qualified retirement plans.
    B. Learning less and less.
    C. Less and less interested in their investments.

4. You can safely make 300 percent each year …

    A. If you base your stock investments on your horoscope.

    B. If you only buy stocks with eight letters in their names.

    C. If you are completely insane.

    D. None of the above.

5. Critical thinking skills can …

    A. Help you spot frauds and scams.

    B. Make you unpopular at the water fountain.

    C. Cause you to miss some great investment opportunities.

6. Predicting market highs and lows is …

    A. A great gift.

    B. Impossible with any consistency.

    C. Easier than you think.

7. Advertising made to look like information …

    A. Rarely happens.

    B. Is easy to spot.

    C. Can look very objective, despite hidden agendas.

8. Companies selling investment products often …

    A. Concoct stories that look like information, but are really about selling their product.

    B. Downplay their products' good points.

    C. Work hard to be objective about their products.

9. *The Wall Street Journal* is …

    A. The financial equivalent of the National Enquirer.

    B. A leading source of baseball news.

    C. Considered the best and most reliable financial news source.

10. The Internet has …

    A. A large number of reliable financial sites.

    B. A large number of unreliable financial sites.

    C. A large number of frauds.

    D. All of the above.

QUIZ

HOUR 8
Picking a Broker

CHAPTER SUMMARY

LESSON PLAN:
In this Hour you will learn about ...

- Reasons you need a broker.
- SIPC insurance.
- Stock certificates.
- Full-service brokers.
- Discount brokers.
- Online brokers.
- Technological problems with online brokers.
- Evaluating a broker.

Before we spend a lot of time discussing how to pick the right stockbroker for you, we need to answer a broader question: Do you even need a broker?

If you plan to put your investment dollars into no-load mutual funds exclusively, then you are dismissed from this class. You don't need a broker to buy mutual funds. By the way, investing exclusively in mutual funds is a common and sound strategy.

However, many people want a more hands-on involvement with investing decisions and are interested in owning individual stocks as well as mutual funds. This is a fine strategy also.

I would caution against beginning investors owning just individual stocks. Mutual funds provide a diversity of investment that a beginning investor owning just individual stocks cannot achieve, especially on a modest investment budget.

With those cautions in mind, let's look at the wacky world of stockbrokers.

WHY DO I NEED A BROKER?

Brokers provide the link between you and the stock market. Except under unusual circumstances, which we'll look at in a later chapter, you need this link to buy stocks, bonds, and many other financial instruments, but not no-load mutual funds.

One of the reasons you don't need a broker to buy mutual funds is that they, for the most part, are bought from the mutual fund company. When you sell your mutual fund holdings, the mutual fund company buys them back from you. Thus, there is no need for an intermediary.

JUST A MINUTE

As we will see in upcoming hours, no-load mutual funds keep fees low by dealing directly with investors.

When you buy stocks, you are purchasing the shares from another investor, not the company. There are some exceptions, but for the vast majority of trades, this is the case.

Matching the buyer with the seller is a function of a very sophisticated market system. Your access to that system is through a broker. Your broker has the network connections to execute simple transactions in a matter of seconds.

In addition to accessing the market, the following sections will cover some common considerations that apply to all brokers.

SIPC INSURANCE

Securities Investor Protection Corporation (SIPC) offers insurance to protect your account at a brokerage firm. Do not use a broker that is not covered by this protection.

SIPC insurance protects your assets in the event the brokerage you are using fails. Minimum coverage is $500,000 per account, although some firms purchase more. SIPC is like the FDIC protection of your bank deposits, although it is not backed by the federal government.

This insurance won't protect you against bad investment decisions or an errant stock market, so don't try to file a claim when your investment in digital hula hoops goes south. SIPC insurance comes in to play when a brokerage fails or substantial fraud is discovered. Regulators will contact account holders with claim information.

CONSUMER PROTECTION

Consumers do have some protection against brokers who screw up their trades or accounts through neglect, incompetence, or fraud. TheNational Association of Securities Dealers (NASD) is the primary regulatory body for brokers.

You can contact the NASD through their web site: www.nasd.com or one of their district offices. Those addresses and phone numbers are found in Appendix B, "Resources."

The NASD licenses individual brokers and brokerage firms. Individual brokers must pass a series of tests and a background check to be licensed to sell securities. There are several tests that cover different products.

JUST A MINUTE

Don't let a dispute with a broker go unresolved. There are systems in place to make sure the consumer is protected. The NASD has a complaint system in place through their Web site or district offices.

The people who supervise brokers also must pass examinations, and brokerage firms are required to meet certain standards. If a firm fails to maintain its records and accounts or fails to adequately supervise its brokers, the firm could lose its ability to do business.

Consumers who have complaints against brokers or their firms can petition the NASD if their concerns are not properly addressed.

The NASD regularly yanks broker's licenses for a variety of infractions and, more rarely, closes down brokerage firms.

STOCK CERTIFICATES

Some investors want to take possession of the certificates of stock they buy. It may give you some pleasure to drag the stock certificates out every once in awhile to look at them, but it is a bad idea to keep them in your possession.

TIME SAVER

Stock certificates are a relic of the past. You are better off not taking possession and risk losing them.

Most brokers recommend you keep your stock in a "street name," which means they keep the certificates for you. In reality, there may not be an actual certificate unless you request it. Most transactions are recorded electronically.

If you insist on keeping possession of your certificates, put them in a safe deposit box at your bank. Lost certificates can be replaced, but it is a big headache and may cost money.

What Kind of Broker Do I Need?

GO TO ▶
See Hour 20, "Conservative/Low Cost Investing," for ways to buy stocks without using a broker.

Brokers come in two basic varieties: full service and discount. There are some variations within these categories, such as a full-service broker that offers some discounted services, but the lines are fairly distinct.

Prior to the mid-1970s, there were no discount brokers. But as we learned in the previous Hour, in 1975 the commission structure was deregulated. This gave birth to discount brokers who have taken investing from the country club set and made it accessible to almost everyone.

Full-Service Brokers

Full-service brokers provide a variety of services to their customers, as the name suggests. In addition to brokerage services, these brokers offer proprietary research to their customers.

They make recommendations and handle all of the paperwork. Their offices are often downtown in prestigious locations and are decorated with portraits of the late 20th century rich. If you have a large enough account, you will probably be asked to lunch periodically.

Large account holders may have access to IPOs before the general public. Many of the full-service brokers now call themselves financial planners and offer other services besides executing trades.

All of this service comes with a price—sometimes a hefty price.

Do you need a full-service broker? For most people, I would say no. You will learn all you need to know in this book to handle most of the transactions that the average investor makes.

However, some people are so nervous about money that they need someone to help them even if they are smart enough to do it themselves. Don't be ashamed if this is you. It is better to be honest with yourself about money, than to get into something that is emotionally difficult.

Fee-Only Financial Planner

You may also want to consider using a fee-only financial planner, especially if you have a large sum of money to invest. These professionals work to put together a complete financial plan for you that look at your total financial picture, not just your investments.

Be sure they are certified financial planners and work on a fee only. They are pricey, but definitely worth the peace of mind if you are managing a large sum.

A number of folks call themselves financial planners and may have professional designations, but charge a commission for their services. There is an inherent conflict of interest in these cases that should raise a flag of caution. Are they always going to recommend what's best for you, even if it means a low commission for them, or even none at all?

GETTING TO KNOW YOU

There is one function full-service brokers perform that you will not get with a discount broker, and that is qualifying an investment as appropriate for your particular situation. Because full-service brokers make recommendations, they have to know their customer.

PROCEED WITH CAUTION

Brokers cannot recommend investments that are inappropriate for your particular financial situation. One of the prime directives of the securities business is to know your client. Brokers face penalties and possible loss of their license if they recommend inappropriate investments.

This requires them to learn about your financial resources and sophistication before recommending an investment. They cannot recommend, for example, a high-risk investment to an elderly retiree on a fixed income. That investment would not be appropriate for that particular investor.

I think there are probably three circumstances under which you would use a full-service broker or fee-based financial planner:

- If you were managing a large sum of money
- If managing large sums of money is terrifying to you
- If you have neither the time nor interest in managing your own financial affairs

DISCOUNT BROKERS

Discount brokers have come from nowhere to dominating the retail stock brokerage industry in a short 20+ years. I think there are several reasons for this:

- Discount brokers' lower commissions have made investments profitable sooner by taking a smaller bite out of profits.

- They are less intimidating to work with than full-service brokers for many people.
- They have tapped into a strong desire on the public's part to take control of their financial future.

Discount brokers started off looking very much like the full-service brokers, but with some major differences.

Many of them located in suburban areas where rents were lower. There offices often had a much more utilitarian look and, in most cases, customers were not encouraged to visit in person, although some did maintain branch offices.

Their business model for acquiring customers depends almost exclusively on marketing through television, radio, publications, and the Internet. The brokers are, for the most part, order takers who are on a salary. Their job is to execute your orders in a fast and accurate manner.

Contrast this with the full-service brokerage where the same marketing tools are used, but their brokers are required to generate business on their own.

This is done several ways, but one of the most common is for new brokers to make a list of several hundred names, addresses, and phone numbers of people they know. This is sometimes a condition of employment.

The new broker is then expected to get on the phone and contact these people to solicit their brokerage business.

ACCESSING DISCOUNT BROKERS

There are three basic ways to access your discount broker: by voice, over the telephone; by touch-tone, using your telephone; or online, via the internet.

Some discount brokers will allow all three methods, others just one or two. The first two are somewhat self-explanatory, although you may not be familiar with using the Touch-Tone system.

It is not much different than using your phone to access account information at your bank or navigating a voice-mail system. The system prompts you to enter certain codes, such as your account number or social security number. You will need to know the code, often the stock symbol, of the stock you are buying or selling. This system is often slightly cheaper to use than talking to a live broker.

JUST A MINUTE

A discount broker that has multiple ways to access your account may provide a margin of safety when one entry point is not working or you are away from your computer.

Most, if not all, discount brokers now have a presence on the Internet. In fact, many discount brokers are almost exclusively accessed via the Internet. It is here where you will find the cheapest trades and, potentially, the most problems.

All three means of access depend on the telephone for contact. Don't leave risky positions (selling short) open without some limits, if you are going to be away from a phone for an extended period or live in an area with frequent phone outages.

ONLINE DISCOUNT BROKERS

The latest craze in the discount broker world is online investing via the Internet. The brokerage firms are drawn to this means of trading, because it further reduces costs.

This means of trading has caught on like wildfire, in part, I believe, because it is a further extension of the hands-on experience investors and Internet-savvy consumers want.

Online investing offers many advantages for the consumer. It is quick and user friendly. It is anonymous in the sense you will not have to talk to another human to complete your transaction. Investors who may have been intimidated by a broker can now trade with confidence.

SERVICE WITH A MODEM

The online brokers offer many services with their sites, including quotes, news, charting, and research, most often provided by a third party. The different online firms offer varying mixtures of these products and services. Not surprisingly, their fees reflect the depth of their services.

We will go over some ways to evaluate online brokers to find the one with the right mix of products and services for you. For right now, let's look at the "dark side" of online investing.

Online investing is not without its problems. Some of these problems can be dangerous, while others merely annoying.

TECHNOLOGICAL PROBLEMS

The Internet is basically held together with chewing gum and bailing wire. One problem anywhere along the network and all sorts of bad things can happen.

If you cannot connect to the Internet because of a problem with your Internet Service Provider (ISP), you cannot connect to your broker. If a major link in the Internet becomes overloaded or breaks, you cannot connect to your broker. If your broker is swamped with attempted connections due to some radical market activity, you cannot connect to your broker.

If you cannot connect to your broker and have a risky position or you need to dump a stock in a nosedive, you could lose a lot of money. This has happened more than once, and it almost always happens when everyone needs to connect the most.

SECURITY PROBLEMS

Although there have been no massive cases of security breaches at online brokers, the potential is always there that someone could hack into the system and begin trading out of your account, however you also face the risk from traditional full service brokers that your hard-earned retirement fund may just pay for your broker's hide-away on some Caribbean island.

PROCEED WITH CAUTION

For the most part, doing business on the Internet is safe and secure, but don't let your guard down. Avoid sites where extensive personal information, such as Social Security number, credit card number, and so on, is required for no apparent reason. Online brokers will require your Social Security number for tax purposes, but a site that sells books has no need for it.

This is why it is important that your broker has SIPC insurance. There are a lot of new players in the online discount broker game. Make sure the one you are playing with is legitimate and will stand behind their service.

PROCEED WITH CAUTION

Be careful that you don't get addicted to online investing. It is as addictive as gambling for some people and just as ruinous.

EVALUATING A BROKER

In this section, we are going to walk through some of the considerations in picking a discount broker.

I am not going to do the same with full-service brokers for two reasons: first, very few of you will want to use a full-service broker; and secondly, the quality of service will largely depend on the individual broker assigned to your account, and that quality can vary even within the same company. If you want to use a full-service broker, it is best to get the name of one from someone you trust.

TIME SAVER

A helpful source for evaluating online brokers is www.gomez.com. This site evaluates online brokers on several levels including price, performance, easy of use, and quality of service. They also tell you what to expect if you are an occasional trader or more active.

COST

The primary reason for using a discount broker in the first place is to take advantage of their lower costs. However, some discount brokers are more discount than others.

Before signing on, be sure you understand the whole fee structure. For example, one discount broker may charge a fee for wire transfers, while another does not.

PROCEED WITH CAUTION

Commissions, fees, and any other costs take money out of your investment pool. Be sure you keep your trading costs as low as possible.

Advertised rates are often for their best customer (those who trade often). Be sure your anticipated trading volume is not at a significantly higher rate just because it doesn't match their ideal customer profile.

Some brokers offer premium services for a monthly fee. Weigh the value of these services carefully before signing up.

On the other end, there are deep-discount brokers who have stripped their offerings down to the bare bones. These are typically online brokers. If you are confident of the technology and want a broker to execute your trades and nothing more, these may be the brokers for you.

EXECUTION

Execution refers to the actual trade transaction and how it is handled. You want a discount broker that is directly connected to the market so you can get the fastest executions.

Be wary of fly-by-night online vendors that appear to have those connections, but in reality you are filling out an e-mail form that is sent to the firm. They turn around and reenter it into the system, often through another broker.

There is too much danger your order will get screwed up and it will be slowed because of the extra steps. Ask your broker what level of service they have to the market. You want them to have a direct connection to the market and not through a third party.

SERVICE

Although discount brokers are not employed to provide a lot of hand-holding, there are times when you will need their assistance filling out a form or resolving a conflict on your statement.

PROCEED WITH CAUTION

Discount commissions don't mean you should settle for discount service. If you are considering a discount broker, call its customer service number and see how quickly and professionally your call is answered.

Brokers should have toll-free phone numbers to their customer service departments and real people on the other end to answer your questions. If you pick the least expensive broker in the world, don't have high expectations of service.

EXTRAS

Many discount brokers offer extra services such as research and analytical tools for you to use. You need to evaluate these services for their usefulness to you. Many are quite good and can be very helpful.

Some of these extras are free and some will carry either a one-time fee or monthly subscription. Online brokers may offer extras for a fee that are available elsewhere on the Internet for free.

With legitimate discount brokers you usually get what you pay for in commissions. The more extras and perks that are offered, the more the fees and commissions are going to cost you.

WHAT CAN YOU DO?

The following is a list of five things you can do today:

1. Using the worksheet below, decide what type of services you will want from your broker. Decide if you need more than a discount broker can offer and contact friends who might be able to recommend a full-service broker or a fee-based financial planner.

2. Honestly assess your comfort with using a broker via the Internet. If you feel insecure about investing this way, check out your yellow pages for the names of discount brokers in your community or look through business publications for possible candidates. Request information packages for evaluation.

3. Some discount brokers maintain offices you can contact for information. If you would feel more comfortable establishing a relationship with a broker in person, call to see if they will accommodate you.

4. If you are comfortable with using the Internet, check out www.gomez.com for information about online brokers. This site rates brokers and provides a good overview of their services.

5. Visit several of the online broker sites for a feel of how easy or hard it is to use and how comfortable you feel with the organization. Not all online brokers are the same. It pays to shop.

WORKSHOP

Here are some of the services offered by brokers. See where your needs fall and use this as a guide to picking a broker. (y = they offer the product or service and n = they don't)

Service	Full-Service Broker	Discount Broker	Online Discount Broker
Research			
Proprietary research	y	n	n
Third-party research	n	y	y
Service			
Product recommendations	y	n	n
Help with IRA forms	y	y/n	y/n

Service	Full-Service Broker	Online Discount Broker	Discount Broker
Wire transfers	y	y	y
Extended hours	n	y	y
Comprehensive statements	y	y/n	y/n
Execution of trades			
Prompt attention	y/n	y	y
Complicated trades	y	y/n	y/n
Direct connection to market	y	y/n	y/n
Fees			
Low commissions	n	y	y
Transaction fees	y/n	y	y

This is just a guide to get you started in evaluating a broker. There are other considerations, which you can find at www.gomez.com.

HOUR'S UP!

A broker is your entry into the stock market. They aren't all the same, so finding the one that is right for you is an important step in the investment process. This short quiz will let you know if you are on track.

1. You need a broker to …

    A. Buy and sell securities.

    B. Make a lot of money.

    C. Buy no-load mutual funds.

2. Full-service brokers …

    A. Usually will work for free.

    B. Have extensive proprietary research.

    C. May need your help selling stocks.

3. Discount brokers …

    A. Offer quick executions, but no research.

    B. Offer cheap commissions, but no advice.

    C. Offer coffee mugs when you open an account.

4. You can access discount brokers …

    A. Your computer and/or by telephone.

    B. By smoke signal.

    C. Invitation only.

5. Online brokers …

    A. Cost more than other brokers.

    B. Don't want small accounts.

    C. Are eager for your business.

6. Technological problems may …

    A. Cause you to lose your job.

    B. Make it difficult to connect to the Internet.

    C. Make it difficult to make money.

7. Addictive trading is …

    A. A good thing.

    B. A real possibility if you like to gamble.

    C. Can be used to your advantage.

8. Online brokers …

    A. Are pretty much the same.

    B. Offer the same services.

    C. Offer different services for different prices.

9. Discount brokers …

    A. Must all charge the same commissions.

    B. Only want large accounts.

    C. Should be compared before making a decision.

10. Discount brokers offer …

    A. Third-party research.

    B. Valuable stock recommendations.

    C. Convenient "trade-by-mail" service.

Quiz

PART III

Mutual Funds, Stocks, and Bonds

HOUR 9

Mutual Funds—Part I Classifications

CHAPTER SUMMARY

LESSON PLAN:

In this Hour you will learn about ...

- Sales fees.
- Load funds.
- No-load funds.
- Expense ratios.
- Actively managed funds.
- Index funds.
- Closed-end fund.
- Unit investment trusts.

Choosing a mutual fund is like walking into a candy store with a pocket full of change. So many choices, so little money.

Actually, this is good news for the investor. Not too many years ago, there were very few choices in mutual funds. It was pretty much a one-size-fits-all kind of world.

Times have changed for the better, but now instead of too few choices, one could argue that there are too many choices. How do you sort through the hundreds of choices and make an intelligent decision?

That process is not as hard as it might initially seem. The first step is to classify mutual funds several different ways.

For this chapter, we are going to focus on sales fees and types of management.

SALES FEE OR NOT

The broadest classification of mutual funds involves sales fees. *Sales fees* are like commissions on stock purchases; they are paid to the broker who sold you the fund.

LOAD

These funds are said to be load funds, because they have a fee that you pay up front when you invest in the mutual fund. If you remember the table on mutual funds from Hour 6, "Understanding the Numbers," in the Newspaper

Mutual Fund Tables there was an entry for one fund where the offering price was higher than the net asset value (NAV). This difference is the *load*.

Another way to identify a load fund is they are most often sold by brokers or financial advisers. No-load funds, on the other hand, are available directly from the mutual fund company.

BACK-END LOAD

I have heard two sayings about details in my life:

"God is in the details."

"The devil is in the details."

I'm not clear who is in the details, but I know that if you don't read the details closely, you may be in for a rude surprise if you bought a mutual fund you thought was a no-load fund, only to be hit with fees when you sell.

These funds are known as back-end load and can give someone who is un-aware a real shock. *Back-end load funds* may charge a sales fee when you cash out of the fund. Some suggest that if you leave your money in for a long period, say five plus years, some or the entire fee may be waived.

Of course, these funds seldom use the term "back-end load" to describe themselves. Most often it is called a "deferred" something or a "contingent" something else. The words are carefully chosen to seem harmless. They may even be called "class B" shares of the mutual fund.

LEVEL LOAD

One more type of load we need to expose is called a *level load* fund. This sneaky little trick may or may not involve a very small front-end load, but flat fee appears every year in the form of 12b-1 fees (more about those to follow). These often end up being very expensive for a long-term investor, because a fee comes out of your investment every year. If you remember our discussion on compounding, reducing the amount compounded every year will have a dramatic effect on your total return.

Remember, someone has to pay the high sales commissions, and that person is you. Whether it's pay me now or pay me later, you still pay, either in sales fees or operating expenses or wherever they can hide the fee.

JUST A MINUTE

You don't need a broker to buy a no-load fund. The fund companies sell them directly. You can do all your business over the phone after you have been sent the prospectus and have opened an account.

You need to read the fund's prospectus (we'll cover that later, in Hour 17, "Picking a Mutual Fund") for any hidden fees. The mutual fund industry has become very clever in disguising fees and figuring out ways to capture more of your money.

Why would you want to buy a load fund, you ask? The salespeople will say their performance is superior because the sales fee means they can hire the top talent to manage the fund. As a rule, load funds perform no better than their no-load counterparts. Besides, the sales fee goes to the broker who sold you the fund, not the mutual fund company managing the fund.

Which gets us back to the original question: Why buy a load fund? The short answer is you shouldn't. There are too many good or better alternatives that don't charge a sales fee to consider a load fund.

However, you should always look at the whole picture. If a load fund was dramatically outperforming its no-load counterparts, it might make sense to consider the investment. You should always look at the total return of an investment before making any decisions. We'll show you how to get to that figure in the section "Total Return" found toward the end of this hour.

NO-LOAD MUTUAL FUNDS

As we have already learned, no-load mutual funds do not charge a sales commission when they are bought (or sold, for that matter). This doesn't mean the fund is free of any charge, just no sales charge.

Let's focus just a few more minutes on sales charges and how they can impact fund performance. Let's compare two funds, one a fund with a 6 percent load (about average) and a no-load fund.

You invest in an IRA for 25 years. What would be the difference between the two investment choices?

	Load Fund	No-Load Fund
Amount Invested Annually	$2,000	$2,000
Sales Commission	($120)	$0
Net Invested Annually	$1,880	$2,000
Annual Return	10 percent	10 percent
Balance in 25 years	$223,700	$238,000
Difference		+ $14,300

I know I violated my own rule and only looked at part of the picture, but I think the point is still valid. All things being equal (operating expenses, taxes, and so on), a load fund is not a good investment. After 25 years, you have paid a $14,300 penalty. I don't know about you, but I am sure an extra $14,300 will come in handy during my retirement.

I am going to leave load funds behind at this point. Through the next steps we will be looking at fees of all kinds and how they impact your return. If you want to analyze a load fund, you can add the sales fees into the mix, but you will be hard pressed to find a load fund that will outperform a comparable no-load fund.

EXPENSE RATIO

Now, there is a scary term: expense ratio. It conjures up all sorts of images of men with green eyeshades, hunched over adding machines, furiously working away. It's not that bad at all. The *expense ratio* is simply how much money (what percentage) the mutual fund company takes off for itself to cover operating, administrative, and other expenses. This is the cost of owning the fund.

There's not much math involved here. All of the numbers that go into this figure are readily available through a variety of sources, but primarily the prospectus.

GO TO ▶
See Hour 17, "Picking a Mutual Fund," for a detailed look at the prospectus.

Once you have the numbers, you add them up and that gives you the expense ratio. This number is mandatory if you are going to consider different funds. If two funds have similar performance and tax consequences, then obviously the one with the lower expenses is the winner.

We can minimize tax consequences by picking the right category of fund or housing it in a tax-deferred account, like an IRA. We don't have any control over performance.

Expense ratios on the other hand, represent the amount of our money that is not invested. The lower the expense ratio, the more money is actually invested. You don't have to be a genius to see that picking a fund with a low expense ratio makes a lot of sense.

COMPONENTS OF THE EXPENSE RATIO

Thanks to modern technology, I can see your eyes at this very moment, and they are glazed over. You may pretend to be reading, but I know the truth. "Components of the Expense Ratio" sounds about as exciting as watching your fingernails grow.

However, stick with me on this one because if you understand what goes into this ratio, it will help you make better investment decisions. Like my dad used to say, "If this weren't important, I wouldn't make you do it."

JUST A MINUTE

Management fees are high so fund managers can drive nice cars. Actually, most fund managers are compensated based on their fund's performance.

ADMINISTRATIVE EXPENSES

These are the keep-the-doors-open kind of expenses including rent, technology, mailings, printing, and support staff (like customer service and representatives that take phone orders). A well-run fund will have administrative expenses around 0.3 percent and lower. This doesn't sound like much, but if the fund has $500 million in assets, 0.3 percent is not chump change (that's $1.5 million).

MANAGEMENT FEE

The *management fee* may also be called the investment advisory fee and is used to pay the fund's manager. A fund manager is responsible for making sure the fund meets its investment objectives and makes lots of money. These folks are followed by some investors the way horseracing fans follow jockeys.

These fees usually run 1 percent or less (again, that would be $5,000,000 if a fund had $500 million in assets). This is a lot of money and fund managers are under intense pressure to make sure the fund performs well. Actively managed funds (we'll discuss them next) tend to pay their managers the most, mainly because the success or failure of the fund is more directly tied to them; index funds, on the other hand, would pay less because the investment decisions are fewer.

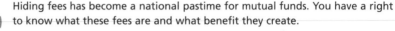

PROCEED WITH CAUTION

Hiding fees has become a national pastime for mutual funds. You have a right to know what these fees are and what benefit they create.

12B-1 DISTRIBUTION FEES

The 12b-1 fees are for marketing and advertising costs and distribution services and can range up to 1 percent per year (again, that would be $5,000,000 if a fund had $500 million in assets). They are often used instead of or in conjunction with load funds. More and more load mutual funds are shifting away from front-end loads and hiding fees in the expense ratio.

Be wary of 12b-1 fees in a fund. Not all funds charge the fee, and it would be worth your effort to find one that doesn't.

TRANSACTION FEES

Although they are not included in the expense ratio, transaction fees can eat into your return. These are extra, usually one-time fees for a variety of services the mutual fund company provides.

PROCEED WITH CAUTION

Read the prospectus carefully for transaction fees or other fees. One fee that is fairly common is a low-balance fee, meaning if your account falls below a certain balance, you may be charged a fee.

For example, if you want to redeem (sell) $1,000 from your account and have the money wired to your bank, the fund company may charge a transaction fee for that service. Read the fine print carefully, and you will avoid funds with high fees for services you frequently use.

TYPICAL EXPENSE RATIO

Now that you know what goes into the expense ratio, let's look at what a typical expense ratio is for different funds.

For actively managed funds, expect an expense ratio in the 1.5 percent range, while true index funds will sport an expense ratio in the neighborhood of .25 percent. As we look at different types of funds, I'll give you some guidelines about where the expense ratio should be.

The other thing to remember about expense ratios is they are paid to the mutual fund company regardless of the fund's performance or any other factor. That is why it is so important to consider the expense ratio in evaluating a mutual fund.

FUND MANAGEMENT

GO TO ▶
See Hour 11, "Mutual Funds – Part III Investment Objectives," for more information on investment objectives of mutual funds.

How a fund is managed is another way to classify funds. There are two basic approaches, actively managed funds and index funds, although like many other aspects of mutual funds, there are a number of variations.

ACTIVELY MANAGED FUNDS

Actively managed funds have specific investment objectives that are met by buying and selling stock and/or bonds. They are often measured against market indicators like the S&P 500 Index.

These funds may target a particular segment of the market, such as healthcare or Internet stocks. They may be growth oriented or income driven, combining stocks and bonds. In the next hour we will look more closely at the different fund objectives.

To hit these objectives, managers buy and sell stock holdings frequently, often turning over the portfolio 100 percent in a year. All of this buying and selling costs money. Even though big mutual fund managers pay very minimum commissions because of the volume of business they do, the cost still translates into a lower return for you.

The idea is that hotshot managers will beat the market. The embarrassing truth is that during the last couple of years of the 1990s, in the middle of the greatest economic expansion in our history, many of the actively managed funds didn't beat the market.

TIME SAVER

Actively managed funds should not be dismissed because their fees tend to be higher than index funds. Measure their performance against a common yardstick for comparable results. For example, a mutual fund that specializes in stocks of large companies should be measured against the S&P 500.

As we have seen with expense ratios, actively managed funds tend to be more expensive to own. When we look at the tax consequences of actively managed funds, we find that those that turn over a big percentage of their portfolio each year are creating big tax headaches for their investors.

Does this mean actively managed funds are to be avoided? Absolutely not. Some of the hotshot fund managers do, in fact, beat the market—and beat it rather soundly. The question you must answer as an investor is this: Can the manager duplicate this performance year after year?

Here's where past performance can be a big help. How has the fund fared in the past? This question is really only relevant if you compare it to comparable funds of that time period.

A well-managed fund will consistently be at or near the top of its classification. Since our goal is long-term success, we want to see a consistency of performance. This certainly doesn't guarantee future success, but if a fund has been successful (that is, better than the market) for eight out of the past ten years, for example, you could conclude that the odds are good it will be successful in the future.

A fund that is hot this year for the first time in 10 years may just have gotten lucky. It's like my grandfather used to say, "Even a blind pig finds an acorn once in awhile."

On the other hand, a lot of new funds don't have that kind of history, so it is somewhat harder to predict future success.

Sometimes the best place for one of these actively managed funds is in a tax-deferred account—IRA, 401(k), and so on—to minimize the tax consequences.

Again, I repeat the basic rule: Look at the total picture before making a decision and you will save yourself a lot of headaches and a substantial amount of money.

INDEX FUNDS

Index funds have been the darlings of those online pundits, The Motley Fools (www.fool.com). They love index funds and strongly recommend them to investors as low-maintenance, tax-friendly investments.

What are index funds, anyway? *Index funds* seek to replicate the movement of major market indicators, such as the S&P 500 index. Their goal is not to beat the market, but to stay even with the market. For most of 1990s, this was a winning strategy.

An S&P 500 index fund will try to mimic the index's reaction to the market. The fund does this by replicating the index's underlying holdings. For example, as we learned in Hour 3, the S&P 500 is an index that measures the movement of the 500 largest corporations in America.

The people at Standard and Poor's who maintain the index don't just take one share of stock from each of the 500 companies and call that the index. They give more weight to the true leaders in the market; the bigger, more dominant companies make up a larger proportion of the S&P 500 than smaller, weaker companies.

For example, Company XYZ may be the dominant leader in its industry and thus has a greater effect on the market than its smaller competitors. The S&P 500 may allocate 4 percent of its total index to this one company, while another company might only merit 0.5 percent of the index.

An index fund will match these proportions in its holdings so that any movement by the market leader will be equally felt in the S&P 500 index and the index fund.

"What's so great about matching the market? I thought the idea was to beat the market?" you ask.

That would be great if you could beat it all the time. The problem is, no one has come up with a system that will consistently time the market in order to buy low and sell high.

Since experts have been keeping count, stocks have historically returned around 10–11 percent. That is what the market has done. If you own an actively managed stock, you may or may not have matched that figure. If you own a good index fund, you will be very close to matching that return (or whatever the future market return will be).

We also have learned that index funds tend to have very low expense ratios, many times under 0.20 percent, compared to actively managed funds that can top 1.5 percent. One of the reasons is that an index fund will turn over only a very small portion (often in the 5 percent neighborhood) of its portfolio each year while an actively managed fund may turn over 100 percent of its holdings. Those turnover fees can add up.

Another benefit of the index fund strategy is a very friendly year-end tax figure. When we look at taxes in more detail, you will see the advantages of tax-friendly investing.

Tax consequences of your mutual fund's buying and selling will reduce its actual return. Index funds tend to generate fewer tax bills than actively managed funds.

One final benefit of an index fund is they are very low maintenance and fit a buy-and-hold strategy. You don't need to worry about how it's doing everyday and whether you should get out or put more in. You should never buy any investment and forget it, but a good index fund comes very close to no maintenance.

TOTAL RETURN

You need to look at the major financial components that can impact the return of a mutual fund before you can make an informed decision. These components are: sales fees, the expense ratio, and taxes. When you put these all together you come up with a "total return."

If you only look a one or two of the financial components, you may not get an accurate picture. For example, a fund may be a gang buster in performance, but at the end of the year you may have to give a substantial amount to Uncle Sam in taxes. A fund with a lower return, but much lower tax consequences may actually return more to you.

Most funds do not report their returns as after taxes, so you are left to be surprised when you get a big tax bill at the end of the year.

ODD DUCK MUTUAL FUNDS

Mutual funds come in a wide variety of shapes and sizes, so we will only cover the major classifications. However, there are a couple of odd ducks that will pop up on the investment radar screen from time to time.

CLOSED-END MUTUAL FUND

A *closed-end mutual fund* is one of those hybrid investments you'll find in various corners of the market. While it has many characteristics of a regular or open-end mutual fund, there are some striking differences.

A closed-end fund should not be confused with a closed fund. A closed fund is a regular, open-end fund that has decided not to accept any more investors. For example, when a fund is very popular and becomes too large it is difficult for the managers to keep all the inflow of money invested. At some point, a fund's popularity may become its worse enemy and the managers will close the fund to new investments.

There are a number of reasons a fund may close itself to new investment, but it is not the same as a closed-end fund.

JUST A MINUTE

Despite their higher fees, closed-end funds can be attractive investments, but they are probably not suited for the beginning investor.

A closed-end fund is financed by a group of investors who have pooled their money to accomplish certain objectives. It is professionally managed, and one share is called the net asset value. All of these are characteristics of a regular mutual fund.

However, the closed-end fund only offers shares for sale once in an initial public offering. Regular mutual funds constantly sell and redeem shares, unless its managers decide to cease sales. The mutual fund company facilitates these new sales and redemptions.

With a closed-end fund, an investor must use a broker to find a buyer for their shares. Closed-end funds can only be bought and sold through brokers, so there are no no-load, closed-end funds.

Closed-end funds trade on the open market and have a market price, which is the price you pay when you buy shares. Regular mutual funds are bought at the NAV in the case of no-load funds and at the offering price for load funds.

Closed-end funds trade at their market price, plus you pay a regular commission to the broker just as you would pay if you were buying stock.

Many times the market price of a closed-end fund is lower than the NAV, meaning its assets can be bought at a discount. Closed-end bond funds are popular for this reason. Income is paid out based on the NAV, not the lower market price.

Closed-end funds are probably most appropriate for a buy-and-hold strategy, since the commissions paid may eat into short-term returns. Operating expenses tend to be lower than open-end funds, since the mutual fund company does not have to deal with a daily flow of money in and out of the fund.

Unit Investment Trusts

Another hybrid type of investment, *unit investment trusts (UITs)*, will buy a fixed portfolio of stocks or bonds and never sell or buy more, except in unusual situations.

Like a closed-end fund, brokers sell UITs and the sales charges can be steep; however, their ongoing costs are usually very low. UITs can invest in either bonds or stocks. UITs can be bought in very small chunks, making them attractive to folks who can't buy individual bonds, for example.

The bond UITs offer a consistent income stream and are suitable for people needing that feature. However, because of the high sales charges on bond UITs, they should be held until maturity.

Stock UITs are also known as a focused portfolio and will buy a specific group of stocks and hold them for a specified length, and then liquidate the UIT. This can cause big tax headaches, which makes stock UITs better candidates for tax-deferred accounts. In addition, UITs can be bought through most brokers.

What Can You Do?

The following is a list of five things you can do today:

1. Get your copy of *The Wall Street Journal* and turn to the "Markets" section. Depending on which day of the week you picked, there will be a table called "Mutual Fund Scorecard" at the top of one of the mutual funds pages that looks at a particular segment of mutual funds (for example, large cap). Look over the table and see what it tells you about the funds.

2. In the same section is a table titled "Performance Yardsticks" that offers a wealth of information for mutual fund investors. The table shows how the various funds categories (more about those in upcoming hours) have done over several time periods. Observe which sectors have done the best and worse.

3. This section also gives you benchmarks for fund performance. This information is invaluable when evaluating a fund's performance over time and especially helpful when considering two funds with different objectives. These benchmarks provide a point of common reference. For example, if you can't compare two funds because they have different objectives, you can compare them both to the S&P 500. This will tell you how the funds did against this external measure.

4. If you have Internet access, go to www.morningstar.com and check into some of the funds listed in the table as "Fund Leaders and Laggards." Do you see a difference in the two lists in terms of how Morningstar classifies them?

5. If the prospectus I asked you to order has arrived, look through it with special attention to the fees. They are often listed in the front of the publication. Notice how easy or difficult it is to read and understand the prospectus. Mutual funds have been trying for a number of years to make their information more user friendly, but some have done a better job than others.

WORKSHOP

Reading the mutual fund tables in your daily newspaper or *The Wall Street Journal* can ruin your eyes in a hurry. You can get more complete information in an easy-to-read format on the Internet.

Using your list from *The Wall Street Journal* of "Leaders and Laggards" in the mutual fund table, look up several from each category at www.morningstar. com and note how they are rated in terms of investment objectives. Morningstar also uses a gauge of 1 to 5 to apply its own rating to funds.

Did the leaders get high marks from Morningstar and the laggards get poor marks? Newspapers are good for summary information, but if you want a detailed look at a stock or mutual fund, nothing beats the Internet.

HOUR'S UP!

Mutual funds come in all shapes and flavors. Breaking them down into groups will help you focus on those funds that meet your objectives. Here's a short quiz to see if you are on track with mutual funds.

1. A loaded fund …
   A. Charges only sales fees.
   B. Charges a sales fee in addition to other fees.
   C. Charges fees when you ask for information.

2. Some sales charges …
   A. Are called deferred sales charges.
   B. Are never reported.
   C. Are over 20 percent.

3. Never judge a fund …

   A. By its sales fee only.

   B. By its tax consequences.

   C. By its 12b-1 fees.

4. No-load mutual funds never …

   A. Charge any fees.

   B. Grow as fast as load funds.

   C. Charge sales fees.

5. Expense ratios …

   A. Tell you how much the management company is taking for running the fund.

   B. Are not important.

   C. Mean nothing to the average investor.

6. Administrative expenses …

   A. Pay for the stock exchanges.

   B. Cover the cost of utilities, rent, etc.

   C. Are never paid by the investor.

7. Management fees …

   A. Are not paid by no-load funds.

   B. Pay the manager responsible for investment decisions.

   C. Are paid by the mutual fund company.

8. Actively managed funds …

   A. Are managed by former athletes.

   B. Never lose money.

   C. May generate high expenses due to excessive buying and selling.

9. New funds with little operating history …

   A. Should be approached cautiously.

   B. Will almost always make money.

   C. Must be good because they are new.

10. Index funds …

   A. Seldom make any money.

   B. Charge outrageous fees.

   C. Are a low-cost alternative to actively managed funds.

QUIZ

HOUR 10

Mutual Funds—Part II Types of Funds

LESSON PLAN:

In this Hour you will learn about …

- Stock mutual funds.
- Growth funds.
- Income funds.
- Value funds.
- Cyclical and sector funds.
- Bond funds (taxable and tax-free).
- Money market funds (taxable and tax-free).
- Real estate investment trusts.
- International funds.

In the previous hour we looked at several ways to classify mutual funds—for example, whether or not they charged a sales fee, and active management vs. passive management (index funds). We also took our first look at expenses associated with different types of funds and how those fees (or the absence of fees) affected the fund's performance. A couple of odd ducks—closed-end funds and unit investment trusts—were introduced.

This Hour we are going examine funds from the perspective of what instruments they use to achieve their goals. This is another way of classifying funds. In the next hour, we will look at investment objectives and how funds position themselves to achieve these goals.

The classifications we are going to examine in this chapter may be no-load or loaded funds. They will be open-end (regular) funds unless I specifically note otherwise, and may be actively managed or index funds. The emphasis will be on what investment instruments (stocks, bond, cash, other) are used to build the fund.

STOCK FUNDS

Stock funds are the biggest sector of the mutual fund industry. Their numbers have exploded in the last 15 years, as more and more consumers want a piece of the stock market.

Fueled by the growth in popularity of personalized retirement plans like 401(k)s and IRAs, stock mutual funds have worked hard to capture a portion of the billions of dollars flowing into the stock market.

PROCEED WITH CAUTION

So much money has poured into the mutual fund market, some funds have simply closed their doors to new investors. If this becomes widespread, watch out for mutual fund fees to rise again.

Stock mutual funds fill a big need among consumers: access to the equities in an affordable and relatively safe environment. All of the attributes of a mutual fund work in favor of stock funds:

- Diversification
- Professional management
- Liquidity
- Relative safety
- Low entry costs

My mother used to caution me about the dangers of putting all your eggs in one basket, which I thought was strange because we didn't have any chickens. She could very well have been talking about diversification with mutual funds.

Stock mutual funds will typically own a large number of different stocks (although there are exceptions), and often in different industries. This spreads out the risk so that one company going south will not dramatically affect the fund's performance.

Unless you have a large sum (I'm talking seven figures here) to invest, you could not hope to spread your risks over as many different stocks as a mutual fund.

In the next Hour, we'll see how some funds turn the notion of diversification on its ear and go the other way.

GO TO ▶
See Hour 11, "Mutual Funds— Part III Investment Objectives," for more information on sector funds.

The attribute of diversification can also work against you. Funds that invest in a large number of stocks may buffer themselves against a couple of turkeys, but they also buffer themselves against the eagles. A fund may have a few real winners, but because the rest of the fund is just average or below average, it will not rise with the stars.

Stock funds often characterize themselves by investing in a certain size of company. The most common way to label a company is by its market capitalization, which is large, mid-size, or small.

Evidence of the booming economy in the 1990s is that at the beginning of the decade, $5 billion in market capitalization was considered a large-cap stock. Today, $8 billion or more is large-cap.

Market capitalization is the product of multiplying the number of shares of a company's stock by the current market price of the stock. For example, if XYZ Company has issued 20,000,000 shares of stock and that stock is worth $25 per share, then its market capitalization or "market cap" is $500 million ($20,000,000 \times \$25 = \$500,000,000$).

There is no one standard defining market capitalization, but many consider these ranges to be accurate:

- Large cap $8 billion and over
- Mid-cap $1 billion to $8 billion
- Small cap   less than $1 billion

Any stock under $250 million is often called a micro-cap.

We'll talk more about market capitalization in the chapters on individual stocks, but for now know that some stock mutual funds invest in one size only. The reason is that different size firms will react differently to changes in the market, the economy, competition, and so on.

GO TO ▶
See Hour 13, "Stocks—Part II Size," for more information on market capitalization.

Smaller companies tend to offer more opportunities for rapid growth, but also may suffer more acutely in a bad economy or if a larger competitor decides to have them for lunch.

Large-cap stocks are usually more stable and are likely to be market leaders in their industry, but their growth may be slow if anything at all.

You get the idea. When we look at individual stocks in the various market capitalization ranges, you will see why mutual funds often focus on a particular size.

Another way stock mutual funds distinguish themselves is by what the manager hopes to accomplish with the fund. In the next chapter, we will look into investment objectives in more detail.

The different types of stock mutual funds are:

- Growth funds
- Income funds
- Value funds
- Cyclical and sector funds

GROWTH FUNDS

Growth funds invest in stocks that are expected to appreciate over time. These stocks often don't pay dividends, electing rather to plow profits back into the company to finance further growth.

Stock mutual funds look for companies that have the potential to grow at a steady rate for many years. Companies in dying industries or companies with management out of step with the market will be rejected. For example, the U.S. steel industry, led by the company U.S. Steel, was an icon for America's manufacturing greatness, but high energy costs, high labor costs, and foreign competition doomed the industry.

GO TO ▶
See Hour 12, "Stocks—Part I Classifications," for more information on growth stocks.

Basically, the fund looks for firms with consistent growth in sales and earnings. These companies are often small- or mid-cap emerging businesses in industries with significant growth potential.

When you invest in a growth fund, you are expecting your returns to come over a long period of time in the form of price appreciation. A well-managed growth fund will not have a large turnover in its portfolio. If the manager has chosen correctly, the fund will ride a good growth stock for the long term.

JUST A MINUTE

Growth funds that don't grow often find money leaving the fund, which forces the manager to sell in what may be a stagnant or declining market for the fund's particular holdings, further driving down the fund's value.

However, most growth funds have criteria that say when a stock has failed to meet certain parameters for a specified period it may be dropped from the fund, even if it has produced a gain. These events will trigger tax consequences for the investor, so many choose to put growth funds into tax-deferred (retirement) accounts.

INCOME FUNDS

Income funds are fairly self-explanatory. These mutual funds buy stocks that show consistent dividend growth and high dividend yields. *Dividend yields* are calculated by dividing the stock price per share into the dividend per share.

For example, XYZ Company sells for $20 per share and its annual dividend is $1.50 per share. Its dividend yield would be 7.5 percent ($1.50/$20 = 7.5 percent).

Some of the favorite targets for investment by income funds include utilities and real estate investment trusts (REITs). We'll talk about REITs more a little later in this Hour.

Most income funds contain a mixture of bonds and stocks.

A person looking for supplemental income in retirement years, for instance, might be attracted to income funds. Since income funds produce taxable current income, investors need to be conscious of tax consequences.

VALUE FUNDS

Value funds are the bargain shoppers of the market. They look for stocks that are trading below the value of the company's assets. There can be several reasons for this discrepancy.

The stock may be in an industry group that has fallen out of favor with investors. Many times this happens by default. Investors get excited about an industry group and other investments are forgotten.

Value funds seek out this type of stock and look for situations that have the potential and probability for turning around. The fund manager believes this forgotten child will return to favor with investors and experience catch-up growth.

CYCLICAL AND SECTOR FUNDS

Cyclical funds invest in stocks that are riding a market boom for whatever reason. The stock may be in an industry that has suddenly caught on fire with investors and the fund hopes to capitalize on a volatile market.

Sector funds focus on one particular segment of business, such as technology, healthcare, and so on.

Bond Funds

If you like bonds, you'll love bond funds. In Hour 14 we will cover bonds in detail; this section concerns itself with bond mutual funds.

JUST A MINUTE

Bond mutual funds offer the same advantages of diversification that stock mutual funds offer. By spreading the risks over a large number of issues, they reduce the risk and impact should a bond default.

The real killer for bonds and bond funds is the rise in interest rates. The longer a bond's maturity is, the more sensitive it is to interest fluctuations, and usually the deeper the discount.

GO TO ▶
See Hour 14, "Bonds," for more information on the tax consequences of bonds.

Like all mutual funds, a *bond fund* offers the investor a chance to invest in bonds and spread the risk out over a collection of selected bonds. Bond funds are usually divided two ways: by the length of maturity of bonds they buy and by their tax status.

Short-Term Bond Funds

Short-term bond funds invest in bonds which mature in just a few years or less. Some argue that you're better off putting money into a short-term bond fund than a money market account or a bank certificate of deposit, because the yield will be better.

Usually people employ this strategy when they are saving for a purchase in the near future. The downside of this strategy is that spikes in interest rates will not only reduce your yield, but may cut into the principal value.

You may not earn as much with a bank CD, but your principal will be intact when you need it. The decision rests on how much risk you are willing to take.

Retired people in low-income tax brackets might favor such a short-term fund for its current income.

JUST A MINUTE

Because bonds with longer terms are more risky, keep an eye on funds that invest in these issues for swings in price.

MID-TERM BOND FUNDS

Mid-term bond funds (5–10 years maturity) offer a great chance for higher returns than short-term bond funds, but have a corresponding higher risk of being hurt by rising interest rates.

Mid-term bond funds are more volatile and should be watched closely. Because of this volatility, it has become popular to trade in and out of bonds. Investors in bond funds should be careful that fees don't eat up any gain they hope to make.

LONG-TERM BOND FUNDS

Long-term bond funds invest in bonds with maturities out past 10 years as a rule and are the most volatile of all the bond funds. This volatility comes through exposure to interest rate fluctuations. The longer the term, the more chance rates will move up (or down).

Long-term bond funds are often put into retirement accounts to defer the current income created by the bond, where the owner is willing to chance the market fluctuations.

TAX-FREE BOND FUNDS

One advantage bonds have over many other investments is the ability to offer tax-free income. Tax-free means exactly that, as opposed to tax-deferred. Bonds and bond funds do this by investing in city, state, federal, and special governmental agencies' bonds.

JUST A MINUTE

High-income individuals find the triple-exempt bonds an attractive option. Triple-exempt bonds are usually municipal bonds issued in states where there is an income tax and in communities that also have an income tax. As municipal bonds they are exempt from federal tax and, when purchased by investors living in the municipality, are exempt from state and local taxes.

Which tax the bond's income is free of depends on which bonds the fund buys:

- Income from treasury bonds and bills are free from state and local tax, but subject to federal income tax.

- Income from bonds that are issued by a state are free from federal income tax and free from state income tax if the holder resides in the state issuing the bond. Bond funds that seek this double exemption invest in bonds from one state only, so you may find a California bond fund, for instance. If you live in a city where there is an income tax, those bonds will likely be free from local, state, and federal tax.
- Tax-free income from a bond fund only makes sense for people in high-income tax brackets. Whether the state and/or city you live in has an income tax will drive your decision to purchase bond funds that are state-specific.

Average investors probably will do better in stock funds, either deferring taxes by putting them in retirement accounts or investing in tax-friendly funds (more about those later in Hour 17, "Picking a Mutual Fund").

Corporate Bond Funds

Bonds issued by corporations as opposed to governmental agencies are, obviously, not tax-free, but often pay a better return than their public-sector cousins. Bonds issued by highly regarded companies are considered relatively safe investments.

Bond funds that buy highly rated (more about ratings later in Hour 14) bonds generate a steady stream of taxable income and are more appropriate for people in a low-income tax bracket or housed in a retirement fund.

Money Market Funds

Money market funds are vehicles for investing in extremely short-term cash or cash equivalent instruments. They typically pay a higher interest rate than regular bank accounts.

A money market fund's value is a relatively safe place to park money temporarily awaiting investment or a pending expense. Its interest rates are not going to take your breath away, but it is better than a savings account.

Because the Securities and Exchange Commission has tight regulations about where a money market fund invests its money, there is not much difference in interest rates. Look for funds that have low operating expenses, certainly below 0.5 percent.

Many stock mutual funds offer money market funds as part of their family of funds. They will often let you sell shares in one of their funds and sweep the money into their money market fund while awaiting reinvestment—as long as it's into another of their funds.

Most money market funds have a check-writing feature and other services that make it convenient to move money in and out of the account.

Money market funds also come in two flavors: taxable and tax-free.

TAXABLE MONEY MARKET FUNDS

Taxable money market funds invest in short-term corporate securities, bank CDs, and government-backed securities. Because of strict credit-worthiness requirements, money market funds are considered relatively safe investments.

TAX-FREE MONEY MARKET FUNDS

Tax-free money market funds invest in U.S. Treasury issues and are considered very safe because the "full faith and credit" of the U.S. government that backs the securities the fund buys. These funds are exempt from state income tax.

JUST A MINUTE

Despite the appeal of tax-free income, most investors will do better in regular funds even if they have to pay taxes because the tax-free funds pay such low returns.

Other tax-free money market funds invest in short-term municipal issues, and if you live in the state where the instrument was issued, the dividends from the fund may be exempt from federal, state, and/or local taxes.

Money market funds are suitable for short-term situations where you know there is another purpose for the money in the near future. Whether you choose taxable or tax-free funds, consider alternative investment opportunities if the money is not earmarked for a specific use in the near future.

SPECIALIZED FUNDS

The process of classifying mutual funds is a fuzzy one at best. Ultimately, it is not really important how you classify a fund as long as you know what the fund is about and whether it is suitable for you.

I have included some specialized funds here and others in the next Hour. Attach no significance to this placement. Some people in the industry prefer to stick with defining mutual funds strictly by their investment objectives, and that is probably the best strategy in the long run.

The funds I have included here are specialized in their investments, which by definition means they are specialized in their objectives. Bear with me as we push through this and it will all fall into place near the end.

PROCEED WITH CAUTION

Don't worry about specialized funds until you have a firm grip on regular funds. However, many investors find a place in their portfolio for some specialized funds.

The specialized funds we'll discuss here include REITs and international funds.

REAL ESTATE INVESTMENT TRUSTS

Real estate investment trusts (REITs) are specialized investment units that invest in income-producing real estate, such as shopping centers, apartments, and so on. The management takes a fee for doing all the legwork of finding the properties and managing them.

REITs are very much like closed-end funds and, in fact, could have been included in that section we covered in the previous hour. It is an arbitrary decision on my part to place them here.

JUST A MINUTE

Real estate mutual funds have not done well. Real estate often performs better during periods of higher inflation.

Like their closed-end cousins, REITs trade like securities and are bought through a broker. This gives them the liquidity so desperately lacking in straight real estate investments. However, be aware that some REITs are "thinly" traded, meaning there are not many buyers and sellers, so dumping your investment may not be a quick and easy proposition.

A good alternative is to put your money in a mutual fund that invests in REITs. If this seems like you are getting further away from the investment, you are right, but it does give you better liquidity if that is important. REIT mutual funds often specialize in certain types of property, like hospitals or shopping centers, which allow you to target industries or market segments that are growing.

INTERNATIONAL FUNDS

International funds open the door to worldwide investing from the comfort of your living room. "Why," you ask as you settle down in your Bark-o-Lounger, "would I want to invest in some foreign country?"

Overseas markets are some of the most rapidly growing in the world. Developing countries are expanding their economies, and there are good opportunities to participate in the growth. However, here more than ever, you need the expertise of professional fund managers to guide investments through foreign waters.

PROCEED WITH CAUTION

International funds give you the opportunity to participate in the growth of foreign economies with someone else worrying about currency conversion and other details.

These funds come in several varieties; some spread investments all over the world and are known as *global funds* or *overseas funds*. Others may focus on a single region, like Latin America, and are known as *regional funds*. *Country funds* focus their investments in specific countries, such as Mexico.

Many investment advisers suggest you have a portion of your portfolio in overseas investments. While this may be a sound idea, it is one of the last investments you should make after you have all of your other investment goals covered with safer investments.

Overseas investments carry some particular risks—and the opportunity for some spectacular rewards. You should keep in mind that, as goofy as our political system can be, it is stable and predictable. Unfortunately, we have had presidents assassinated, but when it happens it doesn't cause the government to fall.

The same cannot be said of all countries around the world. Political instability and changing attitudes about U.S. investments can make the road rocky.

WHAT CAN YOU DO?

The following is a list of five things you can do today:

1. Investing in mutual funds, especially stock funds, can produce tax bills at the end of the year. If you normally get a refund and aren't planning to invest a huge amount, you probably won't be hurt with a tax bill. However, if you are in a high-income bracket or you are self-employed, you may want to consult a professional tax adviser regarding the potential tax consequences of your investments.

2. Remember the investment goals and dates we worked on at the beginning of this book? Now would be a good time to begin considering how some or all of them might be met using mutual funds. Do you have short-term needs that a bond fund would help? What about your retirement accounts?

3. Common stock has produced the best long-term returns of any investment you could make. Based on what you know up to this point, do you feel you might be more comfortable with mutual funds or individual stocks? Part of that answer needs to relate to a previous hour when I asked you to honestly consider how much time you wanted to spend on your investments. The less time you are willing to spend, the more you should consider mutual funds.

4. Using what you know to date about bonds and bond funds, do you see a way they might fit into your investment strategy? We will spend a full session on bonds later in the book, but I would like you to keep your mind open to all possibilities. Do any of the investment goals seem like they would lend themselves to an investment in bonds?

5. Real estate investment trusts are one way to invest in real estate without the hassle of conventional real estate investing. However, we will see in coming Hours that real estate—at least real estate available through securities—has not been a good investment. If you are interested in investing in real estate, you are probably better off looking for something close to home that you can manage personally.

WORKSHOP

Turn again to your "Mutual Fund Scorecard" in *The Wall Street Journal*. The copy I am looking at shows the "Past Year's Top Performers." One thing stands out immediately to me—the funds are all very small (assets under $250 million) and many are less than three years old.

What does *your* scorecard tell you? Once you get comfortable looking at these tables, you will begin to see relationships and connections. The purpose of this exercise is to help you start feeling comfortable with a page of numbers in small type. Spend some time looking over several issues of the paper in the library or that you purchase and you will find you are able to pick out key information quickly.

Hour's Up!

Mutual funds address a variety of needs with a variety of products. We've looked at some of the basics, and now is your chance to review what you have learned.

1. Stock funds are …

   A. The biggest sector of the mutual fund industry.

   B. Dangerously unpredictable.

   C. For well-heeled investors only.

2. Funds that invest in large numbers of stocks …

   A. May forget what they own.

   B. Often miss gains by some of their holdings because the rest of the portfolio is holding them back.

   C. Are called mega funds.

3. Growth funds seek …

   A. High income from dividends.

   B. Growth through acquisition.

   C. Companies with high growth potential.

4. Income funds seek …

   A. Tax-free income.

   B. High current income through dividends and bonds.

   C. Income from rentals.

5. Value funds seek …

   A. Stocks that have been marked down.

   B. Only investments from the best families.

   C. Companies currently undervalued by the market.

6. Sector funds seek …

    A. Investments in particular parts of the country.

    B. Hot areas of investor interest.

    C. Growth through acquisition.

7. Bond funds …

    A. Invest in privately held companies.

    B. Spread interest risk over a number of investments.

    C. Never do well.

8. Corporate bond funds …

    A. Invest in troubled companies.

    B. Generate predictable income streams.

    C. Grow in periods of high inflation.

9. Money market funds …

    A. Pay more interest than savings accounts.

    B. Invest in high-risk loans.

    C. Are used to park money for long periods.

10. International funds …

    A. Are fronts for the CIA.

    B. Offer frequent flyer miles.

    C. Invest in foreign economies.

QUIZ

HOUR 11

Mutual Funds—Part III Investment Objectives

CHAPTER SUMMARY

LESSON PLAN:

In this Hour you will learn about ...

- Different fund types.
- Investment objectives.
- Different systems to classify stocks.

"Yikes! How many ways can this guy talk about mutual funds?"

You don't want to know. Actually, this is the last chapter on mutual funds—well, there is one more later on, but it is really exciting.

What you are getting here is just the tip of the iceberg, but at least it's the most important part. Out there in the cold, cruel world, there are complete systems for classifying mutual funds.

The reason folks spend so much time on this seemingly meaningless activity is that it is the only way to compare two or more funds. If you want to buy an aggressive-growth, mid-cap stock fund, it would be nice to line up several candidates so you can pick the best one for you.

What we are walking through in this book is not a system, but a survey of what makes one fund different from another. There are several systems out there that will do the classifying for you, but they will be more meaningful if you understand why it makes no sense to compare a large-cap value fund with a small-cap aggressive-growth fund.

JUST A MINUTE

Morningstar.com has an excellent system for classifying mutual funds. We will talk about it later in Hour 17, "Picking a Mutual Fund," but if you want a peek, go to www.morningstar.com and enter the name of a mutual fund in the quote box.

A note of caution: Just as you can't judge a book by its cover, you can't judge a mutual fund by its name. A common marketing trick is to name a fund something that sounds like it is in a currently hot classification, when it really belongs in another based on its holdings and investment style.

In this chapter, we will look at a variety of fund types to get a feel for what makes one different from another.

INDEX FUNDS

Index funds, as we learned in Hour 9, "Mutual Funds—Part I Classifications," seek to mimic a particular stock or bond market index or indicator. They do this by mirroring the holdings that make up the indicator.

For example, an index fund that tracks the Dow Jones Industrial Average (DJIA) would buy the 30 stocks that make up the DJIA in the same proportion that makes up the indicator. An S&P 500 index fund would look like the S&P 500 and would try to hold the same weight of securities as the indicator.

JUST A MINUTE

Index funds track different market indicators, but they don't all do it well. Check the fund against the indicator and see how well they match.

Index funds would seem to be a no-brainer and, in many ways, that would be right. An index fund's investment objective is to follow its indicator. There are, however, numerous index funds for each indicator. Many pundits like index funds because they take a lot of decision-making out of investing, are generally tax friendly, and often produce superior results to actively managed funds.

PROCEED WITH CAUTION

Don't assume that index funds will always beat actively managed funds. In the roaring hot market of late 1999, index funds were routinely beaten.

Their results, however, can be a mixed bag. Index funds that track small-cap stocks are subject to poor results due to the volatility of small-cap stocks. In addition, actively managed funds can and do beat index funds at different times.

The bottom line is that if you want an investment that is basically on auto-pilot, pick an index fund tied to a major indicator, such as the S&P 500. You should have fairly low fees and few ugly tax bills at the end of the year.

On the other hand, a young person would probably do better investing in an aggressive growth fund sheltered in a retirement program where tax issues are not as important.

The reason index funds typically beat actively managed funds is their low expense ratio. Index funds spend considerably less on research, as a rule, and much less in commissions.

PROCEED WITH CAUTION

Low expenses mean the fund doesn't have to work as hard to achieve its return because the expenses aren't eating up the profits.

GROWTH FUNDS

I once was involved in some market research for a mutual fund company. We used a focus group, which is a small number of customers sitting around a table with a facilitator. The purpose of focus groups is to determine what your customer thinks about the product in a casual atmosphere that invites more than "yes" or "no" answers.

We were trying to get information on how our investors viewed us and what we could do to improve their perception, since we were getting ready to roll out some new funds.

Along with several other people, I was behind a large two-way mirror, just like you see in the police shows.

After a short time, it was clear we had a problem. Several of the folks that had invested in our growth fund hadn't done well. One investor summed it up quite succinctly: "Your growth fund didn't."

Ouch! However, that pretty much nails the investment strategy of growth funds. These funds look for companies that are on growth tracks with consistent increases in sales and earnings.

PROCEED WITH CAUTION

Growth funds can be volatile and should be held as a long-term investment because long holding periods smooth out the peaks and valleys in your returns.

Growth Funds hope the company's stock will continue to appreciate, thus benefiting the fund and its investors. When growth companies don't grow, they get dumped from the fund. This demonstrates one of the cautions about growth funds: They can generate hefty tax bills and fees. As stocks are dropped from the fund, there is often a gain. This profit is subject to income tax or capital gains tax.

Growth funds tend to be on the risky side because of the type of companies they buy for the portfolio. Growth stocks can achieve significant gains—and suffer significant losses. The only reason for owning growth stocks (they usually pay no dividends) is their appreciation.

If a growth stock quits growing, it will likely fall out of favor with investors.

Within the growth category are many variations that involve more or less risk, depending of how the managers structure the portfolio. For example, an aggressive growth fund invests in only, or predominantly, small-cap stocks. These types of stocks can be highly volatile.

Significant changes in the economy or the market can have dramatic effects on stock prices and fund NAV.

Growth funds often distinguish themselves by the size of company they invest in and whether they narrow their selection process to particular industry groups or geographic areas.

Growth funds are probably best housed in a retirement account, where they will have many years to grow and tax consequences will be deferred.

JUST A MINUTE

Large-cap growth funds perform very differently from small-cap growth funds. It is important to measure comparable funds to get an accurate picture of how the fund is performing.

INCOME FUNDS

Income funds seek to generate current income by investing in bonds and dividend-paying stocks. As a group, they tend to be less risky than growth funds.

On the more conservative end, they focus on U.S. Treasury issues and agency bonds. Many of these funds offer partial or complete tax-free income. As a rule of thumb, an investment's return will go down in relation to how much of it is tax-advantaged.

As you move up the return and risk scale, income funds focus their investment strategy on corporate bonds from blue chip companies and utilities. These funds seek higher income by moving out of primarily government issue into corporate bonds and high-paying dividend stocks.

PROCEED WITH CAUTION

Income funds are favored by people in retirement because they become a source of monthly income.

Income funds that invest in foreign bonds with a mix of U.S. bonds are seeking a higher level of income than those that stick with strictly U.S. issues. These funds involve more risk and are subject to international economics and monetary policy.

At the high end of risk and potential reward are income funds that invest in low-rated (junk) bonds and municipal bonds from poorly rated communities. Because both the corporate and municipal bonds are considered at risk of default, they have to pay high rates to attract purchasers. These may be the exception to the rule of lower returns for tax-free income because of the risk.

Income funds that generate tax-free income are suitable for persons in high tax brackets, while funds that generate taxable income are more appropriate for retired persons in lower-income tax brackets or sheltered in a retirement account.

BALANCED FUNDS

If you have ever wanted to have your cake and eat it too, then *balanced* or *blended* or *hybrid funds* may be for you. These funds combine growth and income fund characters for an approach that seeks to smooth out peaks and valleys.

PROCEED WITH CAUTION

Trying to achieve a balance between growth and income sometimes means you don't get much of either. Approach balance funds with caution if you are looking for market returns.

How the fund mixes the two different types of stock determines its relative risk and reward. A more aggressive balanced fund will add more growth stocks to the mix and fewer bonds and dividend-paying stocks.

For the most part, these funds seek modest gains while offering some protection in a down market. Like most conservative investments, you will not set the world on fire, but you also won't lose much sleep.

JUST A MINUTE

Capital preservation is the strategy of focusing on maintaining your capital base at the expense of significant returns.

The buy-and-hold strategy is historically successful for investing purposes, but like all other strategies, it has a weakness—in this case, its exit philosophy. Buy-and-hold strategy assumes a long-term commitment that will go through ups and downs. However, what if you are in a "down" when it is time to start distributions out of your retirement plan?

Some argue that as retirement draws closer, you should begin shifting into vehicles like balanced funds to protect you from any last-minute downturns, the theory being that you want to put a floor under your assets.

This strategy targets the investor who is more concerned about capital preservation than big gains. These funds are one logical step out of the buy-and-hold strategy for people approaching retirement.

Because of the interest from bonds and dividends from income stocks, balanced funds are more appropriate for a tax-sheltered account.

SECTOR FUNDS

If balanced funds are the rocking chairs of mutual funds, sector funds are the roller coasters. *Sector funds* focus their investments in one particular area, or sector, of the economy, such as technology.

Their investment strategy is almost an abhorrence to mutual funds that draw their strength from diversification. Sector funds are safer than individual stocks, but would fall in the high-risk zone by almost anyone's measure.

PROCEED WITH CAUTION

 Sector funds tend to be on the high-risk side because they can suffer roller-coaster results.

You can also buy sector funds that invest in specific areas of the world, such as the Pacific Rim or Latin America.

When they're hot, they're very hot; when they're not, nobody remembers their name. It is easy to look backward and spot the shooting stars. Making a correct decision about which sector fund will be the next winner is not so easy.

As you can see from this chart based on information from Morningstar. com, U.S. sector funds have not fared so well in the past three years, with the exception of communications and technology. Real estate, precious metals, and natural resources have all lost money over the three-year period. These figures are averages for all the funds in each sector, so some of the funds have done better and some worse.

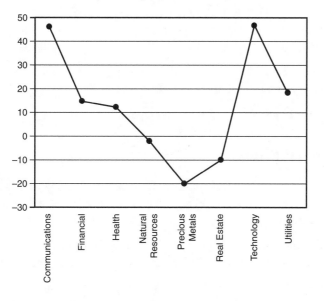

3-year Average Return for Sector Funds

U.S. sector funds chart, based on information from Morningstar.com.

More so than any other mutual fund, sector funds require a close watching for signs that the sector is falling out of favor with the market. Normally, when sector funds fall, it is fast and final.

JUST A MINUTE

Sector funds can be among the most risky of all mutual funds because they don't diversify their holdings.

If you want to roll the dice, this is as good of way as any, but don't bet Junior's college education on a sector fund, unless he will be happy attending a school advertised on a book of matches.

VALUE FUND

Value funds are the bargain shoppers of the mutual fund world. They look for stocks that are selling below the value of their assets.

Don't get the idea that these are junk companies. Hidden under a shabby financial exterior may be a solid company waiting for things to go its way. On the other hand, it very well *could* be a junk company. Knowing the difference is what you pay the fund manager for.

GO TO ▶
See Hour 12, "Stocks—Part I Classifications," for a more complete discussion of value stocks.

There are some very successful investors who have made a career out of investing in value stocks and watching them turn into growth stocks. In the meantime, the stocks tend to be fairly stable, so you might say that value funds are moderately risky.

Some value funds can generate high-expense ratios due to excessive trading, so be cautious of those numbers.

Value funds are a long-term investment.

TAX-FREE FUNDS

Tax-free funds, as I am sure you have guessed by now based on previous hours, are bond funds. I mention them here as an example of how diverse mutual funds can be.

You know by now that bond fund strategy is to generate tax-free income invest in a variety of U.S. Treasury, state, municipal, and other agency bonds.

Not much return here, but a lot of safety (for those funds who focus on highly rated bonds) and tax-free income based on what the fund buys and where the buyer lives.

INTERNATIONAL FUNDS

International funds target investments in foreign stocks and bonds, with some funds adding U.S. investments for balance. They seek out stable and mature foreign markets, as well as opportunities in emerging markets.

There are some risks associated with these funds, but in many respects they are very similar to strictly U.S. funds. Some of the funds add U.S. stocks and bonds to give them a more stable base, while others are out there on the edge looking for big gains and risking corresponding loses.

PROCEED WITH CAUTION

International funds allow you to participate in the growth of developing countries and regions around the world under the guidance of professional managers.

You might ask why international funds are not included in sector funds, since foreign markets were mentioned as a recognized sector. There is no particular reason other than to give a bit more attention to these funds. One market watcher will put them under sector funds and another will hold them separate.

Don't get too hung up on being precise with these terms, because their definitions are very fluid. Toward the end of this Hour we will introduce you to a widely accepted way of classifying mutual funds that is not arbitrary.

PRECIOUS METALS FUNDS

Precious metals funds could also be positioned under sector funds, but are worth mentioning by themselves. Precious metals funds, and particularly gold funds, have been around for a long time. When the U.S. economy was suffering through high inflation back in the 1980s, gold in the form of coins and bullion and gold funds were seen as effective shelters from inflation, and their values soared.

However, when inflation started dropping, so did gold funds. During periods of economic uncertainty and inflation, gold has a magic to attract money like almost nothing else. The 1990s were not kind to the gold funds, as noted in the sector fund chart earlier in this Hour.

A strong economy and low inflation beat them fairly severely. Will inflation come back? Who knows? If it does, expect gold funds to shoot up again.

SOCIALLY RESPONSIBLE FUNDS

Socially responsible funds, also called *green funds,* base their investments on strict ethical, political, and/or environmental guidelines. These funds may avoid tobacco stocks, for instance, or industries with reputations for polluting the environment.

JUST A MINUTE

There are funds for just about any strategy, including funds that are interested in being socially and environmentally responsible. Nonprofit religious groups often favor socially responsible funds because of their investments.

Once considered a novelty, they have grown in recent years. Most analysts still rate them as somewhat risky because of the severe limits on their investment options.

Some politically active groups have started their own mutual funds in response to the difficulty in finding funds that matched their beliefs. If you have strong feelings about certain issues, there is nothing wrong with putting your money where your heart is.

You may have to settle for a limited selection of funds, but you will have the comfort of knowing your pocketbook isn't vetoing your political or ethical convictions.

WHAT CAN YOU DO?

The following is a list of five things you can do today:

1. Make a chart with three headings across the top:

   Value   **Blend**   **Growth**

   Put your investment objectives under the column that seems to fit. Don't worry if this all still seems fuzzy, it will become clearer as we go along.

2. Go to www.morningstar.com and find three mutual funds that fit under each column.

3. Using the "Performance Yardstick" table in *The Wall Street Journal,* pick the fund groups under each column.

4. Using fund names as a guide (not always accurate), look up Vanguard Funds in your *Wall Street Journal.* Notice which funds are doing well and which are not.

5. From *The Wall Street Journal,* compare the Lipper Indexes (a table usually found at the beginning of the mutual fund listings) with fund categories the *Journal* uses in its "Performance Yardstick" table. How do they compare? Which is more useful?

WORKSHOP

List three attributes of the following fund types:

Growth

1. _____
2. _____
3. _____

Value

  1. _____

  2. _____

  3. _____

Income

  1. _____

  2. _____

  3. _____

HOUR'S UP!

Now you know everything there is to know about mutual funds, right? Okay, not everything, but you do know much more now than when you started. Take this short quiz and prove it to yourself.

1. Index funds …

   A. Are a low-cost way to invest.

   B. Seldom make any money.

   C. Don't attract much interest.

2. Income funds …

   A. Make money by selling stocks.

   B. Only invest in income-producing real estate.

   C. Create tax bills.

3. Balanced funds …

   A. Seek harmony with nature.

   B. Try to achieve income and growth.

   C. Mostly vote Republican.

4. Sector funds …

   A. Invest in specific industry sectors.

   B. Can be highly volatile.

   C. Are not for the faint of heart.

   D. All of the above.

5. Value funds …

   A. Invest in Wal-Mart.

   B. Don't cost as much as other funds.

   C. Seek companies undervalued by the market.

6. Tax-free funds …

    A. May appeal to high-income investors.

    B. Invest in foreign currency.

    C. Pay high returns.

7. International funds …

    A. Are sold in foreign countries.

    B. Invest in foreign economies.

    C. Seldom do well.

8. Precious metals funds …

    A. Invest in mining stocks and bullion.

    B. Are great anniversary gifts.

    C. Have done very well recently.

9. Socially responsible funds …

    A. Invest in companies that meet certain ethical and/or environmental standards.

    B. Vote frequently.

    C. Hold great annual meetings.

10. Mutual funds …

    A. Come in many different flavors.

    B. Span the risk spectrum.

    C. Offer something for just about every investor.

    D. All of the above.

HOUR 12

Stocks—Part I Classifications

CHAPTER SUMMARY

LESSON PLAN:

In this Hour you will learn about...

- Growth stocks.
- Income stocks.
- Value stocks.

This Hour we will focus on classifying individual stocks for those of you who want a more active role in their financial future. A legitimate question at this point might be: "Isn't this chapter in the wrong order? Shouldn't it have come before the chapter on classifying mutual funds?"

A fair question, and the answer has more to do with convenience than logic. Mutual funds lend themselves to easier classification because they have stated investment objectives and goals, however fuzzy those may be.

PROCEED WITH CAUTION

The market ultimately decides what classification will be placed on a stock. Stocks don't have stated objectives like mutual funds, so their classification is solely based on performance; the classification changes as the stock's performance changes.

Individual stocks, on the other hand, usually have one objective, and that is to *make money*. No one starts a company with the goal of becoming a value stock or growth stock. The market will determine where stocks fall in any classification system.

Therefore, this section is, in some ways, a deconstruction of the previous hour. It will go quicker because you have been introduced to the concepts already. For example, you already know that a growth stock often pays no dividends and reinvests its profits back into the business.

Like mutual funds, classifying stocks can be, and often is, an arbitrary decision by some investors, while others tend to look for quantifiable data so they can create a fair comparison.

There are many services on the Internet that will help you compare stocks that are similar in certain characteristics. It would be very slow work indeed to plow through the 5,000 or so companies regularly followed by major services.

The following classifications will get you pointed in the right direction when considering your portfolio of individual stocks. You will want to look at adding a variety of stocks in different classifications to diversify your portfolio, but more about that later.

Here are the classifications we will look at:

- Growth
- Income
- Value

GROWTH STOCKS

Once again, we step into the murky waters of classifications. Simply labeling a stock "growth" is not very helpful. How much growth? What kind of growth? Over what period of time?

Of all the classifications we will look at, this is the hardest to pin down without some help from the experts. This help is free and readily available if you have access to the Internet. One of the best places to start is morningstar. com. This site has a tremendous amount of information and classifies individual stocks by their own system.

To help us get a handle on the whole growth issue, let's look at two companies that can be classified as "growth" companies. The first is the original Ma Bell, AT&T, which is reinventing itself as a major player in delivering Internet services.

Earlier we noted that growth stocks usually don't pay dividends, yet here is a growth stock that does. What gives? This is another example of the slippery slope of classifications. Many people would put AT&T into the income category, a category that is often pictured as older, mature companies who are paying out most of their profits as dividends.

PROCEED WITH CAUTION

Companies can change the perception of their stock by taking bold and decisive steps to enter new markets and improve their current market position.

AT&T is certainly mature, but toward the end of 1999 this "old" stock gained over 20 percent in three weeks! Does that sound like a dinosaur to you?

Even though the stock pays dividends, the following chart shows a clear but slow growth pattern over the past six years. AT&T has forged some key partnerships and made significant acquisitions to position itself as a player in the future of Internet communications, as well as regular telecommunications services.

Compare that chart to the one that follows it for Amazon.com, the online bookseller that has expanded into many other areas of online sales. If you were to make an investment decision based on growth alone, Amazon.com would seem to be the better choice.

PROCEED WITH CAUTION

Comparing two dissimilar stocks is a waste of time and can be misleading. Use Morningstar.com or one of the other online services to identify peers of individual stocks. This service will also let you compare an individual stock with an average of all other stocks in the same classification.

Yet, this is not the whole picture; it points out a danger when looking for ways to define stocks. One measure is hardly ever enough to get an accurate picture. If you had to invest your life savings into one of these companies, which would you pick?

Based solely on these charts, Amazon.com looks like a place your investment could grow in a hurry. If I told you that at the time these charts were made,

AT&T had $162.8 billion in assets and had been a successful company for many decades, while five years ago nobody ever heard of Amazon.com and it had assets of only $2.2 billion, would that change your mind?

I have chosen these two examples because they fall on opposite ends of the growth spectrum.

Morningstar calls Amazon.com a "speculative growth" stock, meaning it could continue its explosive growth or implode and disappear altogether. The company, as of the date of these figures, had never earned a dollar and there were no profits on the horizon.

PROCEED WITH CAUTION

Not all growth measures are the same. What makes sense for one company may not for another, as these two figures illustrate.

Growth can be defined as growth in sales, profits, dividends, or a number of other criteria. Using sales, Amazon.com would clearly fall into the growth category. If you screened for companies showing growth in earnings, Amazon.com would not even be a blip, since it has no earnings.

Later we look at ways to screen stocks that meet your investment needs (and help you define what your needs are) through a set of parameters. This process will help you compare apples and apples.

AT&T is a blue chip stock by almost anyone's definition—its growth can easily be described as slow growth or mature growth.

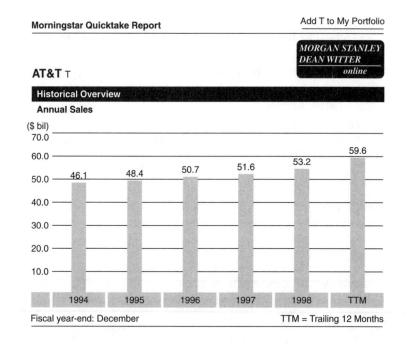

Morningstar Quicktake Report

Add T to My Portfolio

MORGAN STANLEY
DEAN WITTER
online

AT&T T

Historical Overview

Annual Sales

($ bil)

	1994	1995	1996	1997	1998	TTM
	46.1	48.4	50.7	51.6	53.2	59.6

Fiscal year-end: December

TTM = Trailing 12 Months

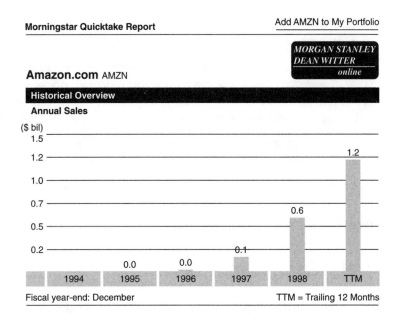

Amazon.com is certainly on a fast-growth trajectory.

As different as AT&T and Amazon.com are, they both have at least one thing in common: potential. Amazon.com is a trailblazer in online commerce. It has obviously experienced explosive sales growth, going from virtually nothing to $1.2 billion in sales in only a few years. In addition, by the end of September 1999, it had over 13 million customers. That's the potential fueling the tremendous investor interest in a company that is broke by most accounting standards.

PROCEED WITH CAUTION

Older companies with significant asset bases tend to be less volatile than young companies without much underlying value.

AT&T, on the other hand, has a huge asset base and a tremendous position in the telecommunications market. It recently bought a cable company, which gives it another entrée to the consumer and business markets for high-speed access to the Internet. When combined with its traditional services, including wireless access, many investors feel they are in a commanding position to participate in the anticipated growth of high-speed Internet access.

On the other hand, Morningstar.com looks at AT&T a bit differently. The service uses a grading system that ranks each stock in the following areas:

- Growth
- Profitability

- Financial health
- Valuation

These grading systems are another way to find comparisons of like stocks. It is also a way to quickly see where a stock may be strong or have some weakness. Morningstar.com arrives at these grades based on fairly detailed financial calculations that do not directly include potential, like I used above.

Let's see how the two stocks do in a head-to-head grading using the Morningstar system:

Stock Grades	AT&T	Amazon.com
Growth	C	A+
Profitability	A	F
Financial Health	A	D–
Valuation	C	—

As we have already surmised, these two stocks are nothing alike, yet they both could be called growth stocks of some sort.

The lesson here is that you shouldn't get tripped up over broad terms such as "growth" when considering stocks. If you want an objective determination, use one of the several systems available, such as Morningstar.com. This will help you compare like stocks and avoid ridiculous questions such as, "Should I buy AT&T or Amazon.com?"

JUST A MINUTE

Picking a potential growth stock out of the bargain bin is not easy, but ultimately very rewarding.

INCOME STOCKS

Finding income stocks is a little more straightforward than deciphering growth stocks. For starters, a stock either generates income or it doesn't. Income is in the form of dividends.

One of the ways to judge whether a company is paying a reasonable dividend is to use the dividend yield calculation, dividing the annual dividend by the stock's price.

JUST A MINUTE

Generating income in the form of dividends only tells part of the story. How do the dividends relate to the stock price? Are they expensive or cheap? The dividend yield tells you the answer.

In the case of AT&T, the dividend yield is 1.6 percent at the time the chart was created. Dividends are set once a year by the board of directors. They can raise, lower, or eliminate the dividend based on the company's financial condition.

As you might have deduced, the dividend yield is not a static number. As the per-share price fluctuates, the dividend yield will change. In our example above, the per-share price was $57 and the annual dividend per share was $0.88. If the per-share price goes up, the dividend yield will go down. For example …

Dividend	Stock Price	Dividend Yield
$0.88	$57	1.6 percent
$0.88	$47	1.9 percent
$0.88	$67	1.3 percent

As you can see, when the price of the stock moves in either direction, the dividend yield changes.

PROCEED WITH CAUTION

Don't latch on to one number or ratio as the key to investment decisions. Looking at an investment in the proper context is the key to sound decisions.

This means that for the price you have to pay to buy the stock, the yield is dropping. If you are thinking about buying this stock for its income, this low yield may seem unattractive.

On the other hand, if you already own this stock you may want the dividend to go up, but you can't be too unhappy that the stock price has taken a major jump.

Morningstar classifies a stock as "high yield" when its dividend is more than twice the large-cap average:

Dividend History AT&T	12/95	12/96	12/97	12/98	12/99
Dividend $	0.88	0.88	0.88	0.88	0.88
Year-end Yield %	2.0	3.0	2.2	1.7	1.7
S&P 500 Yield %	1.1	1.0	0.8	0.7	0.6

*Source: Morningstar.com

As you can see, AT&T has had a steady history of dividends for the past five years. Without seeing the numbers, you can track the fluctuations in the share price by the changes in the "year-end yield percent" from 1995–1999.

Income stocks are much easier to find and rank than growth stocks. Access to information like that from Morningstar.com makes the searching much easier.

VALUE STOCKS

There are many market millionaires (and billionaires) that became that way, in part, by finding stocks that were "ugly ducklings" waiting to blossom into beautiful swans.

PROCEED WITH CAUTION

 Value stocks may be out of favor with investors for no other reason than they are not in the current hot sector.

One of the key numbers in identifying value stocks is the P/E ratio. This number, you will recall, is found by dividing the price per share by the annual earnings per share. The higher this number, the more "expensive" the stock is considered to be and the riskier.

Value stocks fall in the low P/E ranges. The best way to use the P/E ratio is as a measure to compare the stock to its peers and a comparable market indicator.

	AT&T	Industry	S&P 500
Price/Earnings Ratio	27.4	31.4	35.6

Like most ratios, the P/E is just one tool to use in looking for value stocks, but it is a good first cut since value stocks are not going to have high P/E relative to its peers.

The companies listed below are some of the best known in America. They are established, reputable companies that have made a place for themselves in our economy. However, they all have something else in common. Can you guess what?

Ticker	Name	Market Capitalization ($mil.)
BAC	Bank of America	91,547.74
MO	Philip Morris Companies	60,781.37

Ticker	Name	Market Capitalization ($mil.)
F	Ford Motor	60,772.32
GM	General Motors	46,575.14
ONE	Bank One	36,843.53
FTU	First Union	34,817.93
ALL	Allstate	21,206.71
HI	Household International	18,365.08
WM	Washington Mutual	15,587.21
TAP	Travelers Property Casualty A	13,185.53
BNI	Burlington Northern Santa Fe	13,162.88
S	Sears Roebuck	11,787.62

*Source: Morningstar.com

What do all of these companies have in common? Other than the fact that you have probably heard of many of these stocks, you may not guess that these are all value stocks. Morningstar has rated them as value based on their proprietary system, which computes a fair market value for the stock, then compares that number to the actual stock price. If it is higher, then the stock is selling below what it should be worth.

It should also be noted that all of these stocks have very low P/E ratios, many in the single-digit area. Does that mean you should rush out and buy as many of these values as possible?

PROCEED WITH CAUTION

Value stocks should be part of a long-term portfolio. These stocks don't often turn around in a hurry.

Not really. The way billionaires become billionaires using value stocks is by identifying those stocks with the potential to become booming growth stocks at some point in time. When we talk about picking stocks in Hour 18, "Picking a Stock," we will cover some of the ways to find the gems.

However, you can look at this list (this is only part of the list Morningstar's stock screener selected for me) and see that none of the companies listed are in industries that are "hot" right now. Some of these stocks are suffering because they aren't a "dot com" company or a computer maker or some other high-tech offering.

STOCKS ON THE INTERNET

Stocks come in a lot of different flavors. Fortunately, there are a number of services out there that can make your job of identifying and picking stocks much simpler.

Access to this information was once very difficult to get. Thanks to the Internet, people of common means and moderate intelligence can make investment decisions based on good, strong information, and not on whims or "hot tips."

You can't beat the Internet for news and information. Here are some great news and information sites:

The Wall Street Journal (wsj.com)

Bloomberg (Bloomberg.com)

The Motley Fool (fool.com)

About.com (beginnersinvest.about.com)

Morningstar.com (morningstar.com)

Forbes (forbes.com)

SmartMoney (smartmoney.com)

BankRate (bankrate.com)

WHAT CAN YOU DO?

The following is a list of five things you can do today:

1. At the beginning of the stock listings in *The Wall Street Journal* are a large number of charts and graphs detailing market activity. Look at the large table titled "Stock Market Data Bank." Can you see how this information will be helpful? We'll get into this in more detail, but for now, familiarize yourself with the different listings.

2. There are two columns on the opening page. One is "Abreast of the Market" and the other is "Heard on the Street." If you plan on being an active trader or just enjoy following the markets, these two columns are a gold mine of information. Read them to get a flavor of their content and tone.

3. Somewhere in the stock listings of *The Wall Street Journal* (usually at the beginning of the tables) is a small box titled "Annual Report Service." It notes how you can obtain free annual reports and quarterly reports of selected companies. Identify a couple of companies you are interested in and order the reports. We'll make use of them later in the book.

4. Also on this page you will find a box titled "Explanatory Notes." These notes, in very small type, expand on the listings I described in Hour 6, "Understanding the Numbers." Find the listings of several stocks you are familiar with and see how hard or easy it is to decipher the codes.

5. In the section listing NASDAQ market issues, you will find a column called "Small Stock Focus." This column tracks activity in the small stock sector. Read it for a couple of days a week to help you understand how this segment of the market is different from the larger stocks.

WORKSHOP

Using your *Wall Street Journal* stock tables, pick out five value stocks (based on P/E ratio only) in the following categories:

Value:

1. _____
2. _____
3. _____
4. _____
5. _____

Income:

1. _____
2. _____
3. _____
4. _____
5. _____

Growth:

1. _____
2. _____
3. _____
4. _____
5. _____

HOUR'S UP!

Individual stocks are often considered more exciting than mutual funds. However, they share many of the same characteristics in terms of how we define them. See whether you can master this short quiz.

1. Growth stocks …

   A. Pay consistent and handsome dividends.

   B. Never lose money.

   C. Show growth in earnings and/or sales.

2. Growth can be defined …

   A. As growth in sales.

   B. As growth in earnings.

   C. As growth in dividends.

   D. All of the above.

3. Comparing two growth stocks …

   A. Is impossible.

   B. Not very telling.

   C. Must be done on some common basis.

4. Classifying stocks …

   A. Is purely arbitrary.

   B. Is difficult without some standard procedures.

   C. Is not worth the effort.

5. Income stocks …

   A. Are easier to classify than growth stocks.

   B. Defy classification.

   C. Have no classification.

6. Dividend yield tells you …

   A. What the company's profits are.

   B. How expensive or cheap the dividends are.

   C. How much the stock is worth.

7. The dividend yield …

    A. Remains the same all year.

    B. Moves with the price of the stock.

    C. Is never more than 3 percent.

8. Value stocks …

    A. Lack any value at all.

    B. Are more expensive than growth stocks.

    C. Are undervalued by the market.

9. Value stocks have …

    A. No P/E ratio.

    B. A high P/E ratio.

    C. A low P/E ratio.

10. Value stocks …

    A. Are hot investment opportunities.

    B. Have made people rich.

    C. Never lose money.

Quiz

HOUR 13
Stocks—Part II Size

CHAPTER SUMMARY

LESSON PLAN:
In this Hour you will learn about ...

- Market capitalization.
- Large-cap stocks.
- Mid-cap stocks.
- Small-cap stocks.
- Penny stocks.
- Initial public offerings.

You need to know that I am from Texas, and Texans are genetically predisposed to think big. Big houses, big ranches, big lies. I once had a pickup truck that was so big, the back end was in a different zip code from the front end.

When it comes to stocks, size is one primary method for finding the right investment in a particular situation. We use size as a first cut because it is an easy measure that narrows our focus to a smaller group of stocks for further analysis.

The usual way the market measures a company is by market capitalization, also known as market cap. A large company would be known as a large-cap stock, while a small company would be known as a small-cap stock, and so on.

PROCEED WITH CAUTION

Companies are measured based on their assets, sales, earnings, and other marks in addition to being measured by their market capitalization.

If you remember earlier discussions about market capitalization, you know that it is figured by multiplying the number of outstanding shares of a stock by its current price. For example, if XYZ Company has 10 million shares of stock outstanding and the current price is $55 per share, the market cap is $550 million.

You can see from this formula that the market cap of a particular stock can (and does) change every time the price changes or it issues or buys back stock.

Market cap doesn't tell us anything about the company other than this particular way of looking at size. It certainly doesn't tell us anything about the quality of the company. A company can have a high market cap and be broke.

JUST A MINUTE

Even a company that has never made money can be a good investment. Stock appreciation has made Internet companies hot buys.

Near the end of 1999, Amazon.com, the online book-and-everything-else seller, had a market cap of over $32 billion, yet it had never made a penny of profit.

MARKET CAP AND INVESTMENT DECISIONS

So, how does knowing the market cap of a stock help us make an investment decision? One of the things market cap can do is help us compare companies of approximately the same size. This information lets us find peers in size and industry.

For example, if we were looking at communications companies, it might be interesting to compare AT&T ($170 billion market cap) with SBC Communications ($175 billion market cap).

Size is just one factor out of many to consider, but it is important to understand what you should expect of companies in different size groups. If one company is acting in a manner that is quite different from what you would expect, it might mean a buy-or-sell situation.

The numbers I am using in this Hour were generated from a database of 9,351 companies and were captured in late 1999. This database includes almost all publicly traded companies, although most are very small.

TIME SAVER

StockQuest, which can be found at www.marketguide.com, is a valuable tool for screening stocks.

The size stocks we will look at are …

- **Large-cap stocks**—market cap in excess of $8 billion (451 companies)
- **Mid-cap stocks**—market cap in excess of $1 billion, but less than $8 billion (1,259 companies)
- **Small-cap stocks**—market cap less than $1 billion (7,641 companies)

LARGE-CAP STOCKS

Large-cap stocks are important because they are often the "movers and shakers" of the market and their particular industries. Where you cut off large-cap stocks from mid-cap stocks is somewhat open to interpretation.

Some systems use a dollar figure, such as $8 billion and up. Others will use a percentage method that takes all the stocks and says the top 5 percent in number are the large-cap stocks.

A problem with both of these systems is that you have a huge gap between the bottom of the large-cap range and the top. Using either the $8-billion figure or the 5-percent range gets you about the same results in terms of the number of large-cap stocks.

PROCEED WITH CAUTION

Use some common sense when considering large-cap stocks. Huge gorillas should not be compared to large monkeys.

The range from the bottom of $8 billion to the top of $596 billion is significant. These mega-giants all have market caps exceeding $100 billion, with Microsoft at the top. Is it rational to expect an $8-billion company to behave in the same manner as a $596-billion company?

We remember that our focus is on grouping companies of like size, so we aren't going to be comparing Microsoft ($596 billion) with Check Point Software ($7.1 billion). It is not particularly important where you put the mark that designates large-cap stocks, as long as you are consistent in its application.

The Dow Jones Industrial Average, you remember, is made up of 30 of the largest companies in the United States.

Yet, the 30 companies in the DJIA account for only 18.63 percent of the total market value of all stocks (9,351). The S&P 500 accounts for 54 percent of the total market value.

As you become more familiar with the numbers used to value and analyze stocks, you will notice that market cap is only one of many, and not a very important one at that. Why, then, are we spending so much time looking at this number?

Our goal here is not to focus on numbers, but on characteristics. The numbers are just to help us collect stocks in like-sized groups. This grouping gives us some basic characteristics to work with in our stock-selection process.

Notice that the DJIA does not include the 30 absolutely largest companies.

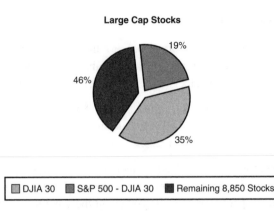

Large Cap Stocks

19%

46%

35%

| DJIA 30 | S&P 500 - DJIA 30 | Remaining 8,850 Stocks |

Large-cap stocks, as a rule, are older, more mature companies with lengthy histories. However, the explosion of technology and the Internet combined with the raging stock market have vaulted some very young companies into the large-cap category.

So even as we approach large-cap stocks to get an understanding of what they are and why they are important, we have to temper our assessment with the realization that some of these young shooting stars may not be around as we know them in the next five years.

In many ways, traditional large-cap stocks are the cornerstones of most institutional investment programs. Known as *core stocks*, these giants may not be nimble, but aren't likely to fall, either.

JUST A MINUTE

Core stocks are the cornerstones of many portfolios. They are held for the long term and provide stability.

Moreover, when they do stumble, many have the resources, both financial and personnel, to get back on their feet. Earlier, I mentioned IBM as a large-cap stock that fell on hard times, but has managed to regain a measure of trust and respect in the market.

Size alone does not guarantee survival, but it certainly helps. Consequently, large-cap stocks are not known for their volatility—that is, rapid swings in price, up and down. Historically, they have added stability to portfolios and income to the bottom line.

I wonder if it irks old-time General Electric Company employees and stock-holders that Microsoft, whose founder wasn't even born when GE was one of the most trusted and profitable companies in America, is valued by the market some $100 billion more.

Blue chip stocks are considered the safest of stock investments because they are felt to be the best of their industry, although some folks will call any company in the S&P 500 a blue chip stock because of its market presence.

PROCEED WITH CAUTION

Back in the days when most brokers managed peoples' money, they were supposed to only recommend stocks appropriate for their clients. Blue chip stocks were called "widow and orphan" investments because the stockbroker could safely invest their money in blue chips without fear that the recommendation was inappropriate.

Others feel that size alone is less important than a long history of growth in earnings and dividends. There is no one "official" list of blue chip stocks, but you would certainly have to consider the 30 stocks in the DJIA as potential candidates, even though one of those stocks is Microsoft, a mere pup in this rarified atmosphere of elder companies.

Large-cap stock characteristics are covered in the following sections.

HEAVY TRADING VOLUME

Large-cap stocks tend to have fairly heavy trading volume day in and day out, regardless of news and market conditions. They are frequently, but not always, among the top trading volume leaders.

This relatively heavy trading volume usually means it is fairly easy to buy and sell the stock. It also means that the market is constantly repricing the stock. This is important because prices are more reflective of the market assessment of the stock when it is heavily traded.

FOLLOWED CLOSELY BY MEDIA AND ANALYSTS

The financial press and stock analysts follow large-cap stocks very closely. Because they tend to dominate the market, it is important news when something happens.

This attention makes it easier to find information about the company and what other people think about its worth as an investment. This access to information will make your job of picking stocks easier.

TENDENCY TO BE LESS VOLATILE

Large-cap stocks, especially the older ones, tend to be less volatile, meaning there is a smaller variation between the high and low during daily trading.

PROCEED WITH CAUTION

Some institutional investors (endowment funds, charities, and so on) are more interested in stability than superior returns.

This does not mean that large-cap stocks can't rise and fall fairly dramatically. During the last quarter of 1999, AT&T's price was up over 20 percent in four weeks on some positive news releases.

In regular markets, where there is no positive or negative news, large-cap stocks will tend to trade in a narrow range. This is the stability institutional managers look for in the large-cap stocks.

DJIA AND S&P 500 MEMBERS

Large-cap stocks will be found in the DJIA and the S&P 500 Index, so these market indicators are important.

Certainly all the 30 members of the DJIA are large-cap stocks. Many of these are core, blue chip stocks as well. The most recent addition to the DJIA is Microsoft.

JUST A MINUTE

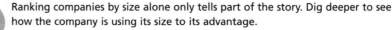

Ranking companies by size alone only tells part of the story. Dig deeper to see how the company is using its size to its advantage.

The S&P 500 is viewed by many as a gauge of large companies in the market, even though some of the members are quite small (under $1 billion market cap). This is because the S&P 500 represents not the 500 largest companies, but the most important 500 companies (in the opinion of Standard & Poor's).

SMALL GROWTH POTENTIAL

Large-cap stocks, especially the older core stocks, are usually characterized by a smaller growth potential than smaller companies. This does not mean they aren't growing and, in the case of the new high-technology members, may not be true at all.

Many of the large-cap stocks grow more by acquisition and merger than increasing market penetration, for example. Mergers and acquisitions don't always work out, but the market often rewards large-cap companies that open new markets or swallow competitors with higher stock prices.

MID-CAP STOCKS

Mid-cap stocks often act like the large-cap stocks' adolescent siblings. They are often characterized by growth spurts, followed by periods of adaptation.

Because they are usually younger than the large-cap stocks, they often struggle with growth that strains management and financial resources. In this fast-moving world, it is not uncommon for a mid-cap company to buy technology, market share, and so on, by merging or buying another mid-cap company.

PROCEED WITH CAUTION

Market analysts watch mid-cap stocks to see which one looks ready to take off. Among the indicators they look for are steady growth in revenues, increased market share, increased earnings or decreased losses, and a management structure capable of handling additional growth.

The market watches these deals closely. If the fit seems to make strategic sense and there is management in place to tackle the new structure, the market will look with great favor on the merger.

It is mid-cap stocks that are sought by growth-oriented investors and mutual funds.

Mid-cap stock characteristics are covered in the following sections.

HEAVY TRADING VOLUME

Mid-cap stocks in hot sectors are often the volume leaders, especially on good or bad news. Everyone is looking for a mid-cap stock that is ready to move up in size and market presence.

MEDIA COVERAGE

As the news media has become more sophisticated about the market, news of mid-cap stocks is now routinely reported along with the market-leading large-cap stocks.

This is due in part to the rapid growth of cable television and the Internet, where huge information markets have been created.

HIGH-TECH AND OTHER HOT GROUPS CLOSELY WATCHED BY ANALYSTS

Stock analysts routinely keep watch over the mid-cap stocks in the hot sectors. They have seen too many young startups zoom through the mid-cap range into the large-cap section without much attention.

The Internet economy has created whole new breeds of companies that the analysts are having trouble following by traditional means. For example, it is doubtful that too many companies have gone from startup to large-cap stock in a manner of a few years.

Many times, traditional methods of analysis don't work as well for companies with market caps in the billions, but that have never made a penny of profit.

HIGH VOLATILITY

To carry the adolescent analogy a little further, mid-cap stocks can be moody and irrational in reacting to market pressures. Consequently, some have wide swings in price each day.

JUST A MINUTE

Trying to figure out a volatile mid-cap stock can be frustrating, but it is highly rewarding when you find one ready to move.

This is not categorically true of all mid-cap stocks, but the potential for some wild swings is certainly greater than the large-cap stocks.

LESSER-KNOWN INDEXES

The growing importance of mid-cap stocks is revealed by the number of indexes used to follow this group. However, these indexes are not as well known or reported as those that follow the large-cap stocks.

JUST A MINUTE

The lesser-known indexes usually tell a better story about the stocks they cover than the broader market indexes.

S&P Mid-Cap 400 index is one of the best known, along with the NASDAQ composite and computer and telecommunications indexes. The Wiltshire 5000 is probably the broadest-based of the indexes.

HIGH GROWTH POTENTIAL

The growth potential of mid-cap stocks is where they really draw a crowd. It is from this group that the new Microsofts and Intels will emerge. Folks who can spot these rising eagles will be handsomely rewarded.

However, it is always easier to spot the winners in retrospect than it is to pick them out of a crowd of wannabes. There will always be many more mid-cap companies that stall at this level or decline than go on to be industry leaders.

JUST A MINUTE

Sometimes a mid-cap stock will move up to the big leagues by merging with or buying a competitor. The resulting large-cap stock may solidify its position in the market.

Mid-cap stocks also face the possibility that one of the large-cap stocks will hear the sound of their footsteps behind them, turn around, and gobble up their potential rival. Life is precarious at this level, but the potential rewards are extremely attractive.

SMALL-CAP COMPANIES

Small-cap stock characteristics are covered in the following sections.

LIGHT TRADING VOLUME

The vast majority of the small-cap companies are traded very lightly, if at all. Many may have no trading for weeks or months. This light volume makes buying and selling difficult and it is often hard to get pricing information.

Many of these small companies are publicly traded in form only. Quite often most of the stock is held by a handful of stockholders. At the bottom end of the small-cap section, it is not uncommon to find stocks with no trading on any given day.

JUST A MINUTE

Small-cap stocks often dwell in obscurity. Almost all of them that survive will remain small, many by design. Despite being "publicly traded," many small companies are closely held, meaning most of the stock is owned by a handful of individuals, frequently family members. This is done so that if the company is sold, each family member who owns stock will receive a fair proportion of the proceeds.

ALMOST NO MEDIA COVERAGE

Except for those companies on the top end of the small-cap limit, most of the companies in this category dwell in obscurity as far as the national media is concerned. Many of these tiny companies never make any national news unless it is scandalous (see the section "Penny Stocks" later in this Hour).

ALMOST NO ATTENTION FROM ANALYSTS

At the very top of the small-cap range, you will find some attention from analysts and reporting organizations, but most of the tiny companies that make up the bulk of the small-cap sector never receive much attention.

This is understandable, since many of the companies may have virtually no trading activity during the year and are not the subject of any real investor attention.

HIGHLY VOLATILE

The small-cap stocks, if they are actively traded, can be highly volatile. These companies are often extremely vulnerable in their market position and don't have the resources to ride out some of the rough spots.

PROCEED WITH CAUTION

 Small-cap stocks usually have no buffers against adverse market or competitive conditions. This makes them extremely vulnerable.

Because many of the stocks are thinly traded, any burst of activity is likely to send the price jumping.

LESSER-KNOWN INDEX (S&P SMALL-CAP 600)

There are several indexes that follow small-cap stocks. The best known of these is the S&P Small-Cap 600 Index. This index really measures the activity of the upper end on the small cap scale.

The average market cap of the S&P Index is $544 million (as of November 23, 1999).

HIGH GROWTH POTENTIAL, BUT VERY HIGH RISK

The small-cap stocks are ripe for explosive growth—or disastrous crashes. They live on the market bubble and any minute can plunge into obscurity or worse.

Stocks with share prices under $2 are ripe targets for manipulation. Use caution when approached to invest.

As we have already discussed, size matters when it comes to riding out market tides. Small-cap stocks are like small boats in the sea. When the sea is calm, they make great racers, but when the wind and waves begin to grow, it is time to look for life jackets.

SPECIAL SITUATIONS

Penny stocks and IPOs are two special situations that deserve attention in this Hour because they are topics of great interest.

PENNY STOCKS

Penny stocks, as the name implies, are a group of unlisted securities traded in the over-the-counter market. There are thousands of these companies, many very respectable.

Subsets of these stocks normally trade for less than a dollar and are often issued by highly speculative companies. When you can find pricing, it is often arbitrary and misleading.

The Internet has given con artists a new venue to run their schemes. Many of these scams target honest but naïve people who think it is possible to get in on hot deals.

Many of these stocks are legitimate, if highly speculative, companies. Unfortunately, they are also the weapon of choice for a particularly unscrupulous breed of stock manipulators.

Here is how this scam works:

You get a call or e-mail from a person who identifies himself as a broker with a hot deal. He may reference someone you know or use some other trick to gain your confidence. He encourages you to invest in this great, new, "undiscovered" company or some other come-on.

The great thing about this deal is that you can lock up 10,000 shares for just $5,000, again because the "big boys" haven't discovered this gem. If you can't afford $5,000, he'll try to get you in at a smaller amount.

You send him some money and, for the most part, that's the last you will see of it. You may get an update a few weeks after your check clears telling you things are going right on schedule, and wouldn't you like some more stock before it really starts to soar?

JUST A MINUTE

People incorrectly assume that because the stock market is highly regulated, they are safe from illegal stock scams. Most of these scams operate without regulatory knowledge until someone complains.

Behind the scenes, this broker and maybe 50 others are all calling prospects that are known or suspected of being gullible. The company they are touting may in fact be a legitimate company with no knowledge of this activity, or it can be a sham designed just for the purpose of parting you from your money.

The brokers own a big chunk of the stock and use the money you send to generate a lot of activity in the stock, which causes the price to rise. When the price gets where they want it, they dump their stock and walk away from the deal.

The stock crashes when the brokers' shares are dumped on the market and all the investors who thought they were getting in on a hot deal get burned instead.

These schemes have many variations, but result in the same conclusion: You lose your money.

Part of the problem is the market in penny stocks is virtually unregulated. If a broker from a licensed and registered dealer misleads you or does something fraudulent, you have regulatory bodies that can step in and set things right.

However, most of the penny stocks trade in an unregulated market, and many of the brokers who sell them are known securities law violators.

The bottom line is: Don't buy penny stocks.

IPOs

Initial public offerings (IPOs) occur when a company first issues stock to the public. They are the subjects of intense interest because their prices can jump so radically if the market takes a liking to the company.

JUST A MINUTE

IPOs are the legal equivalent of stock manipulation. The only people who consistently make money in IPOs are investment bankers.

When a company wants to move into the publicly traded sector, it plans to issue (sell) stock to the public through an offering. This offering is highly regulated and must meet a number of requirements before the stock can be sold to the public.

The company picks an investment banking firm or firms to handle the offering. Once the offering is priced and packaged, a target date is set for the public sale.

However, before the public gets a shot at the stock, it is often sold to the investment banker's real customers, the retail stock brokerage firms. They in turn will offer it to their best customers before the public has a shot.

PROCEED WITH CAUTION

People make money in IPOs by getting in and getting out at the right time. Most people can't figure this out and buy too high and sell too low.

As you can see, there are several steps along the way; at every step the stock price goes up so that by the time it hits the streets for public sale, it may already be way above the initial price listed in the IPO documents.

All of this is perfectly legal and an accepted way of doing business, although there are a couple of Internet-based organizations that are trying some different methods. One company, Wit Capital (www.witcapital.com), allocates IPO shares on a first come, first served basis and also does the underwriting itself.

IPOs are not generally good investments. Most of them are trading at or near their offering price within a year of going public, no matter how intense the interest for the first offering.

The people who make money on IPOs generally are big customers of retail brokers and get the good offering price. They usually will sell all or part of their original purchase for a hefty profit and, if they think the company is going to be a significant player, hold some for future appreciation.

JUST A MINUTE

Even the folks who get in early face some obstacles. If they sell immediately after the stock is made available, their broker may cut them off from future offerings. Selling so quickly is called "flipping," and the brokerage houses don't like to see it because it can erode confidence in the offering if holders sell so quickly.

Most of us won't get an IPO at or near the original offering price. We have to buy when the stock actually hits the market. If the company is hot, the price can skyrocket. If you can get in early and then get out, you may make a profit.

The bottom line on IPOs is that they are not good investments for the most part. If you want to chase them, do so with the understanding that it is a highly speculative activity and is not consistent with a sound investment strategy.

WHAT CAN YOU DO?

The following is a list of five things you can do today:

1. *The Wall Street Journal* publishes a "Stock Market Data Bank" in every issue. The top portion of the feature lists various market indexes. How do the indexes for smaller issues compare with the major indexes?

2. Scan the NASDAQ listings in the stock market tables for smaller issues. Look at the trading volume. Can you see why trading in small-cap stocks is risky?

3. If you have access to the Internet, go to one of the stock-screening sites listed in Appendix B, "Resources," and get familiar with the terminology.

4. Go to your public library and see if it carries the Value Line Investment Survey in the reference section. If so, look over it in preparation for a future hour.

5. If you did not finish your goals set earlier in the book, finish them—you will need them in a few chapters.

WORKSHOP

Using information you can find in *The Wall Street Journal,* make a chart with the following headings:

Large-Cap	Mid-Cap	Small-Cap

Note the number of stories and charts devoted to each size. You will not always be able to tell, but make a guess. This exercise will illustrate the relative attention each receives.

HOUR'S UP!

Crunching your way through all the different characteristics of stocks in particular size groups is an invaluable exercise that will prove itself when you are ready to buy your first stock. Take this short quiz as a way to review your progress:

1. Market capitalization is …

    A. A way to place a value on a stock.

    B. Measure of a company's size.

    C. Not relevant.

2. Large-cap stocks …

    A. Have more than 10,000 employees.

    B. Grow faster than average.

    C. Have market caps exceeding $8 billion.

3. The media …

    A. Pays no attention to large-cap stocks.

    B. Follows large-cap stocks closely.

    C. Considers large-cap stocks silly.

4. Large-cap stocks account …

    A. For most of money in the stock market.

    B. For all of the Dow.

    C. Most of the growth in prices.

5. Mid-cap stocks …

    A. May have heavy trading volume.

    B. Are very stable in price.

    C. Cannot be expected to grow.

6. Mid-cap stocks …

    A. Are usually older manufacturing companies.

    B. Have spotty media coverage.

    C. Grow slower than average.

7. Small-cap stocks …

  A. Are extremely safe investments.

  B. May experience rapid growth.

  C. Lack any potential for success.

8. Small-cap stocks …

  A. Are mostly sold on the New York Stock Exchange.

  B. Have heavy trading volume everyday.

  C. Are extremely vulnerable to market and competitive pressures.

9. Penny stocks …

  A. Are great buys for new investors.

  B. Are subject to manipulation.

  C. Never lose money.

10. IPOs …

  A. Are easy investments to make.

  B. Always rise and stay up.

  C. Are often not good investments for the long term.

HOUR 14

Bonds

CHAPTER SUMMARY

LESSON PLAN:

In this Hour you will learn about ...

- U.S. Treasury Bonds.
- U.S. government agency bonds.
- Municipal bonds.
- Corporate bonds.
- Worth of a bond.
- Figuring yield.
- Junk bonds.
- Risks.
- Subordinated bonds.
- Convertible bonds.
- Rating services.

In this Hour we are going to look at bonds in greater detail than in previous hours, when we introduced you to some of the basics of "fixed-income securities," as bonds are known.

The total worth of bonds owned by Americans is more than that of stocks and mutual funds. Bonds occupy a huge role in our economy and continue to be an attractive source for corporate financing, as well as for governments.

TYPES OF BONDS

In previous hours, we have touched briefly on different types of bonds. Now it is time to dig deeper for a better understanding of their relative strengths and weaknesses. The types of bonds we will be discussing are as follows:

- U.S. Treasury
- U.S. government agency
- Municipal
- Corporate

U.S. TREASURY BONDS

The U.S. government through the Department of Treasury issues debt instruments of various maturities to finance the day-to-day and long-term needs of the government. They come in three basic flavors:

- T-bonds have the longest maturities ranging from 10 to 30 years
- T-notes have mid-range maturities ranging from 2 to 10 years
- T-bills are short-term issues ranging from 90 days to 1 year

All of the Treasury issues come with the full backing of the U.S. government, meaning they are the benchmark for safety. The absolute assurance that they will be paid back comes with a price in the form of relatively lower interest rates.

The bond market watches these issues very closely because they represent the absolute in safety if held to maturity. When interest rates change on new Treasury issues, it usually signals a movement in interest rates on other issues.

The Federal Reserve Bank sells new issues at auction, but sales in the secondary market must be done through a broker.

New T-bonds and T-notes are issued in denominations starting at $1,000 and ranging up to $1 million. T-bills are issued in denominations of $10,000 and may be bundled for much larger investments.

T-bonds and T-notes pay periodic interest just like other bonds and are redeemable for face value at maturity. T-bills, on the other hand, are sold at a discount off the face value. The difference between the face value and the discount price is the interest. No interest payments are made; rather, the bills are redeemed at face value.

For example, a $10,000 T-Bill pays 5 percent interest. You would buy the bill for $9,523.81 and redeem it for the full $10,000 face value. The difference of $476.19 is your interest.

All three of the U.S. Treasury issues are exempt from state and local taxes, but not federal tax.

U.S. GOVERNMENT AGENCY

U.S. government agency bonds are often used to finance mortgages provided under various government programs. The best known are Ginnie Mae (GNMAs), Fannie Mae (FNMAs), and Freddie Mac (FHLs) bonds. These bonds are taxable.

There are also bond programs that support student loans, loans to farmers, and other agencies. These bonds are reported in *The Wall Street Journal* under "Government Agency & Similar Issues." These bonds are exempt from state and local taxes.

Some of these issues may be rated by the standard rating services. They usually pay higher rates than Treasury issue, with just slightly more risk. Their maturities range from 1 month to 20 years in some cases. Most are sold in very large denominations of $100,000 or more.

JUST A MINUTE

U.S. government bonds feature lower yields than other bonds because of the absolute safety they provide. Agency bonds that are backed by mortgages may suffer during economic downturns when foreclosures rise.

In December 1999, a Treasury note carried a yield of 5.94 percent, while a Freddie Mac issue of the same maturity was quoted at 6.04 percent.

MUNICIPAL BONDS

Municipal bonds is a catchall phrase for bonds issued by state, county, city, or other local authorities. Most people are familiar with "munis," as they are called, because local governments use them to pay for schools, roads, and other construction projects.

Municipal bonds are rated for the creditworthiness of the issuer. Usually, the issuer needs to show how the bonds will be repaid. The most common way is through existing or increased taxation. The tax money pays the periodic interest rate and builds a pool of money to retire the bonds at maturity.

Munis are exempt from federal income tax and, in some cases, when the purchaser lives in the jurisdiction of the issuer, may be exempt from state and local taxes, the so-called *triple tax-free bond*. High-income taxpayers are especially attracted to these bonds.

JUST A MINUTE

Triple tax-free bonds or mutual bond funds sound great, but only make sense if you are in a fairly high tax bracket. Most middle-income investors will do better in regular funds.

Mutual bond funds that offer the triple tax-exempt status are sold in individual states because the buyer has to reside in that state to qualify for the triple exemption. You can identify these funds in the newspaper tables easily because they often are named for the targeted state.

For example, if you look under mutual funds listings in your *Wall Street Journal,* you will notice that the USAA Group offers funds titled "CA Bd, NY Bd, and VA Bd." These funds target muni investments in California, New York, and Virginia, respectively, and are sold to the residents of these states.

Munis are usually issued at a lower coupon or interest rate than corporate bonds with the same rating because of the tax-exempt feature and are sold in denominations of $5,000 and up with maturities ranging from 1 month to 40 years.

Like most bonds, munis usually require a large minimum investment and are sold through brokers. Investment bankers often buy up blocks of the bonds and resell them to dealers and brokers who hold them in inventory to sell to their customers.

PROCEED WITH CAUTION

Municipalities guard their bond ratings carefully. A lower rating can mean millions of dollars in extra interest.

While not as safe as U.S. Treasury issues, top-rated munis are considered a minimal risk. Of course, this relative safety and tax-exempt status significantly reduce the interest rate.

Municipal bonds that do not earn a good rating often pay a much higher interest rate to compensate for the higher risk of default. There are a number of mutual bond funds that specialize in high income from these higher-risk bonds.

Munis, especially those issued with high interest rates, may have a call provision. This provision, which is covered in the "Prepayment" section later in this Hour, allows the issuer to redeem or buy back the bond at certain points in the bond's maturity.

CORPORATE BONDS

Corporations issue bonds to finance a wide variety of business-related needs, from expansion of physical plants to financing acquisitions. Bonds are often preferred over bank loans, because the company may be able to structure the bonds to fit its needs at a lower interest rate.

Corporate bonds are rated by the top services based on much the same criteria as munis: creditworthiness, ability to repay, and so on. The bonds are issued at $1,000 par value (that is, full price), but are usually sold in large bundles.

Corporate bonds come in three maturity lengths:

- Short term for 1 to 5 years
- Mid term for 5 to 15 years
- Long term for 15 years+

PROCEED WITH CAUTION

Corporations find bonds an attractive way to finance growth and acquisitions. Commercial loans are usually more expensive, and issuing stock may dilute shareholder positions.

Corporate bonds are at the top of the risk scale when compared to U.S. Treasury Bonds, agency bonds, and municipal bonds of the same rating. The reason is that corporations are more vulnerable to the ebbs and flows of the economy, market conditions, and competitions.

Highly rated corporate bonds offer very little risk and are often used in income mutual funds for their stability of income streams. Some corporate bonds have a call feature, so be sure you understand this status before you invest (see the section "Prepayment" later in this Hour for more information on calling).

What's a Bond Worth?

One of the problems with bonds is the language and math used to describe how they work and are traded. So let's jump right in and get a handle on common bond terminology and math.

Bonds, like stocks, are sold on two venues. The first is at original issue and the second is in the secondary market.

Original Issue

When a bond is issued, it is at par value. Since most bonds are issued in $1,000 denominations, the par value is $1,000. The bond is also issued at a fixed interest rate, or *coupon rate*. The bond also has a maturity date, which is the date when the bond must be paid in full.

For example, XYZ Corp. might issue a 10-year bond with an interest rate of 6 percent and a par value of $1,000. The owner of this bond would receive $60 per year in interest, and at the end of 10 years would receive the full $1,000 back.

Under this scenario, the yield of the bond would be the same as the interest rate.

PROCEED WITH CAUTION

Many issuers of new bonds will absorb the sales commission themselves, making new bonds more attractive. However, you must always look at the total return, which includes not only fees but also yield and any discount.

Secondary Market

The secondary market for bonds works much like the stock market in that buyers and sellers are matched for a fee. It is in the secondary market that a bond's yield may fluctuate.

Since bonds are issued for a specific interest rate, they react to changes in interest rates. If interest rates rise, the older bond will not be as valuable and must be sold at a discount. When the bond's price falls below par, the yield will drop also. Here's how it works:

XYZ bond is bought at issue for $1,000 with a fixed interest rate of 6 percent for a 10-year term, giving it a yield of 6 percent. After two years, the bond-holder wants to sell, but interest rates have risen to 7.5 percent. No one will buy a 6-percent bond at par when they could buy a 7.5-percent bond at par. Translation: Why buy a bond that yields only $60 a year, when you could buy one that yields $75 a year? The answer is discount.

The bondholder will have to reduce, or *discount,* the face value to make the bond attractive in this market.

The complicated nature of figuring a bond's worth often discourages investors from adding individual bonds to their portfolio.

The formula for calculating a bond's yield follows: annual interest divided by price equals yield.

For the bondholder to match the current yield of 7.5 percent, the par price is discounted to $800. To calculate the yield on the discounted bond, divide the annual interest ($60) by the price ($800) and you get the yield.

Why would you want to buy an older bond with a lower interest rate? Take a look at this chart from the buyer's perspective:

	Original bond issued @ 6 %	*2 year-old 6 % bond bought on secondary market*
Interest Rates	6 %	7.5 % (2 years later)
Par	$1,000	$1,000
Total Interest	$600	$480
	$1,600	$1,480
Less Original Cost	–$1,000	–$800
Return	$600	$680
Yield	6 percent	7.5 percent

Under the two-year-old bond, we see that, if held to maturity, the bondholder would collect $480 in interest ($60 × 8). Added to the $1,000 face value the bondholder will receive at maturity, that gives a total gross return of $1,480. Subtracting the discounted cost of the bond ($800), that leaves the bondholder with a return of $680, or 7.5 percent.

See the advantage? Our bondholder invests $200 less than the original owner and makes more in yield and return.

Here's what the transaction looks like from the seller's perspective:

	Original bond issued @ 6 %	2 year-old 6 % bond sold on secondary market
Interest Rates	6 %	7.5 % (2 years later)
Par	$1,000	$800
Total Interest	+$600	+$120
	$1,600	$920
Less Original Cost	–$1,000	–$1,000
Return	$600	–$80
Yield	6 percent	

Rising interest rates have produced an $80 loss. This points out one of the risk factors in bonds: If you have to sell before maturity, you may suffer a loss if interest rates have climbed.

This is a simple example, although not necessarily representative of real market conditions, which shows the importance of understanding yield. Yield is the primary way you can compare bonds.

JUST A MINUTE

Since bonds are tied so closely to interest rates, it is important for bond investors to know what is happening with interest rates and to be especially alert when the Fed board meets.

Professional bond traders use a more sophisticated version of the yield calculation called yield to maturity. *Yield to maturity* is a complicated calculation that takes into account relationships between price and interest rates. It assumes your coupon or interest payments are reinvested at the same interest rate and compounded. This gives you a way to look at return over time.

There are online tools that will help you with this calculation, or your broker can figure it out for you. You can find calculators at About.com's bond site (www.bonds.about.com).

In summary, understanding bond pricing is not difficult, but it is somewhat counter-intuitive. Here are the key points:

- Bonds have fixed interest rates.
- Higher interest rates make lower-interest bonds less attractive, which lowers their price on the secondary market.

- Lower interest rates make higher-interest bonds more attractive, which raises their price on the secondary market.

EXCEPTIONS

Now that we all completely understand how bond prices and interest rates move in opposite directions, I am going to throw a wrench into the works by talking about bonds that are sold at a discount when issued.

JUST A MINUTE

Like just about everything else in investing, bonds have their own twists and turns. Be sure you completely understand standard bonds before jumping into the exceptions.

There are two popular versions of this type of bond. One is called a zero coupon bond and is usually issued by corporations, and the other type is known as a Treasury strip, which is a U.S. bond.

Both are marked by the deep discounting of face value when issued, unlike most bonds that are issued at par or face value.

ZERO COUPONS

Zero-coupon bonds do not make periodic interest payments like regular bonds (remember that coupon equals fixed interest rate). Instead, the interest builds up during the life of the bond. At maturity, the accrued interest and the principal equal the face value of the bond.

Zeros are popular with corporations (and other issuers) because they have use of the money without having to make periodic interest payments. They have been used in the past to finance mergers and acquisitions.

Investors like them because they can be bought at a deep discount and maturities can be matched with known future expenses. Your payout is predictable if the zeros are held to maturity; however, they are highly volatile in the secondary market, so if you have to sell them to meet an expense you may not be able to predict what you will receive.

Corporations often issue zeros, also known as junk bonds, when there is a high chance of default. Bond issuers with very low ratings often have to offer junk bonds to attract buyers. We'll talk about ratings later in this Hour.

TREASURY STRIPS

Treasury strips have many of the same characteristics as junk bonds with one big exception: They are still backed by the full faith and credit of the U.S. government.

They are not priced as aggressively as low-rated junk bonds, but are usually close in yield to regular bonds. They also can be bought with maturities that match upcoming expenses.

Since the U.S. Treasury backs them, they are not as volatile as civilian zero-coupon bonds. This means you may have a better chance at a good return if you plan to sell them before maturity.

THE BAD NEWS

If you were thinking that zero-coupon bonds sound like a great idea, leave it to the IRS to pop your balloon. There are some important tax consequences to consider when thinking about zero-coupon bonds.

Even though you don't receive periodic interest payments, as with other bonds, you have to pay taxes on the interest anyway. So every year you will have to pay taxes on the interest you haven't received. (The Treasury strips are still exempt from state and local tax, but not federal tax.)

To avoid or at least defer these taxes, zero-coupon bonds should be in a tax-deferred retirement account of some kind.

BOND RISK AND REWARD

While bonds may not be all that exciting, don't get the impression they are without risk. In fact, under certain conditions, bonds can be very risky. What are the risks associated with bonds and how can you mitigate those risks and still make a respectable return?

There are three major risks that are assessed for each bond. These risks are all considered when pricing a bond before issue and subsequently in the secondary market:

- Default
- Inflation
- Prepayment

PROCEED WITH CAUTION

The risks associated with bonds can be a little confusing. For example, the longer term the bond, the more risky it is considered. This is unlike stocks, whose risk decreases with a longer holding period.

DEFAULT

With the exception of U.S. Treasury issues, all bonds are subject to some degree of risk that the issuer will default and not be able to pay back the loan. This has happened with corporate and municipal bonds.

The bond market depends on two main rating services—Moody's and Standard & Poor's—to tell them the likelihood of default. The rating services give each bond a grade. The grade tells the investment community how much risk there is of default. The rating is given at issue and may be changed throughout the life of the bond.

If one of the rating services downgrades the issuer's credit, the issuers will have to offer a higher yield to attract buyers who will want a better return in exchange for the risk they are taking.

The best protection against default is to buy U.S. Treasury issues and high-grade corporate and government bonds.

INFLATION

High inflation rates are a killer of long-term bonds. The longer the maturity of the bond, the greater the likelihood of inflation eating away yields.

There is no rating for inflation as such, so bond traders and issuers watch key economic indicators for signs of high inflation. Interest rates are set by the Federal Reserve Board and are used to control the economy. The board meets quarterly to consider where key interest rates ought to be to maintain a healthy economy.

If the Fed, as the Federal Reserve Board is known, feels the economy is overheating and in danger of sparking inflation, they may move to raise interest rates in hopes of slowing down the economy and heading off inflation.

Bond traders fear inflation because it can erode the value of money locked up for a fixed period, often for 30 years or more. Even a modest rate of inflation will suck the life out of a 30-year bond. That is why the longer the maturity, the higher the yield. The higher yield compensates for the inflation danger.

PREPAYMENT

Although it may seem odd, prepayment of a bond is considered a risk. Some bonds have a feature that allows the issuer to buy back or call the bond before the maturity date.

While it is certainly better than a default, where you might get nothing, prepayment defeats one of the purposes of buying a bond: a predictable income stream and/or money to meet a known expense in the future. When the bond is called, you have to find something else to do with the money.

Why would a bond be called? One reason might be that the bonds were issued during a period of high interest and now the interest rate has dropped (which, incidentally, makes an older, high-interest bond more valuable).

The issuer may be able to refinance the bonds, with other lower-interest bonds, so it makes sense to save the additional interest expense. Unfortunately, if your bond is called you may be stuck buying a new bond at a lower interest rate that might not meet your need.

Like mutual funds and IPOs, new bonds are sold with a prospectus. The prospectus will tell you whether the bonds can be called. Bonds that can be called, should probably be avoided if possible, unless you enjoy having the rug pulled out from under you.

PROCEED WITH CAUTION

Don't let the confusing nature of bonds turn you off to their possibilities. Although some financial professionals eschew bonds, many others find a place for a bond's special attributes in their portfolios.

ODD DUCK BONDS

Like most products in the financial market, bonds come in a variety of shapes and sizes. Two types that are worthy of special mention are subordinated and convertible bonds.

SUBORDINATED BONDS

Subordinated bonds are second-in-line bonds that are paid after a senior bond issue has been repaid. This junior position makes them somewhat more risky, and as such they carry a higher coupon.

CONVERTIBLE BONDS

Convertible bonds carry a feature that allows the bond to be converted to stock rather than be paid out in cash. This option lets the issuer get by with a lower coupon rate. It also makes the bond somewhat less sensitive to interest-rate changes.

HOW BONDS ARE SOLD

Bonds, with the exception of new issues from the U.S. Treasury, are sold through a broker. Some new-issue, non-U.S. Treasury bonds are sold without commission because the issuer is paying the broker directly.

All bonds on the secondary market are sold through a broker, and a commission is paid. What amount is charged in commission is governed by market competition, but it can be substantial if you are not careful. Always get the commission structure spelled out before engaging a broker.

Almost all bonds are sold through the vast electronic over-the-counter market where buyers and sellers are matched.

Although bonds usually have a $1,000 face value, they are often sold in bundles, making them expensive for the average investor. Many individual investors find mutual bond funds an attractive alternative, since initial deposits are often just a few thousand dollars.

Mutual bond funds also provide a degree of liquidity for the average investor that individual bonds do not. In addition, the mutual bond funds are quoted just like regular mutual funds, avoiding all the confusion over yield, return, and so on.

On the other hand, a mutual bond fund is not a bond. It does not have the certainty of maturity that people sometimes need to meet a known upcoming expense.

BOND TABLES

GO TO ▶
See Hour 6, "Understanding the Numbers," for a discussion on newspaper tables and online services.

Bond quotes are reported in *The Wall Street Journal* and many daily newspapers. Since the quotes are often for blocks of $1 million or more, they are not necessarily helpful to the individual bondholder, who will probably not get the same price. If you are interested in the bond tables, most newspapers provide explanations, or some online services can give you quotes.

RATING THE BONDS

One of the most important pieces of information about a bond is its rating by one or both of the major rating services. These ratings tell you about the relative risk in a bond and let you compare bonds of similar risk.

The two rating services are Moody's and Standard & Poor's. Both use similar criteria for rating bonds and report the rating using a key. Below is a chart comparing the two services and the ranking systems they use.

Standard & Poor's	Moody's	What the Ratings Mean
AAA	Aaa	The highest rating of all. Issuers are stable and well able to meet their obligations. Lowest risk.
AA	Aa	Only slightly more risk than highest rating. Considered a top-quality bond with excellent prospects of repayment.
A	A	Still considered low risk, although the issuers may be slightly more susceptible to adverse economic or political risks.
BBB	Baa	Bonds are considered to have adequate security and repayment prospects. May lack strength to be consistent of longer maturities.
BB	Ba	These bonds are considered to have speculative elements due to less than strong protective elements.
B	B	These bonds are a higher risk due to vulnerability to adverse business or market forces.
CCC	Caa	Bonds rated at this level are nearing default and will avoid it only if everything goes their way.
CC	Ca	Highly speculative. Bonds may be in or near default.
C	C	Bond issuer may be in bankruptcy or near collapse, but payments are still being made. Extremely high risk.
D		Obligation is in default and payments are not being made. Small chance of repayment.

Moody's may use numeric modifiers for top ratings to indicate a high, medium, or low ranking within a specific rating. Standard & Poor's ratings may carry a + or - modifier. Note that C is Moody's lowest rating, which is why there isn't a comparable Moody's rating to Standard & Poor's D rating.

Other than U.S. Treasury issues, which are assumed to be safe, almost all other types of bonds are rated. Moody's and Standard & Poor's ratings are based on extensive research into the issuer's financial health, including other debt and ability to make repayment.

JUST A MINUTE

The two major rating services maintain high standards of objectivity to avoid any hint of favoritism.

Issuers are very careful about their rating status. A lower rating can cost millions of dollars in interest since the issuer will need to compensate investors with higher coupons to offset the increased risk. Issuers will even pull a new bond back if they don't get the rating they need to make the issue work.

The rating services monitor the issuers' financial well-being and, if adverse conditions warrant, may downgrade the issuer during the life of a bond. This will obviously have a bad effect on bonds in the secondary market and force the issuer to offer an even higher interest rate on new bonds.

A bond's rating will be found in the prospectus or can be obtained through a broker. These ratings are another way of comparing bonds of similar risk.

WHAT CAN YOU DO?

The following is a list of five things you can do today:

1. Don't give up on bonds just because they may be difficult to understand. Read the bond commentary in *The Wall Street Journal.* Does it sound like gibberish? The more you immerse yourself in bonds, the easier they are to grasp.

2. Check your local newspaper or other news sources for any bond issues in your community. What is the rating? How will the bonds be repaid?

3. Using online sources or *The Wall Street Journal,* order a prospectus from a mutual fund company that looks interesting to you. We will be using it in a later chapter.

4. Also order an annual report from a company you may want to invest in. *The Wall Street Journal* has a free service you can use. Look for the ♣ symbol in stock listings and in an explanation box, where you will find a toll-free number to order the reports. We will be using the annual report in later chapters.

5. Either online or using *The Wall Street Journal,* check out mutual bond funds for their change in NAV for the day. Were many up or down? Did they move in the opposite direction of stock funds?

WORKSHOP

The Wall Street Journal runs a "Credit Markets" column daily. With the column is a chart showing yield for various bonds from Treasury to corporate. Read the column and study the chart, noting the price you pay for the safety of Treasury issues. Does it seem out of line? Do the other yields make sense based on what you learned in this Hour?

HOUR'S UP!

Maybe by the end of this Hour you've become convinced there is more to bonds than meets the eye. Bonds, like any investment, are appropriate for some investors and not for others. This quiz will check your progress.

1. U.S. Treasury Bonds …
   A. Are completely tax-free.
   B. Frequently default.
   C. Are considered the safest of investments.

2. New-issue U.S. Treasury bonds are …
   A. Sold by brokers.
   B. Sold on Ebay.com.
   C. Sold at auction by the Federal Reserve Bank.

3. U.S. government agency bonds …
   A. Are used to finance mortgages, student loans, and other government programs.
   B. Are free of federal income tax.
   C. Pay more than corporate bonds.

Quiz

4. Municipal bonds finance …

    A. New roads and schools.

    B. Oil wells.

    C. New acquisitions.

5. Corporations use bonds to …

    A. Pay their taxes.

    B. Finance acquisitions.

    C. Pay their employees.

6. A bond's worth …

    A. Is not much on the secondary market.

    B. Depends on the yield and current interest rates.

    C. Rises as interest rates rise.

7. Zero-coupon bonds are …

    A. Also known as worthless.

    B. Pay no periodic interest.

    C. Are exempt from federal income tax.

8. Treasury strips …

    A. Are nightclubs in Washington D.C.

    B. Are when the IRS takes all your money.

    C. Pay no periodic interest.

9. Junk bonds …

    A. Still incur income tax liabilities even though they don't pay interest.

    B. Finance landfills.

    C. Are sold at par.

10. Dangers to bondholders are …

    A. Inflation.

    B. Default.

    C. Prepayment.

    D. All of the above.

Quiz

PART IV
Making Choices

HOUR 15

Investment Strategies

CHAPTER SUMMARY

LESSON PLAN:

In this Hour you will learn about ...

- Components of an investment strategy.
- Passive investment strategies.
- Active investment strategies.
- Dogs of the Dow.
- Growth strategy.
- Income strategy.
- Balance strategy.
- Capital-preservation strategy.
- Risk tolerance.

Investing is an active use of your money to accomplish certain goals. These goals may be short, medium, or long range, and most folks will have one or more from each range.

An investment strategy is simply a plan of how you are going to accomplish your goals and what tools will be needed for the job. In an earlier hour, I asked you to begin working on some investment goals. Now would be a good time to get those out.

There are two main components besides the amount of money available of any investment strategy:

- **Time**   The remaining time before you need to complete your goal. It might be 30 years to retirement, but only 12 years until your kid's college education bills start. How much time you have to work with will, in part, suggest some of the tools that are available.
- **Risk tolerance**   An important psychological price of investing. Investing by definition is perceived as risky. How much risk you are willing to take will also suggest some investment tools.

PROCEED WITH CAUTION

Risk is a part of investing. You cannot separate the two. Information will give you the tools to understand risk and the potential rewards.

We are going to spend the next hour looking at risk and its relationship to reward in much more detail. *Risk tolerance* is your emotional reaction to risk and how much risk you can tolerate before investing becomes painful.

The simple formula for risk is "the higher the potential reward, the higher the risk." Notice in this formula that the reward is conditioned as "potential," while the risk is certain. You must take the risk without any certainty of success.

How much risk you are willing to take to possibly reach your goal is the essence of risk tolerance.

YOUR ROLE

There are almost as many names for investment strategies as there are people talking about them. Everyone seems to have a different way of looking at the same process.

TIME SAVER

How involved or uninvolved you want to be in your investments is not a reflection of your character. Give yourself a chance to enjoy it, but if you just can't get interested, find a passive way to invest—but don't stop investing.

Like just about everything else we have explored so far, investment strategies are multilayered. The first decision regarding investment strategies involves what role you are comfortable with and willing to play in the process.

These are the two roles you have to consider:

- Passive
- Active

As the names suggest, these roles define how involved or uninvolved you are in the decision-making process. Either role is perfectly acceptable and will have about the same chance for success.

The real world is never just black and white, and neither is investing. Most folks end up taking both roles at some point in their investing experience.

THE PASSIVE ROLE

The passive role turns most of the decision-making over to professionals with periodic checkups on performance. Your 401(k) retirement plan is one variation of the passive role.

You may choose how to allocate your investment among several choices, then professionals, usually mutual fund managers, take it from there. You may make adjustments in the allocation from time to time, but you pretty much turn over control to professional managers.

GO TO ▶
See Hour 19, "Asset Allocation," for a more complete discussion about adjusting the allocation of your investments.

Another example of the passive role is the selection of index mutual funds for your primary investments. An index fund, you will remember, is a fund that seeks to mimic the performance of certain stock market indicators. Its goal is to match the market.

The most popular of these index funds are those which track the S&P 500. These funds are as close to autopilot investing as you can get. If you have neither the time nor the interest in regularly monitoring your investments, index funds are for you.

Index funds beat most actively managed funds for several years in the late 1990s, a time when the stock market was roaring. Index funds are a fairly conservative approach to investing, but sound ones with proven results.

THE DOG PLAN

Another passive approach is called *Dogs of the Dow* or the *Dow Dividend* approach. This approach takes less than one hour per year and is purely mechanical, meaning there is no interpretation or analysis to do. You follow the formula and let the market do the rest.

The Dogs of the Dow operates on the theory that the 30 stocks that make up the Dow Jones Industrial Average represent the best large companies in America. The method is to find the highest-yielding stocks in the Dow and invest in them. The assumption is that, over time, high-yielding stocks will do better than the market in general.

The yield is calculated by dividing the annual dividend by the stock's current price (but you knew that from previous hours, right?). What this formula gives you is the lowest-priced Dow stocks (that pay a dividend). Obviously, as a stock's price changes, the yield will change. To solve this problem, you buy and sell only once a year.

The yield can be obtained from many places, including the daily stock tables in many newspapers or from a number of Internet sites. Rank the 30 Dow stocks in descending order of yield—in other words, from highest to lowest. (You can find a list of the Dow stocks in Appendix B, "Resources.")

Take the top 10 stocks and invest an equal amount in each one. Many proponents suggest you do this in January for best results, but any time will work. You hold those stocks for one year. At the end of the year you recalculate the yields, and any stock(s) from your original list that are no longer in the top 10 you sell and buy the stock(s) that are on your new list.

It is that simple. Does it work? You bet! This strategy has outperformed both the Dow itself and the S&P 500 for 25 years!

This chart shows what the Dogs of the Dow looked like in late December 1999.

Dividend

Ticker	Yield	Name
MO	8.44	Philip Morris Companies
JPM	3.12	J.P. Morgan & Co. Inc.
CAT	2.89	Caterpillar, Inc.
EK	2.88	Eastman Kodak Company
GM	2.82	General Motors Corp.
MMM	2.36	Minnesota Mining & Mfg.
DD	2.04	E.I. DuPont de Nemours
SBC	1.9	SBC Communications, Inc.
IP	1.87	International Paper Co.
MRK	1.74	Merck & Co., Inc.

I know, you remember that this is an odd-lot trade and may incur additional commissions fees. For this strategy, you need the cheapest broker you can find, because you are only going to be placing orders once a year.

This process is mechanical and doesn't require any analysis or decision-making. There are several variations on this strategy, but the basic concept is the same.

An important note: If you need to sell any stocks at the end of the year, be careful to hold the ones with capital gains (a profit over what you paid) for at least one year and one day. This will bump the profit into long-term capital gains, which is taxed at a lower rate for most folks than ordinary income.

Even though this investing type is passive in the sense that it requires nothing more than following the formula, it is an aggressive growth strategy and should be followed over a long period for best results.

It is possible to have a passive investment type and an aggressive growth strategy. Whether you use the Dogs of the Dow plan or simply invest in aggressive growth mutual funds, your investment type is still basically passive. I guess this makes you passive-aggressive.

THE ACTIVE ROLE

Investors with the time and inclination often want a more hands-on approach to their investment program. They want to pick their own mutual funds and/ or individual stocks.

Their goal is to beat the market, and they use aggressive tools to accomplish their goals. Actively managed mutual funds are more attractive to them than index funds. Even though index funds can and do beat actively managed funds, they don't beat them all.

Investors interested in a more active approach are generally more risk tolerant and willing to look at more aggressive plans.

Taking an active role in your investments requires some discipline and commitment of time. It is important to be honest with yourself. If you don't have the time or commitment to do some homework, you are better served with a more passive approach to investing.

Whether you choose the active or passive role in investment decisions, you still need to decide on a strategy (or strategies) for reaching your goals. The amount of time you have to reach your goal and your tolerance for risk suggest a strategy for each investment goal.

SHORT- AND MEDIUM-RANGE GOALS

I have spent a lot of time talking about long-term investing. Funding our retirement is the most expensive goal most of us have, and it is best achieved by long-term investment strategies.

However, all of our goals don't fall in a far distant time, so we need to have some strategies to deal with investment objectives that are in the short to medium time frame.

INVESTING FOR SHORT-RANGE GOALS

Investing for a short-term goal requires a different strategy than long-term investing. Because you have only a short period in which to work, you can't afford to be very aggressive.

Short-term investing, which I define as two to five years, is more concerned with reaching a specific goal than beating the market. For truly short-term goals, investing will probably give way to savings.

For example, if I want to buy a car in three years that will require a $5,000 down payment, I must be sure it will be there when I need it. If I don't have any money saved, then I will need to invest about $130 per month at 5 percent to reach my goal.

A 5 percent return is certainly possible in today's market, but we need to be sure we reach our goal, or no car. Investing in stocks or mutual funds is too uncertain over a short period like three years. We could lose money if the market goes south at the last minute.

In this case, the safest and surest strategy is a savings instrument like a savings account. If your bank offers a money market account with a low initial fee, you can switch from a savings account when you hit that number.

What if you have the $5,000, but won't need it for three years? You have some better choices in this situation. A bank CD with a maturity date close to when you will need the money is a good, safe choice. Another alternative would be to buy a high-quality bond, also with a maturity date close to your "needed by" date.

If you go the bond route, make sure you buy a bond you can hold to maturity, either a new issue or on the secondary market. You will remember from previous hours that bonds are interest rate sensitive. If interest rates go up after you buy your bond, you may be forced to sell at a loss because the value of the bond has dropped.

INVESTING FOR MEDIUM-RANGE GOALS

Medium range goals of 5 to 15 years are a little easier to work with than short range goals because you have enough time to be slightly more aggressive.

For example, in 15 years you want to have at least $25,000 in a college tuition account for your three-year-old child. You could invest about $95 a month at 5 percent for 15 years and get there.

However, because you have some time to work with, you might choose to be more aggressive in the early years and less so the closer you get to your goal.

For example, you could take that $95 and put it in an aggressive growth fund. If the fund returned 10 percent for the 15 years, you would have almost $40,000 in the account.

That may be a little too optimistic, but if you keep an eye on the fund and move into something less aggressive if the returns don't stay up, you can still reach your $25,000 goal.

If you get nervous that the growth fund isn't going to sustain its growth, you can pull out and lock your profits in a bond or a bank CD.

The concept to remember is that the closer you get to your goal in time and money, the more protective you need to be.

TYPES OF STRATEGIES

I have broken the spectrum of investment strategies down into four parts. Although these distinctions are somewhat arbitrary on my part, people familiar with investing will understand what they mean. As you become more sophisticated, you will recognize variations and combinations of these strategies.

JUST A MINUTE

Blending your personal strategy with particular and appropriate investments is the heart of investing.

GROWTH STRATEGY

If you remember our discussions on growth mutual funds and growth stocks, we defined growth as seeking investments that will increase in value (share price and/or dividends), but primarily focused on companies with tremendous growth potential.

Growth stocks are typically characterized by a history of growth in all or many areas of financial measurement including profits, sales, and so on.

They usually do not pay dividends, although this is not an absolute. Growth mutual funds invest in growth stocks.

Growth strategies, whether by mutual funds or individual investors, look for those companies that are about to move up to the next level in market prominence. This growth potential is worth a lot to investors if you consider the number of Internet and technology stocks that are selling at a huge premium profit to earnings or no P/E at all because they have yet to make a profit.

It might be helpful if we are more specific in defining growth and then examine how and when a growth strategy is appropriate.

Defining Growth

It may have occurred to you by now that our definition of growth lacks any way to quantify how much or what kind of growth. Without some measurable key, growth is a very subjective measurement.

Is a growth stock one that appreciates at X percent per year? Is it a company that shows a Y percent increase in profits? Moreover, how do you measure potential?

Rather than picking an arbitrary growth figure out of the air, what if we measured growth against a benchmark? Which benchmark would be best?

Whoa! Defining growth turns out to be a little more complicated than it looks. This is where I put in another plug for doing your research online; whether you buy a computer or use one at the library, you can perform some very sophisticated screens using Internet tools.

These resources, called *screens*, are available from a number of Web sites. Some of the better ones are listed in the Resource appendix at the end of the book. The great thing about using screens is that you can look at thousands of stocks and mutual funds in seconds.

TIME SAVER

Screening software makes looking at various strategies easy work. Take some time to get acquainted with some of the ones listed in Appendix B. They are all free.

An even greater benefit is that most of the screening Web sites have predefined screens already set up, so all you have to do is run them. For example, Morningstar.com has a number of predefined screens in its free section and even more powerful screens in the premium area.

The experts at Morningstar.com have put together some logical screens based on a number of criteria. Their growth screen, for example, compares stock growth to the S&P 500 and industry peers in order to pick out the best.

The folks at Marketguide.com, another screening service, look at growth from several perspectives. Their growth screen looks at stock's price, the company's earnings per share, trading volume patterns, and other factors to arrive at the stocks that fit the best. Their process, called StockQuest, screens almost 10,000 stocks in seconds to produce the answer. In addition, their service is free.

There is no way you could accomplish this amount of work in weeks if you did it manually. This is another of the many reasons you will have much better success as an active investor if you learn to use the Internet and the many services it offers.

In Hour 18, "Picking a Stock," we will go over the important numbers you need to look at in making an investment decision. Most of these important numbers are already calculated for you by the online services. There are several more conventional services that offer detailed analysis of stocks (such as Value Line) and many of their offerings can be found at your library.

So, we have decided that growth is something we can quantify and define. This gives us a tool to pick out stocks and mutual funds. Now, we need to decide how to use those stocks and mutual funds in a strategy that is appropriate for our particular goals.

USING A GROWTH STRATEGY

My grandfather was a carpenter and my father was pretty handy around the house, too. The one thing I could do that would drive them both straight up the wall was to use a tool in an inappropriate way—like trying to drive a nail with a pair of pliers.

A growth strategy is an aggressive approach to investing. Most growth candidates are going to be younger companies just beginning to reach their stride. You are counting on the stocks and mutual funds to grow over time. The operative word here is "time." A growth strategy is not an appropriate tool to achieve a short-term goal.

PROCEED WITH CAUTION

Time is your best friend or worst enemy, depending on how much you have to work with to meet your investment goals.

A growth strategy assumes there will be time to allow the investment to mature. Companies that are in strong growth modes tend to be more volatile (meaning wider price fluctuations) than more stable or mature companies. This means that over the course of your investment there will be times when the stock is up and times when it is down.

The market is not kind to growth stocks that stumble. Short-term investors will jump in and out of stocks on minor changes in price. This is not a long-term strategy. The long-term investor expects some ups and downs. However, you certainly don't want to be so wedded to a stock that you ride it into the ground. Things change and if you are going to be an active investor, you need to know when to hold 'em and know when to fold 'em.

A growth strategy is probably most often used to fund or supplement a retirement program. Given the long-term nature of this goal, we can make some observations based on the age of the investor.

This is for illustration only, but it does raise some interesting points worth noting.

Most financial advisers recommend very aggressive investing for the very young; after all, they have 45 years in front of them to correct any mistakes. More importantly, an aggressive growth strategy at this age has an excellent chance of assuring a retirement with a seven-figure nest egg.

Age and Aggressive Investing

This scale shows the relationship between age and the appropriate percent of aggressive growth investments.

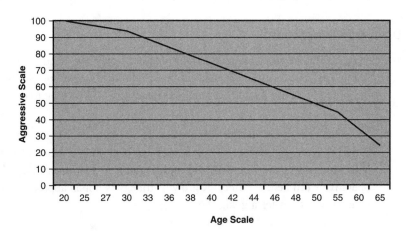

An aggressive growth strategy is likely to produce some capital gains, especially if invested in mutual funds, that should be sheltered in a tax-deferred retirement account. This, of course, allows the account to grow without paying any tax on current earnings.

TIME SAVER

Stock screening Web sites can make short work of identifying potential growth candidates for investments.

What to Invest in for Growth

We have determined that growth investing is most appropriate for long-term goals, but what type of investment instruments make sense for this strategy? Many financial advisers suggest you consider something like a small-cap growth mutual funds if you are more comfortable with that type of investing.

For the active investor, technology stocks have been where some dramatic growth has occurred in the past decade, with no firm end in sight. A stock screen service may pick out some other possibilities, such as companies poised for a potential turnaround, companies that are underpriced, and stocks moving with momentum. (Momentum in this case means stocks that have a strong wind behind them in terms of recent stock price increases.)

Income Strategy

An income strategy shifts the focus from long-term gains to nearer term results.

While an aggressive growth strategy is appropriate for the very young, its usefulness begins to decrease as you approach retirement. The reason is the volatility I mentioned earlier. You don't want to be caught in a down market when it is time to begin living off your investments.

JUST A MINUTE

Your investment strategy is always under review. As your life circumstances change, so will your investment goals. Be flexible.

As you approach retirement, it makes sense to begin shifting some of your assets out of aggressive growth vehicles and into more moderate growth and income instruments.

The reason you do this is to even out those ups and downs so you will have a more predictable income stream when you need it to live on. Think of this as turning down the volume on your car radio rather than hitting the off-on switch.

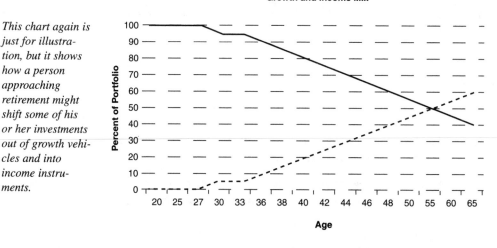

Growth and Income Mix

This chart again is just for illustration, but it shows how a person approaching retirement might shift some of his or her investments out of growth vehicles and into income instruments.

At a very young age, 100 percent of your investments are in aggressive growth instruments. That percentage changes as you age and ends up, in this illustration, with a mix of 60 percent income and 40 percent growth by age 65.

An income strategy is also appropriate for those shorter-term goals, such as investing for a child's college education. You don't want to risk a dip in your holdings just as school is starting and those tuition bills are staring you in the face.

Finding investment vehicles for an income strategy is easier than working with a growth strategy. Our growth strategy looked forward to anticipated growth. An income investment vehicle can be found by looking more at history than at the future.

Obviously, if a company has been paying dividends with regularity, it is a potential candidate. The folks at StockQuest have a screening selection that looks at dividends and their growth, but also at the overall health of the company to see if it will be able to continue paying dividends.

However, many investors may choose to use bonds to satisfy the need for stability of return. As we learned in Hour 14 on bonds, you can match maturity with a specific expense on a certain date.

For example, if you knew that your child needed $5,000 tuition in September 2005, you could purchase a bond that would hit or be very close to this mark.

This same principle applies for people nearing retirement. Their goal horizon is now short- or mid-term and no longer long-term. It will be safer for them to begin the transition to a more certain income stream.

PROCEED WITH CAUTION

A constant source of concern for investors is the trade-off between predictability and return. You will make those decisions your whole investment career.

So what should you invest in for income? Your investment choices for income are fairly simple: bonds or large-cap stocks. Bonds have the advantage of targeting maturity and need, while stocks may provide a better return, since many stocks that pay excellent dividends also show moderate growth.

If you combine stock appreciation with dividends, stocks are going to beat bonds. What you sacrifice is predictability and the chance your stock could go in the dumpster for a variety of reasons.

BALANCED STRATEGY

A balanced strategy seeks—guess what?—balance in its execution and goals. You could make the argument that a balanced strategy is nothing more than that area between growth and income, and you wouldn't be wrong.

However, I have targeted it for the purpose of looking at how we can use a strategy that seeks a combination of growth and income. This is the subject of much debate in the investing community, because it looks for the best answer where there may be none.

JUST A MINUTE

Self-knowledge is a powerful tool in building an investment strategy because it builds on your strengths and works around your weaknesses.

The problem is, there is no one best answer. The investment instruments we have to work with are not nearly as predictable as we would like to think. When you add in varying levels of risk tolerance and feelings about passive or active management, it becomes very confusing, very quickly.

No one knows you better than yourself. It is my hope that this book will get you started on a quest for knowledge that will enable you to figure out what mix is best for you.

If you have access to the Internet, there are a number of sites that will let you set up theoretical portfolios and test them against real market data. This trial and error, done with pretend investments, will give you an opportunity to see how changing the mix works.

Folks who have entered retirement are good candidates for a balanced strategy, which might not be very distinguishable from an income strategy, depending on how it is configured. In addition, there are numerous balanced mutual funds that seek that balance for you.

CAPITAL-PRESERVATION STRATEGY

I have included this strategy to look at how one might want to adopt an ultra-conservative stance that sought only to preserve existing capital. (Hiding your money under the mattress doesn't count.)

PROCEED WITH CAUTION

Removing risk from investing is to remove return. Except for the super-wealthy, this is a losing strategy because inflation and taxes will soon put you in the hole.

These folks have forgone growth and income in exchange for the security that their capital will remain intact. Often this investor has a high net worth and is interested in passing on the "corpus" of an inheritance or trust. The *corpus* is the principal underlying the trust.

For example, if you inherited $100,000,000 with the family duty to pass on the corpus to the next generation, you would want to make sure nothing touched the principal. Investing in government-secured bonds and other low- or no-risk investments would be your strategy.

Since most of us aren't going to inherit a bundle from Uncle Fred, the widget king, we need a more practical application. One such application might be a very short-term need that had to be met.

For example, you are investing for your child's college education and $10,000 is your goal. You meet that goal with your income strategy, but still have six months to go before school starts. Do you leave the money in the income strategy hoping it won't go down?

My guess is that you would be more concerned about locking away that $10,000 than earning a few more dollars over the next six months. You might consider a high-quality bond, but frankly, what makes the most sense is to sock the money away in a savings account, a bank certificate of deposit or a Treasury bill.

In either case, you are locking up your capital so you know it will be there when you need it.

FIGHT INVESTMENT FEAR WITH INFORMATION

Investment strategies provide you with a way to reach your goals in the time allotted for each. The longer the time frame for reaching your goal, the more aggressive you can be. Moderate your investment strategies by carefully considering how much risk you are willing to take. Investing shouldn't be a painful process.

Risk tolerance is simply a measure of how much risk you are willing to take with your investments. Money is an emotion-laden part of our lives. You would be wise not to ignore your feelings about money and risk.

The best tool against investment fear is information. Always know what you are investing in and what the possibilities of loss are for this particular product. The next hour will look at risk and reward in more detail.

Later, we will look at the process of asset allocation, which we have touched on briefly in this Hour. In a nutshell, *asset allocation* is the process of spreading your investments over a variety of investment products to meet your goals and be responsive to your risk tolerance.

For example, the following figures show how people in their late 40s or early 50s might allocate their assets based on risk tolerance.

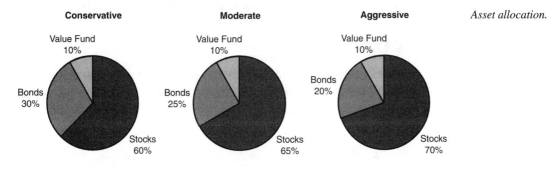

Asset allocation.

As we discussed earlier, moving from a strictly growth (stocks) strategy into a more predictable income stream is a common move for people approaching retirement. The charts above show how people with varying degrees of risk tolerance might approach this transition.

The most important thing to know about risk tolerance is that your particular comfort with your investments is the correct one. Any level of risk that is outside your tolerance level, no matter how attractive it might initially seem, is incorrect.

WHAT CAN YOU DO?

The following is a list of five things you can do today:

1. Sit down with your partner or someone whom you trust will be honest and discuss your tolerance for risk. An honest assessment of risk tolerance is one of the most important steps you can take.

2. List five things you find attractive about a passive investing strategy.

3. List five things you find attractive about an active investing strategy.

4. Look at the online resources, like Morningstar.com, for their perspective on defining growth and income strategies.

5. Take some of the risk tolerance tests listed in the resource section. Do the results match what you found in No. 1 above? If not, in what areas is there disagreement?

WORKSHOP

Get out your list of financial goals we began earlier in the book. Based on what you know now, which investment strategies would you use to reach your goals?

HOUR'S UP!

Your personal investment strategy should address your emotional and psychological profile as well as your particular financial goals. Check out your progress with this short quiz.

1. The two main components of any investment strategy are …

   A. Time and risk tolerance.

   B. Time and luck.

   C. Time and a rich uncle.

2. A passive investment strategy …

   A. Is for sissies.

   B. Can be as successful as an aggressive strategy.

   C. Costs more money.

3. An active investment strategy …

   A. Means you make more investment decisions.

   B. Is foolish.

   C. Always makes money.

4. Dogs of the Dow …

   A. Is an active investment strategy.

   B. Works with small stocks.

   C. Is based on stocks of the Dow.

5. A growth strategy is …

   A. Appropriate for retired persons.

   B. A conservative strategy.

   C. Especially suited for persons under 45.

6. An income strategy …

   A. Can be used to achieve a short-term goal.

   B. Is always tax-free.

   C. Never makes money in odd years.

7. A balance strategy …

   A. Works better as you approach retirement.

   B. Relies on stocks and bonds being equal.

   C. Hopes nothing changes.

8. Capital preservation …

   A. Opposes remodeling the White House.

   B. Is risky by nature.

   C. Is more concerned with preserving the principal than earning a return.

9. Risk tolerance is …

   A. How much you bet at Las Vegas.

   B. The emotional price you pay for investing.

   C. How well you handle skydiving.

10. Risk tolerance …

    A. Suggests ways to meet your goals that are comfortable to you.

    B. Makes you immune to risk.

    C. Is a dangerous habit.

Quiz

HOUR 16

Risk and Return

CHAPTER SUMMARY

LESSON PLAN:
In this Hour you will learn about ...

- Components of the investment formula.
- Economic risk.
- Inflation risk.
- Market-value risk.
- The danger of caution.
- High-risk investments.
- Medium-risk investments.
- Low-risk investments.
- No-risk investments.

"No pain, no gain" is the weight lifter's lament.

The suggestion here is that muscles don't get bigger without being pushed beyond the comfort point.

While the analogy is not 100 percent right on, it does get us moving in the right direction when discussing the relationship between risk and reward in investing. First, let's look at the major components of the investment formula and how they relate to each other. Meanwhile, keep the following in mind:

Risk is certain. Reward is not. How you minimize risk and maximize return is your investment strategy.

YOUR PERSONAL INVESTMENT FORMULA

The investment formula has three components:

- Amount invested
- Time
- Risk

The amount you are able to invest, either in one lump sum or over time, is an obvious predictor of the investment's outcome. Investing $500 per month will get you to your goal quicker than investing $50 per month.

How long your investment grows also has a dramatic effect on the outcome. The more time you can leave your money invested, the better chance you have of success.

The amount of risk you are willing to take will affect how quickly you reach your goal. The more risk you are willing to take, the less important are the components of time and amount of money. The following chart shows this relationship.

Relationship of Time, Risk, & Money

	More Time	Less Time	More Risk	Less Risk	More Money	Less Money	Odds of Success
More Time			x			x	High
Less Time		x		x			Low
More Risk		x				x	Low
Less Risk	x				x		High
More Money			x		x		High
Less Money		x		x			Low

This relationship is not equal, because the more risk you take the higher the odds are that you will fail. When you are forced or choose to take more risk, you increase the volatility of your investments and the predictability of the outcome.

As you can see from this completely arbitrary chart, every time the "Less Risk" category is checked, the higher the odds are for success. This gives you a general idea about the relationship, but is too simplistic to be the complete answer.

JUST A MINUTE

Risk is relative. What is risky for a 55-year-old, may not be for a 25-year-old. Flat assertions that "X" is risky are not particularly helpful.

RISK/REWARD RELATIONSHIP

The relationship between risk and reward is fundamental to the understanding of investing. Investing is inherently risky. In addition, the perception of risk is inherently relative.

If this sounds like double-talk, you are not far off the mark. But both statements are true. The definition of investing places risk as a component.

Most of us would consider skydiving a risky hobby, yet many people eagerly participate. My perception of the risk of skydiving is high. People who do it all the time do not share my evaluation of the risk of skydiving.

Is skydiving any more risky because of my perception? Is it any less risky because people choose to do it as a hobby? The answer is clearly no. There are certain risks associated with skydiving that are not enhanced or diminished by people's perceptions.

PROCEED WITH CAUTION

You are more likely to stick with an investment plan you are comfortable with than one that keeps you up at night.

This is my way of suggesting to you that when you begin to evaluate risk and your tolerance of it, be sure to be honest with yourself. Don't let the media frenzy over day trading or your friend's futures' scheme convince you to take risks you would not normally take.

The goal of this book is to empower you to make your own investment decisions. I also want you to sleep well at night. Worrying about the negative possibilities of an investment is not worth whatever gain you may think can be achieved.

Understanding what the risks actually are will go a long way toward helping you decide what your risk tolerance is. On the theory that we are afraid of that which we do not know, let's take a look at what your investment risks are.

This is not to be confused with risky investment products. We will discuss those later. This section is focused on those risks, real or perceived, that are a fundamental part of investing.

ECONOMIC RISK

Economic risk is the danger the economy could turn against your investment. Although the 1990s were a period of unprecedented growth in the stock market, there have been many times in the past, and undoubtedly will be more in the future, when stocks decline.

JUST A MINUTE

There are plenty of investors in the market today who have no memory of a protracted bear market.

Even in this period of growth, there were losers in the stock market. Check the stock market tables in your local newspaper, a national business journal, or the Internet, and you will find that there are stocks that suffer significant losses even as the market is soaring to new heights.

Political clichés aside, a rising tide does not lift all stocks. What seemed like a good investment idea at the time may find itself out of favor in a super-heated market. Industries like construction that are sensitive to high interest rates often suffer significant stock losses although there is nothing fundamentally wrong with the company.

JUST A MINUTE

Inflation or the threat of inflation often drive investors to hard assets like gold and real estate. Gold is almost never a good investment except during these times. Real estate may be a good investment, but it will depend on the individual property and its location.

Foreign imports can flood a market and drive prices so low that domestic companies cannot compete. The economic stability or instability of foreign markets can have negative effects on companies that export their product to these markets or rely on them for parts, and so on.

Obviously, there is not much you can do that will influence global economy. However, you can use some common sense when it comes to your portfolio.

The first and most important rule of managing risk is *diversification*. Spreading your investments out over different companies in different industries and even different countries is your best defense against economic risk.

Inflation

Inflation is the great value killer. The simple definition of *inflation* is when too much money is chasing too few goods. When this happens, prices increase and workers demand higher wages to buy goods and services.

At some point, prices become so high that consumers quit buying all but the essentials. When this happens, it is like slamming on the brakes in a car.

Consumer demand for products drops, so companies cut their purchases and reduce payrolls by laying people off.

PROCEED WITH CAUTION

Our understanding and control of an ever-increasing global economy is dangerously lacking. While we would like to think we are in control, it seems unlikely all the right answers will be immediately apparent in the event of a global economic disaster.

This is called a *recession*. Prices fall, people are out of work, and businesses close. If it keeps up for too long, a recession will turn into a depression. In this global economy, many countries will soon feel the effects.

To prevent a recession from becoming a depression, interest rates are lowered to make borrowing more attractive and affordable. Businesses stabilize and begin rehiring workers and workers become consumers again.

In a very simple fashion, what I have just described is called an economic cycle. Economists spend a great deal of their time worrying about such cycles and trying to come up with ways to smooth out the peaks and valleys.

Rising inflation triggers interest rate increases, which undermine investor confidence. When their confidence is shaken, investors often look for places to put their money where it will have some shelter from inflation's acid effects.

JUST A MINUTE

Inflation may be the single worst economic problem. Our global economy means we can feel the effects of inflation, even if it is not a problem here.

In the past, investors have run to gold and gold mutual funds, as well as real estate and some exotic investments, to protect their assets from inflation.

The 1990s were a period of overall lower inflation. The last half, in particular, remained virtually inflation-free despite a roaring economy and high employment. Interest rates were raised several times in preemptive strikes against inflation.

Those of us who remember the 1980s and the horrible effect of inflation on our economy are still nervous that it could come back. I am not so confident that our economic controls can provide protection against the devastating effects of inflation.

MARKET-VALUE RISK

Market-value risk refers to the market turning against or ignoring your investments. It is not uncommon for unexciting industries to get lost in the mad rush to technology like we saw in the late 1990s.

Many of these stocks languish, not because there is anything fundamentally wrong, but because the money was chasing something sexier with promises of greater returns.

PROCEED WITH CAUTION

 Just as beauty is in the eye of the beholder, value is in the eye of the market. The market may find a certain sector more attractive even though there is nothing fundamentally wrong with another sector.

If you had run a stock-screening program in December 1999 like I did, you would have found the category of value stocks contained some of the most familiar names in American industry:

- Bank of America
- Ford Motor
- Philip Morris Companies
- General Motors
- Bank One

Do these look like bargain basement companies to you? Nevertheless, they were selling under their intrinsic value as defined by Morningstar.com. Contrast this with the high-tech wonders selling with P/Es in the 30s, 40s, and up, such as Cisco Systems, Microsoft, and Sun Microsystems.

Many of these wonder companies were not in existence at the beginning of 1990, and their combined assets wouldn't equal any one of the stocks listed above.

At this moment, the high-tech stocks have caught the market's imagination, and small wonder. The leaders have posted almost incomprehensible gains, growing from a project in someone's basement to companies with market capitalization in the hundreds of billions of dollars.

PROCEED WITH CAUTION

The great stock market expansion of the 1990s was primarily carried by the technology sector, especially the last few years. Analysts worry about a market balancing on one leg.

One of the major concerns professional market watchers have is that we ended the 1990s with tremendous gains in all the market indicators, but the advances were largely driven by one sector: technology.

If the technology sector was taken out of the equation, the market would have experienced an advance, but probably not on the scale we have seen. What happens if the technology stocks collapse? Will they drag the rest of the market down with them?

This is another danger of market-value risk: The whole market will reverse. It is not uncommon and, as we have already learned, it is actually to be expected for high-growth stocks to have peaks and valleys.

One Internet company I am familiar with experienced a high of around $100 and a low of $24 per share in a four-month period. That kind of roller coaster is not for the faint-hearted and may be a little more exaggerated than most, but it points out how vulnerable a stock can be.

When a few of the leaders in the technology sector have a bad day, you can rest assured the market will have a bad day also. Although there are a lot of younger investors out there who have no real knowledge of declines, the market can, does, and will lose ground at some point in time.

JUST A MINUTE

Diversification is your best protection against market bounces, but carried too far it will eliminate any chance for significant gains by diluting your holdings.

Long-term investors should be prepared to ride out the valleys. Shorter-term investors need to protect themselves because they don't have a large number of years to ride the market back up, as it will surely go.

Again, the best protection against market value decline is diversification. We all want to be invested in the current stars of the market, but those stars have a habit of falling. Diversifying your portfolio to include a broad selection of sectors and industries can cushion the fall.

TOO CAREFUL

There is also a danger in being too careful. Investors, especially those near or in retirement, who get nervous over price fluctuations in stocks and bonds will often jump into something safe like bank certificates of deposit or Treasury bills.

The problem here is that if you retire at age 65 you may have to finance 20+ years of retirement. Living a long time is not a bad thing—I hope I do. The problem is if you are too careful with your retirement nest egg, you may find it does not earn enough for you to live on for 20+ years. Now you are dipping into the principal and in danger of outliving your money.

PROCEED WITH CAUTION

 Advances in medical care and preventative medicine are extending our lives at a greater rate than ever. Unfortunately, these same medical benefits are also eating away our nest eggs.

My grandfather used to call this "being between the dog and the fire hydrant."

This is why Little's Golden Rule of Investing is so important:

The best time to start investing was yesterday. The second best time is today. Tomorrow is better than nothing.

Time will smooth out those peaks and valleys. That is why your risk of losing money in stocks or stock mutual funds decreases the longer you hold your investment.

However, don't forget that the less time you hold a bond, the less chance you have of losing value.

RISK AND INVESTMENTS

We have established that risk is made up of several components, including the economy, market value, and time. I would like to tie together risk, investment strategy, and investment products to fit this all together. Using risk rather than investment strategy, I hope this overview will give you an idea of the relationship between risk and reward. I will not cover inherently risky products like options, futures, and other derivatives in this section. That discussion will come in Hour 22, "Aggressive Investing."

HIGH-RISK INVESTMENTS

An investment can be defined as high risk by the product used and the time it is held. Holding virtually any stock for a short period can be risky.

The shorter the holding period, the higher the risk. This is one of the reasons why most day traders, those folks who jump in and out of stocks in minutes or hours, lose money. The shorter the holding period, the more accurate you have to be in predicting a stock's movement.

To take the risk out of a short holding period, you select a fixed-income type of investment, like a high-quality bond or bank CD. This will cost you some gain if the alternative was to stay with a stock that goes up, but it will also protect you against the higher statistical probability that the stock will go down over a short holding period.

Some examples of high-risk investments:

- It would not be prudent to invest your child's college fund in an aggressive growth stock six months before you need the cash.
- It would be foolhardy to invest your retirement nest egg in one stock just prior to retirement (or any time, for that matter).
- It would be equally foolhardy to tie up your retirement account in bonds 15 years before you retire. Over longer periods of time, stocks have always outperformed bonds. You would sacrifice an almost certain superior return for nothing.

Likewise, playing it too close to the vest will also produce a risky investment because you will have to invest substantially more to achieve the same return.

Putting yourself in a position where you have to hit a home run to achieve your goal is a formula for disaster. As one of the online brokers used to say in its ads, "Someone will win the lottery, but it won't be you." This is why I push so hard to begin saving now.

MEDIUM-RISK INVESTMENTS

This is the area where most investors feel some degree of comfort. You are willing to take some risks, but want to minimize your potential downside while allowing your gains to run.

This is not the best of both worlds. You will not hit any home runs in the short term, but you likely won't strike out, either. You give your plan the time it needs to succeed and buy investment products appropriate for the goal, time frame, and your risk tolerance.

JUST A MINUTE

Think of tuning your investments as an ongoing process. The older you get, the less time you have until your goal and the more conservative you need to be in order to stabilize your portfolio.

You adjust your investment instruments as the time frame changes, moving from aggressive growth to a more stable, predictable return as you approach your goal.

Some examples of medium-risk investments:

- You start a college fund when your child is born (good move) and invest aggressively with it for the first 12–14 years. As your child enters high school, you start moving the assets into more stable and predictable instruments to avoid getting caught in a down market when tuition comes due in four years.

- At age 55, you begin to redistribute your 401(k) holdings out of aggressive growth and into income and value holdings.

- Three years from now you plan to buy a house. You have $10,000 in an index fund that is earmarked for the down payment. You cash out of the fund and buy a CD or Treasury note, so you know the $10,000 will be there when you need it.

The bind a lot of people find themselves in is having to double or triple their money in a short period to achieve their goal. There is no safe or even moderately risky way to do that. I wouldn't count on being able to turn $3,000 into $10,000 in three years.

LOW-RISK INVESTMENTS

Some of you will have a very low tolerance for risk. This is fine and there is nothing wrong with you, despite what you might be led to believe by most advertising.

What this means is you will need even more time than most to achieve your goals. I don't consider investing in the stock market through a good index fund a risky investment if held for 10 years or more.

PROCEED WITH CAUTION

Low-risk investments may be riskier than you think. Factor in inflation and taxes when considering return.

In fact, you could make the argument that investing in stocks for any period longer than 20 years is a low-risk investment. Historically, your odds of losing money would be very slim.

Still, you may get queasy with any kind of fluctuation in your investments. If this is the case, plan on getting acquainted with fixed income or cash instruments like bank CDs and money market funds that you can monitor.

You will also need to plan on making more of your money available for these investments since they will grow at much slower rates. If your goal is retirement, make sure your investments are in a tax-deferred qualified retirement account so they can grow without tax on current earnings. You might want to consider a Roth IRA, which allows earnings to grow tax-free (not deferred). You give up the immediate tax reduction, but it might be worth it depending on your situation. We'll examine Roth IRAs in more detail later.

GO TO ▶
See Hour 23, "Retirement Planning," for more information on Roth IRAs.

NO-RISK INVESTMENTS

I am occasionally asked to recommend a no-risk investment. First off, I never make specific product recommendations, but even if I did, in this case, I couldn't.

There is no such thing as a "no-risk" investment. By definition, investing involves some degree of risk. And I think I have shown that doing nothing may be more risky than some investments you could make. If you're still not convinced, here is another example:

If you invest $2,000 a year for 10 years in a bank CD paying 6 percent interest, you might think this a safe investment. However, even at a low 2 percent inflation rate, your investment would suffer considerably over time. Assume it is in a tax-deferred account.

> $2,000 a year for 10 years at 6 percent with no inflation equals $26,361
>
> $2,000 a year for 10 years at 6 percent with 2 percent inflation equals $24,012

This means your investment would only purchase $24,012 worth for goods at their inflated price. In other words, your safe investment earned 4 percent and you will still have to pay taxes on that at some point.

There are no free lunches and no risk-free investments. Find your level of risk tolerance and match your investment strategy and investment products to that level. And, most important of all: DO IT NOW!

WHAT CAN YOU DO?

The following is a list of five things you can do today:

1. Think of ways that you take risks outside investing. I don't mean skydiving, but how about on the job? Do you suggest solutions to problems that are not "safe"? Why do you do it? There must be some reward, either professionally or emotionally.

2. What are some of the risks your employer or profession face? For example, will safe and cheap laser surgery put eyeglass manufacturers and retailers out of business? What are you doing to make sure you aren't put out of business by people with higher skills?

3. Several months, at least, have passed since I wrote this book. Look up the stocks I cited earlier as value buys (in the section Market Value Risk) because of their low P/Es. Where are they now? Have they come back into favor or are they still languishing? Can you think of what might have changed that could affect their price?

4. Reviewing your financial goals, are there any that would warrant a high-risk investment? If the answer is yes, using the Internet or *The Wall Street Journal* and considering only P/E, can you find five high-risk stocks that might meet your goal?

5. Using *The Wall Street Journal*, your local newspaper, or the Internet, can you find signals that inflation is back or may be coming back? What steps have been taken or are being considered to stop inflation?

WORKSHOP

Make a list of five industries that are not hot at the moment. Using the Internet or *The Wall Street Journal*, find a couple of companies in each of the industries. How is the market treating them based on their P/Es? Do any of these look like good values that might blossom if market attention turns their way?

HOUR'S UP!

Wouldn't it be a great world if we could reap all the benefits without risking any losses? Well, no such luck here on Earth. If you can't design the perfect world, the next best thing is to learn how to adapt to this reality. Check yourself on risk and reward.

1. Time frame, risk, and investment …

    A. Make up the investment formula.

    B. Are the components of heartburn.

    C. Are not all equal in investing.

2. Risk is relative …

    A. But always present in investing.

    B. To the S&P 500 index.

    C. And never enters into bond investment decisions.

3. Economic risk …

    A. Is the danger of running out of money.

    B. Is the loss of purchasing power.

    C. Is the possibility of the economy turning against your investments.

4. Inflation is …

    A. Too little money and too many goods.

    B. Too much money and too few goods.

    C. Too little money and no goods.

5. Market-value risk …

    A. Is the danger of deflation.

    B. Is the possibility of recession.

    C. Is the danger of your investment falling out of favor with the market.

6. A danger of being too cautious is …

    A. Not having any fun.

    B. Outliving your money.

    C. Missing some really good deals.

7. High-risk investments …

    A. Are appropriate for short-term investing.

    B. Are appropriate for long-term investing.

    C. Are appropriate for people on fixed incomes.

8. Medium-risk investments …

    A. Are where most people are comfortable.

    B. Never work out very well.

    C. Seldom make more than low-risk investments.

9. Low-risk investments …

    A. Are hard to find.

    B. Often make large returns.

    C. Take longer to reach their goals.

10. Risk is only a frightening issue …

    A. If you don't have all the information.

    B. For people under the age of 30.

    C. To people with no courage.

Quiz

HOUR 17

Picking a Mutual Fund

LESSON PLAN:

In this Hour you will learn about …

- Funds we won't buy.
- Investment objectives for different age groups.
- The effect of taxes.
- Reading a mutual fund prospectus.

Picking a mutual fund to invest in is a lot like going to the candy store with your allowance—so many choices, so little money.

There are literally thousands of mutual funds to choose from when you are ready to invest. How do you go about finding the right one for you?

Many people have their entire investment portfolio in mutual funds. This is a wise and common sense strategy, so for them, the question is which mutual funds (plural) to buy.

As we remember from earlier hours, a mutual fund is a group of investors who have pooled their money and, through a management company, hired professionals to invest that money. Some of the important characteristics of mutual funds are:

- Diversification
- Professional management
- Low initial deposit
- Liquidity

Mutual funds have investment objectives that drive their purchase of stocks and bonds. Investment objectives allow you to compare mutual funds of the same type, which is helpful in sorting through the numerous choices.

However, some mutual funds have investment objectives that are so broadly stated as to be meaningless, or they call themselves one type of fund when they are really a different type.

JUST A MINUTE

Mutual funds have been the darlings of investors for over two decades. They have many attractive selling points, but don't overlook expenses. The lower the expenses, the better chance your fund has for success.

FIRST THINGS FIRST

Before we get any further with the details, let's make some broad statements about the funds we are not going to buy. We are not going to buy:

- Funds with loads, either front or back end. There are too many good choices out there that do not charge loads.

- Funds with high operating expenses. Again, there are plenty of good funds that responsibly manage their business and keep operating costs low. Earlier, we discussed fees for different types of funds. Keep these guidelines in mind.

- Funds not held in a retirement account that create large tax bills at the end of the year. Look for funds that are "tax friendly," that is, they don't turn their holdings over with any appreciable benefit to the shareholder.

- Funds, other than index funds, that own hundreds of different stocks. Even if part of their holdings did very well, the impact on the fund would be minimal.

We will make a conscientious effort to avoid funds with high associated costs in fees and taxes. The fees charged by the fund will dramatically affect your overall return. As we saw earlier (Hours 4, "Investing Instruments" and 9, "Mutual Funds—Part I Classifications"), even a small .5 percent difference can mean big dollars over the long term.

PROCEED WITH CAUTION

Mutual funds sometimes classify themselves a certain way that makes them look better. Don't take their classifications on face value.

INVESTMENT OBJECTIVES

In previous hours, we discussed investment objectives as a way to match investments to your needs and goals. This is the process that guides your selection of a mutual fund, even if only part of your portfolio is in funds and the rest is in stocks and bonds.

A very helpful tool in looking at mutual funds to match your goals is a system that categorizes funds in an objective manner and not according to the fund's sales literature.

Morningstar.com is an Internet site with tremendous tools to help you pick the funds that are right for you. Most of the site is free and the other part is available for a small ($10) monthly fee. However, most of you won't need the advanced features of the premium membership to help you pick your funds.

You can get everything you need through free Internet access at your library. Without this help or some similar assistance, finding the right mutual fund will be a longer process.

TIME SAVER

You can access a tremendous amount of help on the Internet for free. Morningstar.com is only one of dozens of great reference sites. Others include Bloomberg.com, Smartmoney.com, and Beginnersinvest.about.com.

MORNINGSTAR.COM

What Morningstar.com does is look at each mutual fund and categorize it, not according to what the sales literature says, but according to what the fund actually does. In other words, the site looks at the type of investments the fund makes and uses what it does and not what it says to fit it into a category. Essentially, it helps you compare funds like apples to apples. With this information, they created the "Morningstar Style Box" and a category for each fund.

The style box is a way to place funds within a grid so they can be compared to their peers; it's a quantitative way to identify funds.

An example of the Morningstar Style Box.

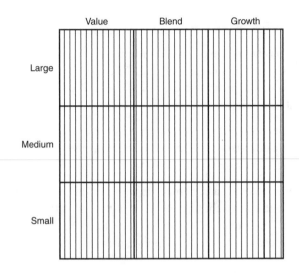

Along the vertical axis is the size designation. This does not refer to the size of the mutual fund, but rather to the size of the fund's holdings. This allows you to compare holdings of the same size. Morningstar used a fairly complicated methodology to arrive at these numbers.

Likewise, the horizontal axis determines how cheap or expensive the holdings are. Using P/Es (price/earnings ratios) and P/Bs (price/book ratios), Morningstar determines whether the holdings are value (inexpensive), growth (pricey), or somewhere in between (blend). The terms "value," "growth," and "blend" do not refer to the mutual fund strategies I listed above.

Once again, Morningstar went through a fairly complicated procedure to get this value. When you combine the two, every fund falls into one of the nine grids. If you want to compare similar funds, you look for those falling into the same grid.

This chart shows how one fund, Vanguard Extended Market Index, fits into Morningstar's grid. If you go to the Morningstar.com site and find Vanguard Extended Market Index fund, Morningstar will show you other funds that fall into the same grid.

The link "Compare investment-style returns" will take you to funds in the same category that fall into the same grid.

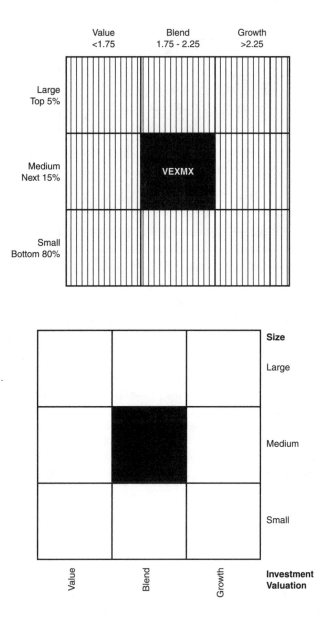

Vanguard Extended Market Index in Morningstar's grid.

Compare investment-style returns for funds in the same category that fall into the same grid.

The style box can also give you an idea about where a fund falls in terms of risk.

Shading indicates a fund's risk.

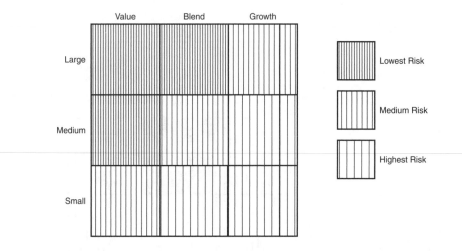

Morningstar has similar systems for bond funds and others. This is one service where access to the Internet will really pay for itself. Morningstar.com has two levels of service. The first level is free, and the next level requires a small monthly subscription. All of the information represented here is from the free portion of the service.

As Morningstar will admit, there is no one system that answers all your questions, but its system at least levels the playing field when determining what kind of fund you are dealing with.

Since all this wonderful information is free and I have nothing to gain by my recommendation, I hope you will check out this fact-filled site. Ask anybody familiar with mutual funds and they will know Morningstar.com.

NOT FOR EVERYONE

Be advised at this point that there are a number of folks who do not think much of mutual funds, especially actively managed funds. Chief among the detractors are the folks at The Motley Fool, a Web site known for insightful advice and unrestrained wit. It suggests that there are only four words you need to know about selecting a mutual fund: "Buy an index fund."

Nevertheless, there are still good reasons for buying mutual funds. Even if your investing tastes run toward individual stocks and bonds, your 401(k) plan may force you to choose a mutual fund.

I will use the Morningstar.com method of classifying mutual funds as we begin our discussion of picking funds to buy. In the previous hour we discussed risk and return, and in the hour before that we talked about risk tolerance with investment strategies. All of these concepts will come into play in this Hour, and in the next hour when we talk about picking stocks.

Let's look at investment objectives by length—that is, long-term, mid-term, and short-term. We will break these down further by age of the investor where appropriate.

LONG-TERM INVESTMENT OBJECTIVES

Long-term objectives are investments of 10 years or more. For many of us, retirement planning will be at the top of our long-term investment objectives. You may have others that are long term.

AGES 20–45

In earlier hours, we noted that the more time you have to reach a goal, the more aggressive you could be in your investment decisions. People within this age range have many years before retirement, so they can be very aggressive in their fund selection, taking into account their own tolerance for risk.

A single person, age 20, would probably want to charge the market with a small-cap growth fund in his or her retirement account. These funds are not normally tax-efficient so they are better suited to tax-deferred retirement accounts.

Small-cap funds have the largest potential for growth, but also carry the highest risk and are noted for their volatility. These are not funds for short-term investing.

A more moderate approach would be to buy medium-cap funds in the growth area and a more conservative approach would consider large-cap growth funds.

If you want to follow the path of least resistance (and least work on your part), pick an index fund, such as one that follows the S&P 500. This type of fund would be considered a large-cap blend, because the S&P 500 index is primarily large-cap stocks. Within the 500 are some value stocks as well as growth stocks.

Ages 45–55

At this point in your life, retirement, while still a long way off, may seem to take on more importance. This would be a good time to consider moving out of the highest-risk funds and into areas of more moderate risk, but still plenty of room for growth.

Trading small- and medium-cap growth funds for large-cap stock funds will begin to bring stability to your portfolio and let you begin planning your retirement with more accuracy.

Income funds in your retirement account toward the end of this period also add a degree of predictability to your retirement.

PROCEED WITH CAUTION

Compounding over a long period is like a ball rolling down hill. The closer it gets to the bottom, the faster it goes. What started out as compounding a small amount is now compounding a large amount. Don't turn off compounding too soon.

AGES 55–65

Although the last 10 years before your retirement should be a time for consolidating your portfolio into a shape that will serve your daily income needs in retirement, most financial professionals caution against pulling too far back.

For one thing, if you have been diligent about funding your retirement account, it is probably quite large by now, and the additional compounding will be significant the last 10 years.

Another concern is that there is a good chance, thanks to modern medicine, that you will live some 15–25 years after you retire. Putting the brakes on your retirement earnings too quickly may put you in the uncomfortable position of outliving your money.

For example, if your retirement fund is $750,000 and it is earning 10 percent per year, you are making $75,000 in interest before taxes. If you pull back to safer investments to protect your retirement and are only earning 6.5 percent, your annual before-tax income is only $48,750, or a loss of $26,250. That can mean a substantial difference in how you live out your retirement.

Many people suggest shifting into more income-oriented funds during this period to smooth out the peaks and valleys. At this point, you probably don't want to be in anything but large-cap funds, with a stronger emphasis on bond funds than stock funds.

HOW DO YOU CHOOSE?

This quick overview of how you might look at your retirement account from different age groups brings us to the heart of the matter: How do you choose this large-cap growth fund over that large-cap growth fund?

JUST A MINUTE

Selecting the right investment is a process of elimination. While this sounds like a lot of work, thanks to the Internet and Web sites like Morningstar.com, most of the hard work has already been done.

There are certain markers that will distinguish good funds from mediocre ones, but understand there are no formulas that will guarantee success. In fact, your educated guess will be about as good as anyone else's guess. Don't jump at headlines on magazines or ads in newspapers or magazines.

No one has a magic answer to picking the winning funds of the future. However, you can improve your chances by following these guidelines for picking an actively managed fund:

- No sales fees of any kind: front end, back end, deferred, whatever.
- Low turnover. You will remember that turnover is the percentage of the fund's assets that are bought and sold each year. A high turnover raises expenses and will probably trigger capital gains taxes.
- Low operating expenses. Shoot for expenses at or under the average for similar funds.
- Consistency of performance. Look for performance records that show returns in a similar range over a period of years.

We have already talked about the first three points in other hours; a fund's expenses (or lack thereof) have a tremendous impact on its performance over time. Keep the expenses low and you've accomplished 90 percent of your task.

PERFORMANCE INDICATORS

Past performance, any fund will tell you, is no guarantee of future success. That is more than a warning from the regulators. It is an absolute truth. Yesterday's hero is today's failure. Basing a decision to buy a fund on past performance only is not much better than flipping a coin.

JUST A MINUTE

Past performance of a mutual fund is no guarantee of future success, but it will pick out the turkeys real quick.

Past performance can tell something about the management of the fund. Wild swings in performance, especially when there is no apparent reason, can signal problems you should avoid. Get to know the manager(s). Their biographies are in the prospectus. A new manager may mean a large turnover in assets, triggering capital gains distributions.

While past performance won't predict future winners, it is pretty good at picking continual losers. Avoid funds that have histories of poor performance—pretty obvious, huh?

Looking at a fund's performance is more useful if you can compare it to some objective standard. This is why measuring performance against some of the leading market indicators, like the S&P 500, is so popular.

This process has some advantages and some disadvantages. The advantages include easy access to the indicators whether it is the S&P 500 or the Russell 2000 or one of the other generally accepted market indicators.

That can also be a disadvantage if the fund is compared to an index that is not reflective of what the fund is about. For example, the S&P 500 is weighted toward large-cap stocks. Comparing it to a small-cap stock mutual fund will yield a distorted picture of the fund, which is what some fund managers want.

It is better to get familiar with the indexes that are reflective of your fund's place in the market.

TAKE A TRIAL WALK

So, how are you going to decide which fund to buy? I suggest returning to Morningstar.com and looking at funds according to their style box category. This will allow you to compare large-cap growth funds with other large-cap growth funds, which is the only reasonable and telling way to compare funds.

TIME SAVER

 There are a number of services on the Internet that will recommend which mutual fund to buy. Save yourself some time and make your own decision. How will that save time? By the time you finish this book, you will have all the tools or know where to find them that you will need to make informed decisions. If you have confidence in your decisions, you won't be checking up on your investments every 20 minutes.

By the way, other services on the Internet offer similar ways to compare mutual funds. They are listed in the resource section.

Let's walk through the process step-by-step:

1. You have established, based on your goal of funding your retirement, that the best product at your age and level of risk tolerance is a medium-cap growth fund.

2. You go to Morningstar.com and use the fund selector to find medium-cap growth funds.

3. If you want, you can follow Morningstar.com rankings to narrow the choices.

4. Examine the funds for fees and expenses and any other characteristic you feel is important.

5. Order a prospectus of your choice. Some funds will let you download a prospectus, while others will mail you one. Confirm the information regarding fees, expenses, and so on.

6. Buy directly from the management company.

Clearly, you can do a whole lot more using the online resources that are available on the Internet than you could accomplish on your own. While it is more cumbersome and time-consuming, it is possible to make your selection using available printed material. You just won't be able to consider as many funds this way.

Your portfolio will obviously consist of more than one mutual fund. How many and what types are topics we will cover in a future hour when we discuss asset allocation.

TAXES

Taxes are a nasty subject, but an important one for mutual fund shareholders. Along with other fees and expenses, taxes affect the total return of your fund.

As a shareholder of a mutual fund, taxes are passed through to you, as well as dividends. These distributions usually occur in December, but check the prospectus of your fund for details.

A capital gain occurs when the fund sells a stock it is holding for a profit. That profit is distributed to you in cash, or it can be reinvested back into the fund. Even if it is reinvested, you still are liable for tax on the gain.

If the fund held the stock for more than a year, the profit is considered a long-term capital gain and is taxed at 20 percent. However, if the fund held the stock for less than a year before selling, the gain is treated as ordinary income and subject to tax at your personal income tax bracket.

The distribution may also be subject to state and local taxes. If a fund is not tax-efficient, you will be giving up a big chunk of the gains to taxes. Funds are reluctant to quote returns on an after-tax basis, so it is up to you to avoid funds that create big tax events each year.

Many of the online services will give you a tax efficiency rating to help you identify known tax offenders.

JUST A MINUTE

After-tax returns are more important than pre-tax returns because they give you a truer picture of your actual return. Few mutual fund companies report their funds on an after-tax basis.

Index fund supporters point out, quite correctly, that they are the most tax-efficient of all mutual funds. The reason is that index funds seldom buy or sell funds, thus there are few gains to distribute. By the way, index funds only trade when stocks that make up the index are bought or merge or are replaced by the index originators.

Of course, many of the unpleasant tax consequences are avoided or at least postponed by containing your funds that generate gains in retirement accounts. Most of us will have to do more than just a 401(k) or IRA to fund our retirement, so part of our retirement portfolio will have to be outside of a tax-deferred home. This makes it even more important than ever to be careful of tax consequences.

PROCEED WITH CAUTION

Where you keep your tax-laden mutual funds can make a big difference. If you only have room for one fund in your retirement account, pick the one most likely to generate tax problems because you will not have to deal with them as long as the fund is in your retirement account and taxes are deferred until withdrawal during retirement.

The biggest fundamental in picking a mutual fund is looking for low expenses. Big returns don't mean much if you give most of that money back in loads, fees, taxes, and so on. Always compare funds of comparable makeup. Remember to compare apples to apples. The Internet is a gold mine of easy-to-access information.

Understanding the Mutual Fund Prospectus

It is a scientific fact that most people would rather poke themselves in the eye with a sharp stick than read a mutual fund prospectus. And who could blame them?

A mutual fund prospectus is a legally required document that the management company must provide to new investors. Many funds have a paragraph somewhere on their application that says you promise that you have read and understand the prospectus. Good thing you don't go to jail for lying on that one. It just keeps the mutual funds from being sued for not certifying that your have read and understand the prospectus and are aware of the risks associated with investing in their fund.

To their credit, many funds are taking steps to making their prospectus easier to understand and look at. Let's walk through a prospectus and see what we find. Not all prospectuses will be structured this way, but they will be close and will contain all the information I cover here.

PROCEED WITH CAUTION

Mutual funds must disclose all their fees in the prospectus. This is one place they can't hide them, because regulators are always looking over their shoulders. Although funds can't technically "hide" any fee, they can make their fees sound sweeter in the fund's marketing materials.

The prospectus usually starts off with a fund profile that describes in semi-vague terms the investment objective, the investment strategy, some of the risks associated with the fund, and some performance numbers.

Often the fund will include a chart showing how the fund did relative to some index, such as the S&P 500; if the fund is a large-cap stock fund, this is an appropriate comparison. Otherwise, look for an index that is closer to the fund's actual investments.

Also included are discussions of fees. Read these carefully. This is where the fund will likely make or break itself. If the total annual operating expenses are out of line with similar funds, then look for a different fund to buy.

We talked about fees in an earlier hour. The prospectus is where you find them listed under "Shareholder Fees" and "Annual Operating Expenses." These two numbers are added together to give you the "Total Annual Operating Expenses." This is a key number you can use to compare this fund with others in its peer group.

You will also find a section called something like "Who Should Invest?" This section lists the attributes of the fund relative to the investor. For example, a large-cap stock fund might suggest that persons "seeking long-term, over five years, growth" would be good candidates to purchase the fund.

The next section concerns itself with the primary investment strategies and how they are implemented. It also will talk about risk, using many of the terms like "market risk" that we learned in the previous hour.

The fund's turnover rate is defined and discussed in nearby sections. Later, in the financial highlights, actual historical data on turnover is given. Remember that this number is important because it tells us how much buying and selling the manager is doing. Excessive buying and selling runs up expenses and may trigger extraordinary capital gains taxes.

The fund's investment adviser(s) are also profiled in this area along with the management company and details regarding their relationship.

JUST A MINUTE

How and when the fund handles distributions of capital gains and dividends is very important to the first-time buyer. Most mutual funds handle distributions in December. If you buy into the fund before a distribution, you may end up with a tax bill. Always wait until after the distribution before buying into a fund.

Next, there is another important section dealing with dividends, capital gains, and taxes. Read this section carefully for policies regarding distributions, and so on.

Right after this is the "financial highlights" section. This is the guts of the prospectus, where the fund's activity for the past several years is compared. Income, expense, and distributions make up the heart of this section.

Many funds publish an easy-to-read guide to accompany the section.

At the end of the prospectus is a section listing all the different types of accounts it accepts and how it handles a lot of the paperwork behind the scenes.

Many prospectuses will also include a glossary at the end.

There, that wasn't so bad, was it?

WHAT CAN YOU DO?

The following is a list of five things you can do today:

1. Read the mutual fund columns in *The Wall Street Journal* (if you haven't bought a new *Journal* recently, now would be a good time).

Does the language sound confusing? Probably not, but you may run into a few mathematical terms. (We will cover the math in a future hour.)

2. Online, go to Morningstar.com and use their fund selector to screen the funds. Notice that if you select individual funds for detailed information, you get a lot.

3. One of the features Morningstar.com provides is a "peer list" of funds with similar investment styles. This is very helpful in choosing a fund.

4. Find yourself in the age ranges listed above. Do these suggestions for your investments make any sense? Can you see any logic in changing your holdings as you move from one age bracket to another?

5. Order a copy of your Social Security Earnings Report. This report will show you where you are and what you might anticipate in retirement. The resource section has the information for contacting them.

WORKSHOP

The Wall Street Journal runs extensive information on mutual funds every day. Their "Mutual Funds Scorecard" is particularly enlightening. It is usually located at the top of the page in the middle of the mutual fund quotes.

The issue I am looking at features large-cap core funds. It lists the top 10 performers and the top 10 performers from last year. None of the top 10 funds from last year are repeated this year. That tells you something about past performance. What does *your* copy of *The Wall Street Journal* feature in this section?

HOUR'S UP!

Picking a mutual fund to invest in is not magic, or an art, or good luck. It is good decision-making armed with the right information and a commitment to invest. Take this short quiz and test your commitment.

1. Mutual funds have many benefits including …

    A. Diversification.

    B. Professional management.

    C. Liquidity.

    D. All of the above.

2. Investment objectives …

    A. Are pretty meaningless.

    B. Direct the fund's buying and selling.

    C. Can change at any time.

3. A fund's investment objectives …

    A. Should match its actual investment history.

    B. Often fail on the first attempt.

    C. Can get in the way of good trades.

4. Actively managed funds …

    A. Are the best investment to make.

    B. Never lose money.

    C. Many times charge too much in fees and expenses.

5. Funds that invest primarily in small-cap stocks …

    A. Almost always do well in any market.

    B. Seldom lose money.

    C. Are extremely volatile.

6. Large-cap stock funds …

    A. Are very risky.

    B. May bring stability to your portfolio.

    C. Lack any real value.

7. Considering only no-load funds with low expenses will …

    A. Seem pretty boring.

    B. Help you meet your goals quicker.

    C. Be an aggressive investment.

8. It is important to compare …

    A. Big funds with little funds.

    B. Funds with similar investment strategies.

    C. Funds with similar names.

9. Taxes can …

    A. Destroy your alleged return.

    B. Can be safely ignored.

    C. Be refunded under certain conditions.

10. A mutual fund prospectus …

    A. Means nothing.

    B. Contains the home addresses of the investment managers.

    C. Contains important information about the fund.

Hour 18
Picking a Stock

- Compare mutual funds and individual stocks as investments.
- Pick stock to evaluate.
- Invest in what you know.
- Invest in what you buy.
- Invest in what a lot of people buy.
- Research without the Internet.
- Read an annual report.
- Read an income statement.
- Read a balance sheet.
- Read a statement of cash flow.
- Read the 10-K report.
- Read the 10-Q report.
- Evaluate a business.
- Define yield-based evaluations.
- Define earnings-based evaluations.
- Define equity-based evaluations.
- Define sales-based evaluations.

Picking an individual stock to buy can be as simple or as complicated as you want to make it. If you make it too simple, you are guessing. If you make it too complicated, you may never get around to actually buying anything.

This Hour will be devoted to looking at ways to pick individual stocks. Be aware: There are people in the investment business that will give you all sorts of reasons why you shouldn't do this by yourself.

Their reasons run from the self-serving (they want you to pay them big fees to do it for you) to the well-meaning but misguided notion that mutual funds are the only way for individuals to invest with any safety.

A common-sense approach to building your portfolio is worth more than all the experts' advice. This approach examines the most critical factor in creating a successful investing program: you.

An honest assessment of your time availability, interest, risk tolerance, and overall goals will tell you what percentage of your portfolio should be in individual stocks and what part should be in mutual funds.

PROCEED WITH CAUTION

How active do you want to be in your investment program? Just because your friends spend hours each week pouring over research doesn't mean that's the approach you should take. If you adopt a strategy that is comfortable and fun, you are more likely to stick with it.

Let's look at a simple side-by-side comparison of investing through mutual funds and individual stocks.

Mutual Funds	Individual Stocks
Professional management	Control of your own investments
Diversification	Focused investing
Require less time	Hands-on analysis
Less risky	Potential for greater gains

This is not a comprehensive analysis by any means, but it gives you an idea of some of the trade-offs. Unless you have a lot of money, investing in individual stocks *only* probably doesn't make as much sense as balancing mutual funds with individual stocks.

Even if you have already made up your mind to invest only in mutual funds, this Hour will help you better understand the whole investment process. So, let's get started.

MATCHING YOUR INVESTMENT GOALS

The first step in picking a stock for investment is to make sure you have a plan. As we discussed in the last hour, a big part of successful investing is matching investment instruments and your goals.

TIME SAVER

Morningstar.com uses the same system to categorize stocks that it uses for mutual funds.

For example, in the last hour we commented that a young person could afford to be aggressive in his or her retirement account. That logic still works with individual stocks. You might want to consider a portfolio of medium- to small-cap stocks with big potential for growth and a corresponding risk. Likewise, a short-term goal should be addressed with a stock that has more maturity and stability to prevent wild fluctuations in value.

If the Morningstar.com system of categorizing mutual funds makes sense to you, you may want to stick with it. Morningstar.com has also done the same thing with individual stocks. Again, this system allows you to compare apples to apples.

In this Hour, I am going to walk through a way of looking at stocks that is commonly referred to as fundamental analysis. *Fundamental analysis* is a way of evaluating not only the stock, but also—more importantly—the company.

There is another form of analysis called technical analysis that is used by a number of investors. I will touch on it briefly later on, but it is too complicated to explain adequately in this venue.

PICKING STOCKS TO EVALUATE

Before you can evaluate a stock, you need to narrow your choices down from the 10,000 or so available stocks. There is no shortage of information on companies; in fact, you may find there is too much.

TIME SAVER

You can find helpful stock screens at many locations on the Internet. Two of the best are morningstar.com and marketguide.com.

The best and fastest way to pick stocks for evaluation is to use a stock-screening service available on the Internet. These tools allow you to set some parameters and narrow the field down to only those stocks that match your "screen."

Many of these services have preset screens that are already set up for you. Others allow you to build your own screens. For example, you can ask the screen to look for companies that have had revenue growth in excess of 15 percent for the past three years and have a market capitalization less than $750 million.

This might give you some potential growth stocks to look at. Morningstar.com has a screening function that will help you focus on the type of company you are looking for and, if you are using morningstar.com categories, allow you to compare this stock to its peers.

There is another screening method that is not nearly so high-tech, but can be just as successful. I call it the "keeping your eyes open" method of screening. Here is an example I remember from years ago, but it is still as valid today.

Years ago, when the financial services industry was going through deregulation, a couple of hotshot brokers were trying to figure out how to make a lot of money by picking the winners in a deregulated market.

Meanwhile, a retired schoolteacher amassed a small fortune (for her) by doing the same thing. The difference? While the hotshot brokers were pouring over research reports and annual reports, the retired schoolteacher noticed that deregulation had permitted the placement of automatic teller machines at sites off of the bank's property. She concluded that this was sure to be a popular trend, so she invested in companies that made the ATMs.

She correctly saw a change in the way cash was distributed by banks and capitalized on it by not worrying about which banks were going to do well in deregulation, but focusing on a machine they would all want and need.

The point is, she kept her eyes open. I am not suggesting you try to figure out what the next ATM phenomenon will be. However, you can make some educated guesses about which stocks to research using the same method.

JUST A MINUTE

Some of the best investment tips come from your own common sense. Keep your eyes and mind open to new possibilities.

Here are some screens to consider:

- Invest in what you know
- Invest in what you buy
- Invest in what a lot of people buy

INVEST IN WHAT YOU KNOW

Are there changes and innovations at your workplace that may indicate potential new markets or other growth opportunities? Maybe your competitors are the ones out front. What about suppliers you work with or observe at your work?

I have missed on a bunch of these, myself. For example, back in the early 1980s, only lawyers had fax machines. They were very expensive and used smelly paper. I couldn't imagine what anyone would do with one. Now everybody has a fax machine, and it is hard to imagine a business operating without one.

Here's my pick for an industry to keep an eye on: delivery systems. E-commerce on the Internet is growing faster than anyone imagined in the beginning. I have bought my last two computers, software, books, and airline tickets, all over the Internet. The weakest link in the e-commerce chain is delivery.

If you are selling a product that can't be downloaded off the Internet, you have to figure out a way to package and ship the product. This means you need to build a warehouse and hire people to do the shipping or you contract with a third party to provide those services for you. Either way, someone has to come to your business to pick up the package and deliver it to your customer. The people who figure out smart ways to do delivery will be worth investing in.

INVEST IN WHAT YOU BUY

Apply the same principles as when investing in what you know. What are you buying now that you didn't buy yesterday? It seems to me that items and services that simplify your life are going to be increasingly important.

PROCEED WITH CAUTION

Consumers drive our economy. Invest in products and services they want and need, and you will seldom go wrong.

In many ways, cellular phones are part of this phenomenon. They make it easy to stay in touch when you are on the go, saving time and money.

However, there may be opportunities worth considering that are not so high-tech. For example, a number of years ago some restaurants tried to market the idea of a "meal to go" that was different from regular "food to go."

The idea was that you could order a meal that was almost ready to eat and pick it up on the way home or have it delivered. You simply put the entrée in the oven or cooked it on the stove. The rest of the meal was already prepared, so you had an almost fresh-cooked meal with virtually no effort on your part.

The idea didn't do well where I was living, but I wonder if it is worth revisiting.

INVEST IN WHAT A LOT OF PEOPLE BUY

Maybe you prefer Pepsi over Coke, but either way, hundreds of millions of people buy both each day. On the other hand, how many supercomputers are sold each day? Not many, I'd guess.

The point is that products used by the masses are usually better investments than companies making a very specific product with a limited market. In our example above, the schoolteacher picked a product that would penetrate 100 percent of its market.

Whether it is consumables or vital infrastructure products, market leaders and up-and-comers are worthy of your consideration.

RESEARCH WITHOUT THE INTERNET

If you choose not to use the Internet, or simply don't have access to it, there are other ways to research companies for investment.

One of the best tools available is called the Value Line Investment Survey. Value Line publishes this comprehensive research tool; you can usually find a copy at your local library. In Appendix B, "Resources," I will tell you how to get your own trial subscription.

The Value Line staff digests tons of information about publicly traded companies and presents it on a single page for easy reference. All the numbers and ratios we will discuss shortly are contained in this summary, as well as important information that describes the business.

The Value Line service is expensive, but if you are going to be an active trader and don't want to use Internet resources, this is the tool you need.

JUST A MINUTE

You will find helpful information about investing at the public library in the reference section.

TONS OF INFORMATION

There is even more information available for free from individual companies. If you find a company you are interested in knowing more about, the next step is to gather some additional information.

If you are using Value Line, this step is still important and, even if you are using the Internet, follow this step for a couple of companies just to get the feel of what is available. You may find that digesting the traditional printed word is easier than reading off your computer screen or printing out everything you are interested in.

Companies will send you annual reports along with other documents they are required to produce for investors. You do not need these to buy the company's stock in the open market, but they contain a wealth of information that will be valuable in your research. If you don't know how to reach the company, call the exchange the stock is listed on for the phone number. You can find the exchange numbers in Appendix B.

You can also go to the company's Internet site; many will let you order annual and quarterly reports online.

TIME SAVER

Companies are eager to share information with you. For one thing, they are required to make most of the information you need available to the public. You do not need to own the stock before requesting this information.

The Wall Street Journal offers a free service that allows you to order annual reports on selected companies. If you look through their listings, you will see that some stocks have a ♣ character next to the listing.

You can order annual reports on these companies using a 1-800 number. The *Journal* claims the reports will be shipped the next working day.

THE ANNUAL REPORT

The annual report is one of several documents the company is required to publish and make available to the public. It is the one that is most often adorned with glossy, color photographs of happy customers, happy workers, happy management, and happy machinery. It projects the company as one big, happy family.

The really important part of the annual report may tell another story, but up front the management will put on their Sunday best to impress current and potential shareholders.

While the up-front material may be forgiven for being a shameless sales job, the financial information inside must adhere to rigid financial and accounting standards. The statements must be audited and prepared by an accredited accounting firm that will testify to their veracity and note any irregularities in accounting or management procedures.

REVIEWING FINANCIAL STATEMENTS

If you are like most people, the thought of poring over financial statements sounds as exciting as watching paint dry. Fortunately, we won't spend a lot of time here because hundreds of analysts have already done that and their opinions are readily available.

PROCEED WITH CAUTION

Financial statements will tell you a lot about a company, but you need to know where to look. For example, in the income section of the Income Statement you may find that a significant portion of the company's income growth came from a wholly or partially owned subsidiary, and not the parent.

However, it is important to get a working knowledge of the three main parts of the financial statement:

- Income statement
- Balance sheet
- Statement of cash flow

Each of these sections tells us something different about the company.

INCOME STATEMENT

The *income statement* tells us about how the business is doing—what it is bringing in and what it is paying out. It also lets us know whether the company is making a profit or losing money. Those conclusions are expressed in total dollars as well as on a per-share basis.

The first part of the income statement is called *revenues*. This is how much money the company took in from customers who bought their products and/or services. It is often broken down by major business centers. For example, an automobile manufacturer might report sales of cars, trucks, parts, and so on. Large multi-division companies may report division revenues in different documents. It is good to look through these to see what products are pushing the company ahead and what is holding it back.

PROCEED WITH CAUTION

An income statement is something like a peek into a company's checkbook. It is probably the most familiar-looking of the financial statements since it reminds many people of their own checkbook.

The next section of the income statement is *expenses,* which is just what it sounds like; like the revenue section, it is broken down into several categories. The expense categories reflect how well the management is running the business. Increases in expenses should be tied to increased revenue. Increasing expenses in the face of declining revenue spells trouble, while the opposite is worth noting.

The third section is a *summary of income,* which will be in parentheses if the company lost money; provisions for taxes; income from other operations that may be partly owned by the company; and finally, net income, or profit. If this number is in parentheses it means the company operated at a loss for the year. These results are then expressed as earnings per share.

What you want to see represented in the income statement is growth in revenues from year to year with a smaller increase in expenses.

BALANCE SHEET

The *balance sheet* is where you will find the real nuts-and-bolts information about a company. The balance sheet covers a one-year period, which is known as the fiscal year of the business. Most companies use a calendar year for their fiscal year, but some will have different periods (for example, May through April). Whether the fiscal year is a calendar year is of no real importance. It may become an issue when comparing two companies with different fiscal years. The reason is that market conditions may have changed and affected one company differently than the other.

The first part of the balance sheet lists the company's *assets,* which include items such as cash, accounts receivable (money owed by customers), real estate, equipment, inventory, and so on. Depending on the nature of the business, some other assets will be reported here.

The next section of the balance sheet lists the company's *liabilities,* which are monies owed to others. These include accounts payable (unpaid bills), income taxes yet unpaid, retirement costs and, when applicable, dividends payable. The company's debt will also show up in this section.

The third section of the balance sheet is known as *stockholders' equity,* which is the liabilities subtracted from the assets.

What you are looking for is a stockholders' equity section that is showing positive growth from year to year.

STATEMENT OF CASH FLOW

This is the most complicated of the three to read, but it does show you where the company's cash is coming from and how this has changed from year to year.

If you are interested in learning more about financial statements, there are some resources listed in Appendix B for further study.

OTHER SOURCES OF INFORMATION

There are several other reports that contain additional information on the company. If you call the company and request an investor's relations packet, it will normally contain at least two other reports:

- 10-K
- 10-Q

THE 10-K

The *10-K* is another of the required reports. It contains all the information in the annual report, plus some additional and expanded categories. Among the most interesting of the expanded categories are detailed income figures from various divisions and subsidiaries. This information is consolidated in the financial statements found in annual reports.

What it doesn't contain is all the pretty photographs and flowery language found in annual reports. If you are interested in digging deep, this is the place to go. A 10-K report can also be obtained over the Internet.

THE 10-Q

The *10-Q* reports are quarterly versions of the 10-K that also include discussions of recent business activity by management, such as new products or new markets for the company's products. These are also available over the Internet.

HOW IMPORTANT ARE THESE COMPANY DOCUMENTS?

The company documents are important in the context that you should never invest in anything that you don't understand, whether it is a mutual fund or individual stock. However, it is unlikely that you will find any information that stock analysts have missed.

One or more analysts follow most companies, and their reports are often available from the company or elsewhere for free. These are worth reading, although I would not pay much attention to their recommendations as to whether you should buy, sell, or hold the stock. Many of these analysts work for the same investment company that helps the company with its finances.

TIME SAVER

Analysts' reports on individual companies are often available for free from the company or over the Internet.

There are many places to get different opinions on companies on the Internet. Review Hour 7, "Market News/Research," for sources and, equally important, cautions about the quality and truthfulness of some sources.

How to Evaluate a Business

Fundamental analysis is about understanding a business and its stock. The two can't be separated. This next section is where you make your choice as to whether you want to invest in the stock or not.

PROCEED WITH CAUTION

Technical analysis is another way to evaluate stocks for buy-and-sell signals. It focuses on price movement, both current and historic.

Although you use different tools, you are already familiar with this evaluation process because you use it every time you buy anything from a car to a commode. Fundamentally, you ask yourself, "Is this a good commode and, for the quality I want, is this a good price?"

These are the same two basic questions you must answer about the stocks (or anything else for that matter) you invest in:

- Is it a good stock?
- Is this a good price?

Defining a good commode may be more subjective than objective (color, shape, size, and so on), while we can be very objective about picking stocks to buy. However, if the truth were known, many people buy stocks based on emotions rather than objective data.

We can measure whether a company is a quality buy by how well it is doing in terms of growth, debt control, market penetration, and so on. We will use objective evaluation tools to reach our decision, so we can apply these same tools to other stocks.

We must also apply the same type of analysis to the stock's price. The price per share is not relevant unless we measure it against those factors we consider important about the stock.

When you buy stock in a company, you are really buying its income, dividends, growth potential, or some other aspect that you find desirable. For example, you might buy a utility stock because it pays a high dividend. You need to relate the price of the stock to the dividend to see if the price is appropriate for the dividend. You can then compare this measurement to other utilities to see whether their dividends are cheaper or more expensive.

Earnings are another key measure most investors use to evaluate price. How does the price relate to earnings? We have already learned that the price/earnings ratio is one way to measure whether a stock is cheap (low P/E) or expensive (high P/E).

VALUATION MODELS

The following are some of the valuation models used to measure a stock for consideration. They examine different parts of a company to draw some conclusions about the relative value of the stock.

JUST A MINUTE

Valuation models address the earlier question of how we use specific indicators to evaluate stocks.

YIELD-BASED EVALUATIONS

Let's start with this one since I introduced the example above of looking for a utility stock based on the dividend it pays. Utility stocks are known for their history of paying solid dividends. Investors looking for current income or income in a retirement account often look to utility stocks.

One of the ways you can gauge how cheap or expensive a utility's dividend might be is using the *dividend yield* calculation. I introduced this calculation to you earlier (refer to Hour 12, "Stocks—Part I Classifications) as one of the figures reported in the daily stock tables of *The Wall Street Journal*.

The dividend yield measures what percentage of a stock's price is being paid out in dividends. The current per-share price is divided into the annual dividend per share. The resulting percentage is the dividend yield. For example, if a company pays an annual per-share dividend of $4 and the current stock price is $64 per share, the dividend yield is 6.25 percent.

$$4/64 = 0.0625$$

Now suppose you found another utility that paid an annual dividend of $4, but its stock price was only $52. Do the dividend yield calculation and see what happens. Which is the better buy of the $4 annual dividend? Consider these situations:

Company A pays an annual dividend of $4.00 and the annual dividend price is $48.

Company B pays an annual dividend of $2.80 and the annual dividend price is $29.

Which of these companies (all else being equal) is the best buy of the dividend?

You can use dividend yield in the stock screening programs I mentioned above to help you narrow your search.

PROCEED WITH CAUTION

A big part of fundamental analysis is relating financial markers to the stock price, just like we did with dividends. This does not give you the complete picture. It does offer a way to not only evaluate the stock, but compare it to another stock.

EARNINGS-BASED EVALUATIONS

The second example I mentioned in the previous section was an earnings-based evaluation. In other words, is the per-share price of the stock in line with the per-share earnings?

The price/earnings ratio is one of the most often quoted calculations investors consider when buying a stock. The mantra is "high P/E equals overpriced stock; low P/E equals bargain stock." Unfortunately, it is not quite that simple.

First, let's review how to calculate the P/E. You need another figure to begin the calculation: earnings per share (EPS). This is found by dividing the dollar amount of earnings by the number of outstanding shares. For example, if a company had $5,000,000 in earnings for the past 12 months and there were 10,000,000 shares outstanding, the EPS would be $0.50.

$5,000,000/10,000,000 = $0.50

PROCEED WITH CAUTION

Financial ratios provide a way to compare two companies from the same or different industries. If you want to buy a stock because of its high earnings, you need to know how much you are paying for those earnings and whether the same level of earnings could be bought for less.

You will often hear EPS referred to as the "trailing EPS." This is because it uses historical data for its computation. In a minute, you'll see why labeling it "trailing" is important.

Once you have the EPS, compute the P/E by taking the stock price and dividing it by the EPS. For example, if a company's stock was $22 per share and the EPS was $0.50, the P/E would be 44.

$22/$0.50 = 44

Without knowing anything else, an investor might assume from this example that the company is considered a growth company that would be expected to show significant earnings growth in the future. Another investor might say, "Whoa! This stock is too risky because it has no proven earnings potential."

While the P/E provides some general information, it is not specific enough to make an investment decision based on it alone. The "multiple" (another term for P/E) of a company is more helpful if placed in a context.

Many investors believe that P/Es should be looked at in relation to future growth. After all, investors pay for future growth and profits, and the P/E is a measurement of the past. To address this concern, it is helpful to look at another earnings ratio, the *P/E and Growth Ratio (PEG)*. The PEG looks forward to future earnings growth.

The PEG is computed by taking the most forward earnings estimates, available from the analyst reports we talked about earlier or on a number of Internet sites, and divides that into the P/E. If our company had a projected earnings growth rate of 15 percent for the next two years, its PEG would be 2.93:

P/E of 44/EPS growth of 15 = 2.93

To put this in context, a PEG of 1 would indicate the stock was fairly priced because the P/E should roughly equal EPS growth. Our example shows the company is priced almost three times over its fair market value. Something else about this stock would have to be very compelling for an investor to consider it.

If you use the Internet, many of these ratios are already computed for you or are a part of a stock-screening service.

EQUITY-BASED EVALUATIONS

Equity is usually defined as tangible and intangible assets held by a company. You may be more familiar with the term in relationship to a loan.

PROCEED WITH CAUTION

 The book value, or equity, is used to evaluate the business and whether the stock is selling at, below, or above its equity.

For example, the equity in your home is what is left when you take the fair market value and subtract any existing debts. The fair market value of your home includes tangible as well as intangible assets. The tangible assets include the house itself and the property it sits on, plus any additional assets such as landscaping, fences, and so on. The intangible assets might include the neighborhood, curb appeal of the house, and proximity to shopping and schools.

A company's assets follow the same general pattern with real estate, equipment, and inventory, which make up the tangible assets. An intangible asset might include the brand name that the consumer knows the company by. This type of intangible asset can be worth a lot.

What would you pay to rename your computer company IBM? It probably wouldn't take long for people to figure out you weren't the IBM they were familiar with, but the point is virtually everyone even remotely connected to computers—and a lot who aren't—would recognize this respected name.

PROCEED WITH CAUTION

 Because companies come in many sizes and flavors, it is important to have several tools to evaluate the business. Some businesses are better analyzed using one tool and other businesses need a different approach.

One of the ways to evaluate a company involves relating equity to stock price. Remember when we looked at a balance sheet earlier and noted that stockholder's equity was the assets of the company minus the liabilities? This is also known as *book value*.

To calculate the book value per share, you take stockholder's equity and divide it by the outstanding number of shares. Next, take the current stock price and divide it by the book value per share. This gives you a *price-to-book ratio*. A price/book ratio of 1 would indicate that for $1 in share price you were buying $1 in book value.

Another way to use equity is to look at a company's *return on equity (ROE)*. This number will tell you how earnings relate to stockholder's equity. It is calculated by dividing annual earnings by stockholder's equity for the same period. This number is useful when comparing a company with its industry peers.

Industries that do not require significant annual capital expenditures in the normal course of business will have lower ROEs than companies that can generate significant earnings without high capital investments. A high ROE among peers may be a sign of excellent management putting the company's resources to the best use. A low ROE among peers might signal the opposite.

SALES-BASED EVALUATION

Sometimes you need a way to evaluate a company that isn't making money for one reason or another. P/E and PEG don't work in this case because there are no earnings.

JUST A MINUTE

Many Internet companies cannot be evaluated with ratios based on earnings or equity, but they can be measured on the basis of sales. The assumption is that growing sales will one day lead to profits.

The fact that a company is not currently earning a profit doesn't mean it is not a good investment candidate. There may be some good, short-term reason for the losses that will be corrected in the near future.

However, the company may be very young and in a very hot industry, such as the Internet stocks. Many of these companies are quite active and have huge market capitalization despite the fact they have never made money.

What many of them do have is sales, and we can use sales as a way to evaluate a company when there are no earnings. The *sales-price ratio* gives us a look at what those sales might be worth relative to the stock's price.

The sales-price ratio is calculated by taking the stock's market capitalization plus any long-term debt and dividing that number by sales for the last 12 months. The closer this number is to 1, the better. The sales-price ratio is also very helpful in comparing the company with others in the industry, some who are making money and some who aren't.

Companies like Amazon.com, which had not made any profits as of the end of 1999, are hot stocks to own; one of the ways you can value its stock is using the sales-price ratio.

FAMILIARIZE, NOT MEMORIZE

Are you completely confused? Well, don't feel bad. I have dumped a lot of new terms on you in this Hour. It is not necessary for you to memorize each of the concepts, but it will be helpful to be familiar with them as we move forward.

PROCEED WITH CAUTION

 This may seem like more math than you ever thought you would see again after that 10th grade algebra class. Don't worry about memorizing these terms; just keep this book handy for reference.

If you are going to use the Internet, all of these calculations are already done for you and you can even use them to screen stocks.

In the coming hours, we are going over specific investment styles that will refer to these terms and numbers. Feel free to look back for reference. As improbable as it might seem, all of this is starting to come together.

WHAT CAN YOU DO?

The following is a list of five things you can do today:

1. Read the various stock columns in *The Wall Street Journal*. Do they make more sense now or less? They will usually cover a large-cap stock and some NASDAQ issues. Look inside the section for more information.

2. Access Morningstar.com on the Internet and use its "quote lookup" feature. It will be in the upper left-hand corner of their Web page. Key in a symbol for a major stock (such as IBM) and look at the wealth of information it gives you. You can do this using a computer at a library.

3. What do you know? Make a list of products, services, etc. that you have more knowledge of than most people. Do any of them suggest investment possibilities? What do you need to know more about before you can make an educated guess about a potential investment?

4. Retrieve the annual report I asked you to order several hours back. With it open, go over the section on annual reports in this Hour. Can you find all the information I mentioned? What other information is there that I didn't mention?

5. If you want to learn more about technical analysis, check out the books and other resources listed in Appendix B.

WORKSHOP

Go to Morningstar.com or any other research site listed in Appendix B and look at their analysis of a stock such as AT&T (symbol: T). Compare that to an analysis of a stock like Amazon.com (symbol: AMZN). How do they differ and how are they similar?

You will notice that the research sites use the measures we have covered in this Hour, plus some of their own.

HOUR'S UP!

Ready for a pop quiz? This Hour might have been the busiest, and if you want to go back and review, please feel free to do so. Take this short quiz to see how much you have learned.

1. A key to successful investing is …

    A. Jumping on hot stocks.

    B. Matching your goals with the proper investment products.

    C. Finding the perfect stock at the perfect price.

2. Stock-screening tools …

    A. Check for missing information.

    B. Only pick the best stocks to buy.

    C. Provide a way to narrow your choices for evaluation.

3. Invest in …

    A. Products you understand.

    B. Companies with broad markets.

    C. Stock that is selling at or below the fair market price.

    D. All of the above.

4. A good place to do research is …

    A. The barber shop.

    B. The public library.

    C. At the beach.

5. Companies will gladly …

    A. Refer you to a broker for information.

    B. Invite you to their annual meeting.

    C. Supply you with lots of important information.

6. Financial statements in the annual report …

    A. Only tell part of the company's financial story.

    B. Are audited by independent accounting firms.

    C. Can be safely ignored.

7. The 10-K report …

    A. Is an expanded version of the annual report.

    B. Describes a company-sponsored race.

    C. Provides key details on all the company's clients.

8. Evaluating a business before you buy the stock is …

    A. Technical analysis.

    B. Business analysis.

    C. Fundamental analysis.

9. The P/E tells you …

    A. How much the stock should cost.

    B. How the earnings relate to the stock's price.

    C. Why the company isn't making money.

10. The sales-price ratio …

    A. Is meaningless for many companies.

    B. Is useful in evaluating businesses without any earnings.

    C. Tells you what the stock is worth.

QUIZ

PART V
Working Toward a Goal

Hour 19

Asset Allocation

Chapter Summary

LESSON PLAN:

In this Hour you will learn about ...

- Asset allocation and diversification.
- Age and risk tolerance.
- Portfolio components.
- Conservative, moderate, and aggressive portfolios.
- Rebalancing your allocation.
- Taxes.
- Other assets.

Have you ever done this with children squabbling over the last piece of cake? One child gets to cut the piece into two pieces, and the other child gets to pick which piece he wants.

Well, this is nothing like asset allocation, but it does cut down on the "his piece is bigger" fights.

Seriously, asset allocation diversifies your portfolio to help you control risk, yet achieve maximum return within your risk tolerance range.

As noted numerous times already, investing is about risk and reward—more specifically, achieving the maximum reward for the minimum risk. Asset allocation spreads your portfolio over several asset classes and is linked to the time horizon of your goals and individual tolerance for risk.

Some studies have indicated that your overall investment success is more closely tied to achieving the correct asset allocation than which assets you actually buy. The historical justification for this is that different classes of assets don't necessarily move in the same direction at the same time.

For example, at the end of 1999 stocks were blazing hot (at least some stocks were), while bonds were in the pits. When 2000 dawned, there were growing concerns about rising interest rates. If interest rates do rise, new bonds will improve and stocks will suffer.

Stocks have historically outperformed bonds, but they have also experienced periods of extreme volatility. Bonds tend to move in a much narrower range.

If you knew when stocks were going to soar or fall, you wouldn't need to worry about asset allocation. You would have perfected the art of market timing—getting in and out of the market at the right times. Unfortunately, as I have previously noted, no one can do that with any consistency.

JUST A MINUTE

The odds are slim that you will never suffer a loss while investing, but thoughtful allocation is your best defense.

WHAT IS ASSET ALLOCATION, REALLY?

Asset allocation allows that we will have less than ideal returns in exchange for some real-world protection against market ups and downs. It should be noted here that asset allocation is no guarantee against losses. The best it or any system can do is reduce the odds against a loss.

Although asset allocation is widely accepted as a prudent measure, it is not universally accepted. In particular, some financial professionals view it with disdain, mainly because they want nothing to do with bonds for any reason. Others dislike both bonds and mutual funds and argue that individual stocks are the only way to go.

As we noted in the last Hour, building a diversified portfolio of individual stocks requires more time, money, and expertise than most people have. Introducing bonds to your portfolio will reduce your return over a portfolio of the correct stocks. However, therein lies the rub. Who can pick the correct stocks for each and every market? The answer is *no one*.

That is the essence of asset allocation: building a portfolio that is appropriate for your risk tolerance, time horizon, and ultimate goal. As you have probably concluded, asset allocation is more important for your long-term goals than for the short-term ones.

Retirement is the biggest long-term goal and financial need most of us face. Our examination of asset allocation will focus on creating a retirement nest egg.

You may already be practicing asset allocation if you participate in a 401(k) plan at work. These plans will typically give you four to six choices of how to invest your money. If the plan is well designed, the choices will cover a range of investments that let you place your money in appropriate instruments on any percentage basis you choose.

ASSET ALLOCATION MODELS

There are a number of asset allocation models available. While most folks agree you need to do asset allocation, there is no universal formula that everyone accepts. Companies that have products that—oh, surprise!—fit the model, generate many of the models.

The asset allocation model consists of two major parts: age and risk tolerance.

AGE

Based on our work together this far, you know that the younger you are, the more aggressive you can be in your portfolio. The more years you have to let your portfolio work for you, the more likely you will go through periods of ups and downs in the market. Time has a way of smoothing out the bumps, but the closer you get to needing your money, the higher the chance that the market may be down when you need to get out. If you look at any short period (three years or fewer) there is a much greater chance the market will be down in one of those years when compared with longer periods (five years or more).

PROCEED WITH CAUTION

Risk is the fuel that pushes an investment forward. The more risk, the faster you go. The faster you go, the more likely you are to crash.

This is why there is no one asset allocation model, but a process that frequently examines where you are and adjusts your portfolio accordingly.

RISK TOLERANCE

I will repeat my earlier cautions about being honest with yourself relative to how much risk you can tolerate. If watching your investments bounce up and down on a frequent basis makes you lose sleep, then a pure stock portfolio is probably not right for you.

Stocks (more accurately, some stocks) have been super investments for most of the past 10 years. If you don't pay attention, you could conclude that it didn't make any difference what stocks you bought. However, the rising stock market tide was built on technology stocks and did not lift every other stock with it. Take a look at the stock tables in any issue of *The Wall Street Journal,* and you will find a list of winners and losers. In fact, many days there were more losing stocks than advancing stocks, even when the media reported the market was up.

Balancing your portfolio with less volatile instruments is a way to smooth out some of the natural volatility in the stock market. Asset allocation provides you some protection from the unknowns.

Remember Little's Golden Rule of Investing:

> *The best time to start investing was yesterday. The second best time is today. Tomorrow is better than nothing.*

PORTFOLIO COMPONENTS

Asset allocation is about spreading risk over different asset classes to even out the peaks and valleys. Most financial professionals feel that your portfolio should consist of a mix of bonds and stocks. Some would add cash to that mix, but most don't.

The obvious questions here are

- Which stocks in what portion?
- Which bonds in what portion?

The answer, like most answers to investing questions, is: "It depends." It depends on your age and risk tolerance. A young, aggressive investor will look at those questions quite differently than a middle-aged conservative investor.

It might be helpful to look at the problem from an age/risk perspective. Again, we are assuming that the investment goal is funding retirement by age 65.

JUST A MINUTE

The suggested allocations do not include a cash component. Many financial professionals do include cash. This is a personal preference. Do what is most comfortable for you.

We will look at age groups starting with the youngest and working forward. Each age group will have three levels of risk tolerance: conservative, moderate, and aggressive with suggestions for each. There is no "official" asset allocation formula, so consider these suggestions as just that: a starting point for your own thinking.

AGE 20–30

It may be hard to think seriously about retirement at this age, but you couldn't pick a better time to start. Not only will you almost certainly build a substantial nest egg, but you will get in the habit of investing that will serve you well the rest of your life.

CONSERVATIVE PORTFOLIO

A conservative approach at this age suggests a stock/bond mix for long-term growth and stability. An additional consideration is that there will not be a lot of money invested in this period, so mutual funds make more sense than individual issues.

Stocks	S&P 500 index fund	80 percent
Bonds	Long-term bond index fund	20 percent

MODERATE PORTFOLIO

A more aggressive approach might stay with a stock/bond mix, but change the portions somewhat.

Stocks	Large-cap value fund	25 percent
	Large-cap growth fund	50 percent
	Foreign stocks fund	15 percent
Bonds	Long-term bond index fund	10 percent

AGGRESSIVE PORTFOLIO

Our young lion wants to roar, so we drop bonds from the mix completely.

Stocks	Small-cap growth fund	40 percent
	Small-cap value fund	30 percent
	Foreign stocks fund	30 percent

AGE 30–40

For many of us, this is the age at which we begin to settle down and start thinking about our future. Retirement is still a long way off, but not so far that it is off our radar screen altogether.

CONSERVATIVE PORTFOLIO

Our conservative investor can stand pat, or if she believes the stock market is looking shaky, move more assets into long-term bonds.

Stocks	S&P 500 index fund	70 percent
Bonds	Long-term bond index fund	30 percent

MODERATE PORTFOLIO

Our moderate friend is happy with the mix, but just to be on the safe side, ups the percentage of bonds.

Stocks	Large-cap value fund	25 percent
	Large-cap growth fund	40 percent
	Foreign stocks fund	15 percent
Bonds	Long-term bond index fund	20 percent

AGGRESSIVE PORTFOLIO

Our young lion still wants to roar but begins to understand the danger of staying heavily invested in one area (small-cap stocks).

Stocks	Small-cap growth fund	40 percent
	Large-cap growth fund	40 percent
	Foreign stocks fund	20 percent

AGE 40–50

As we enter the years of our peak earning capacity, retirement begins to seem like a not-to-distant hill looming larger and larger.

CONSERVATIVE PORTFOLIO

Our conservative investor hears retirement calling more loudly than most. She grows more nervous about stocks and moves more assets into long-term bonds.

| Stocks | S&P 500 index fund | 60 percent |
| Bonds | Long-term bond index fund | 40 percent |

MODERATE PORTFOLIO

Our moderate friend is becoming nervous about the stock/bond ratio and moves to up the bond component at the expense of the large-cap growth fund.

Stocks	Large-cap value fund	25 percent
	Large-cap growth fund	30 percent
	Foreign stocks fund	15 percent
Bonds	Long-term bond index fund	30 percent

AGGRESSIVE PORTFOLIO

Our young lion realizes he is not a young lion anymore, but wants to stay as heavily invested in stocks as is prudent. His move into bonds discards the fund notion and buys bonds directly for a better yield even though the risk is higher.

Stocks	Small-cap growth fund	20 percent
	Large-cap growth fund	40 percent
	Foreign stocks fund	20 percent
Bonds	Long-term bonds	20 percent

AGE 50–60

These are the years we set the stage for retirement, getting our ducks in a row and guarding against any fourth quarter surprises by the market.

CONSERVATIVE PORTFOLIO

Our conservative investor is focusing on calculating what her living expenses will be and how much she will have coming in between Social Security and her retirement. The focus is shifting to income and capital preservation. She will stay in equities but will move out of an index fund and into solid income stocks like utilities. At the same time, she will slowly shift out of a bond fund and into individual bonds (10 years or more) that begin maturing at retirement. At the end of this period, her portfolio looks like this:

| Stocks | High-quality income stocks | 50 percent |
| Bonds | Long-term bonds | 50 percent |

MODERATE PORTFOLIO

Our moderate friend also begins moving toward income and away from growth, but not completely. Foreign stocks look too unstable, so they get dropped. He also begins shifting away from a bond index fund and into high-quality individual bonds.

Stocks	Large-cap value fund	40 percent
	Large-cap growth fund	20 percent
Bonds	Long-term bonds	40 percent

AGGRESSIVE PORTFOLIO

Our young lion's aggressive tendencies are tempered by the reality he is zooming past middle age and headed straight for retirement. He still has faith in equities, but needs more stability in his portfolio.

| Stocks | Large-cap value fund | 70 percent |
| Bonds | Long-term bonds | 30 percent |

AGE 60—??

Even though we may not retire until 65 (and many folks are continuing to work after 65), we are in a retirement mode at this point with our investments.

CONSERVATIVE PORTFOLIO

Our conservative investor continues her shift to current income and capital preservation. However, she is aware that being too conservative may cause her to outlive her money. Because she is so busy, it seems like a good idea to shift some of her maturing bonds back into a bond index fund to reduce the amount of time she spends watching her investments.

Stocks	High quality income stocks	30 percent
Bonds	Long-term bonds	40 percent
	Bond index fund	30 percent

MODERATE PORTFOLIO

Our moderate friend begins the shift to a heavier emphasis on income and away from growth.

Stocks	Large-cap value fund	20 percent
	High-quality income stocks	40 percent
Bonds	Long-term bonds	40 percent

AGGRESSIVE PORTFOLIO

Our now not-so-agile young lion finds golf more interesting than investing, but still keeps his toe in the water.

Stocks	Large-cap value fund	30 percent
Bonds	Long-term bonds	70 percent

WHAT IT ALL MEANS

The previous portfolio examples are for discussion purposes only and do not necessarily represent the best asset allocation for your situation. Use them as a beginning point for further study. This exercise has looked at one situation in isolation without regard to other goals or financial needs.

Those of us who have kids headed for college face some pressing challenges that will surely distort our allocation schemes. Use common sense when working with models like this. They aren't set in stone.

The next section is going to look at some other considerations that may alter your asset allocation plans.

OTHER CONSIDERATIONS

None of us live in a cocoon, isolated from the rest of the world and its nasty habit of intruding in our best-laid plans. We need to be flexible to accommodate whatever challenges come our way, as well as take advantage of the opportunities.

JUST A MINUTE

Once you have found a comfortable allocation, keep an eye on it for slippage, which occurs when one component does exceptionally well and becomes out of proportion with the rest of your assets.

REBALANCE YOUR ALLOCATION

Your retirement account may have grown by leaps and bounds in the last few years if it was heavily invested in stocks. Big run-ups in the stock market have undoubtedly thrown any system you had out of whack.

If you were shooting for a 70/30 stocks/bonds mix and haven't made adjustments in the past five to seven years, you are more likely sitting at 90/10 stocks/bonds or worse. Your stocks have gone up and, I suspect, your bonds have tanked.

It is a fairly simple job to redistribute the mix, but you may be tempted not to given how severely stocks have beaten bonds. This is where discipline is needed most. The reason you allocate assets in the first place is to guard against a "bull run that won't end" ending.

A few short months will pass between the time I finish writing this book and when it hits the street, yet that is an eternity in the stock market. We could be deep in a bear market by then or watching the Dow pass 15,000. No one knows. Rebalancing your portfolio will give you the best chance to do well or minimize any loss.

DON'T FORGET TAXES

Taxes don't retire, unfortunately. Before you reach retirement and begin withdrawals from your qualified retirement account, schedule a visit with a tax accountant to work out a plan.

You will have tax liabilities, and those need to be considered in your plan. For example, it may make sense to look at moving assets coming out from under a tax-deferred umbrella into a tax friendly or even tax-free investment to minimize post-retirement tax bills.

JUST A MINUTE

Asset allocation is not Aladdin's magic lamp, nor is it foolproof portfolio armor. It won't prevent a loss, but it will improve the odds that your investments will be enough to meet your financial goals.

WHAT CAN YOU DO?

The following is a list of five things you can do today:

1. If you have a 401(k) or IRA, do you know how your assets are allocated? If you had a big chunk invested in technology stocks during the 1990s, you may be way over-represented in this sector and vulnerable.

2. Locate your age bracket in the text. Does the suggested allocation seem to make sense for you and your risk tolerance? Remember, the suggested allocation is a starting point for you to reach your own allocation model.

3. Using your financial goals, which of the models seems like it would work best for you: conservative, moderate, or aggressive?

4. Your house is a major resource that should not be ignored. Do you plan to live in your current house until you retire? If so, when will it be paid off? Not facing a monthly mortgage payment may make your retirement more comfortable. If you do not know when it will be paid off, contact the mortgage company for an amortization schedule. If you need to make additional payments to pay it off by retirement, consider doing that.

5. Your taxes after retirement could be a significant liability. Do you know what your current property taxes are and what they might be in the future? As you pull money out of your retirement fund, it will most likely be taxed as ordinary income. Do you plan to work part-time after retirement? If you are going to be self-employed (a consultant, for example), self-employment taxes are significant.

WORKSHOP

Investors buy on the hope of future gain. However, the potential of future gain is always tempered by the potential for loss. It is not a rule that stocks and bonds must move in opposite directions, but that often happens.

If you read *The Wall Street Journal*'s daily commentary on stocks and bonds, you will often see that what moved the market ahead might have been cited as the reason bonds retreated, or the other way around.

However, it is not uncommon for bonds and stocks to move in the same direction. Can you draw any conclusions about the role of balancing stocks and bonds as a hedge against losses?

Hour's Up!

Asset allocation is the process of moving your investment tools around, while dropping some and picking up others. This is all in response to your changing circumstances. Here is a short quiz.

1. Asset allocation is …

   A. Something you do after you retire.

   B. The process of counting your assets.

   C. The process of mixing classes of investments to reduce risk and maximize return.

2. Age plays a roll in asset allocation because …

   A. The younger you are, the more conservative you should be.

   B. Your age will give you the amount of time left to achieve your goal.

   C. The older you are, the more aggressive you should be.

3. Risk tolerance …

   A. Will drive some investment decisions.

   B. Is not a factor in asset allocation.

   C. Is something to overcome.

4. Most portfolios are …

   A. Made up of mutual funds and options.

   B. Stocks and bonds.

   C. Stocks and futures.

5. Conservative portfolios …

   A. Stick with small-cap stocks.

   B. Stick with growth funds.

   C. Mix conservative investments like index funds and bond index funds.

6. Moderate portfolios …

   A. Look for balance in growth and safety.

   B. Stick with bonds.

   C. Never buy large-cap mutual funds.

7. Aggressive portfolios …

    A. Shoot for market returns.

    B. Like short-term bonds.

    C. Are willing to take extra risk for potentially greater gains.

8. You should consider rebalancing your allocation …

    A. When one component has had a big increase or decrease.

    B. When you feel like it.

    C. Every 15 years.

9. Following the crowd …

    A. Is usually the right thing to do.

    B. Is usually the wrong thing to do.

    C. Doesn't matter one way or another.

10. Taxes during retirement …

    A. Are not a factor.

    B. Are deferred.

    C. Make a big difference in your standard of living.

Quiz

HOUR 20

Conservative/Low Cost Investing

CHAPTER SUMMARY

LESSON PLAN:

In this Hour you will learn about …

- Dollar cost averaging.
- Low-cost mutual funds.
- Automatic deduction.
- DRIPs and DIPs.
- Buy-and-hold strategy.
- Market timing.
- Staying in the market.
- Market cycles.
- Holding periods.

I vaguely remember a poem I learned in high school about a young couple that wanted to get married, but first they had to finish school, then get jobs, then something else came up and they kept postponing the wedding.

When everything was perfect for them to wed, they both were very old people. Although I don't remember much of the poem, obviously, the message stuck with me: If you wait until everything is perfect, you may never do anything.

Remember Little's Golden Rule of Investing:

The best time to start investing was yesterday.
The second best time is today. Tomorrow is better
than nothing.

PROCEED WITH CAUTION

Sometimes it is easier to think of excuses about why something won't work than it is to do it. We all suffer from the tendency to put off the uncomfortable. I hope by now you are starting to see that investing need not be uncomfortable.

One of the frequent laments I hear is from people who feel they don't have enough money to invest. Certainly your basic needs come first, but don't let the lack of a large investment stash prevent you from getting started.

This Hour I am going to show you how you can start investing with just a few hundred dollars. I will also show you some conservative investment strategies that will feel comfortable for just about anyone.

Conservative investing and low-cost investing are not synonymous, but many of the conservative strategies also happen to be low cost. I have grouped them in this Hour to avoid duplication.

Conservative investing in this context means a style that is long-term in nature and focused on investments that are conventional. The fact that many of these strategies are low cost helps conservative investors achieve decent returns because less is lost to fees, commissions, and so on.

DOLLAR COST AVERAGING

Dollar cost averaging is the single most powerful investment strategy that most individual investors can use to achieve their financial goals. It works because it takes full advantage of compounding and a continuous presence in the market.

With dollar cost averaging, you are buying no matter what the market is doing. That may not sound like a conservative investment strategy on the surface, so let me explain what dollar cost averaging is and does.

TIME SAVER

Monthly investing of a fixed amount deducted from your checking account is a way to bring discipline to investing and save time, too.

The essence of *dollar cost averaging* is putting a fixed amount of money into the market every month. If you have a 401(k) or 403(b) plan at work, you are practicing dollar cost averaging right now.

I will use mutual funds as the investment target for this explanation, but you can do this with individual stocks; I will show you how later this Hour.

Say you have $100 a month to invest, whether it is through your retirement plan or your own investment program. Every month $100 is invested in a mutual fund regardless of whether the fund is up or down.

The dollar cost averaging philosophy isn't concerned with the price of a fund when it is time to invest. The result is when the fund is up you buy less and when the fund is down you buy more. Over time, you will achieve a good average cost basis for the investment.

It will not be the ideal return. The ideal return depends on buying heavily when the fund is at its lowest, while avoiding buying when it's at its highest. If you recognize this as market timing, go to the head of the class.

Your bonus question: Who can consistently time the market correctly? That's right: no one.

PROCEED WITH CAUTION

A benefit of long-term investing is the extraordinary affect of compounding on even the most modest of investments. Start now with however much you can put together.

I also want to emphasize that dollar cost averaging works best over a long time frame. This is where you need courage to ride out the low spots even if they occur right after you get started. Few investment strategies work well over a short period of time, and dollar cost averaging is no exception.

It is also important to note that if you buy a turkey, it will still be a turkey even if you buy it using dollar cost averaging. If you buy a stock for its growth potential, but it is not showing any signs of growth, follow up with a check on morningstar.com of their analysis of the stock. When no one believes in the stock it is probably time to cut your losses and move on to another opportunity.

If you read investment books or wander around the Internet, you are likely to find discussions about using dollar cost averaging to invest a large sum of money. For years, it has been suggested that if you have a large sum to invest (an IRA rollover or inheritance) that it is best to invest it over a period of time rather than all at once.

Now folks are saying that may not be a good strategy. We will explore this use of dollar cost averaging a little later this Hour, but for now let's assume we don't have a lot of money to invest at once. A number of sources raise the question: "Would it be better to invest $2,400 at once or $200 a month for 12 months?"

PROCEED WITH CAUTION

For the most part, money for investing is better in the market than out. Avoid holding large amounts of cash for extended periods.

That is not a question that many of us in the real world care about, because we don't have $2,400 sitting around. What we can do is free a sum of money each month to invest. It is my feeling you are better off in the market than out, and it is better to invest money as it is available rather than wait until you have saved a big chunk.

INITIAL DEPOSIT

Most mutual funds require you to come up with an initial deposit of $2,000–$3,000. This amount is often less for IRA accounts, but may still be $1,000. If you have the money to make this size of initial deposit, your choice of mutual funds is fairly broad.

However, we noted that many of us don't have an extra $3,000 lying around. You can still get in the market, because there are mutual funds that will let you open an account for a couple hundred dollars. These aren't crummy funds because they have low entry points, but there are fewer out there so your selection is not as large.

AUTOMATIC DEDUCTION

Once you are in a fund, plan on setting up an automatic deduction from your checking account each month. Almost every fund out there will do this for you, and many actively encourage it. Some will lower their initial deposit if you set the account up this way from the beginning.

The automatic deduction from your checking account enforces a disciplined approach to investing that is sometimes compromised when you have to write a check each month.

JUST A MINUTE

You should be less concerned about finding the perfect investment and more concerned about getting the process going.

When your account is large enough, you can move to another fund if you aren't happy with the fund you're currently in.

When you have more money to invest on a monthly basis, consider increasing your monthly deposits or opening another account with a different fund. Appendix B, "Resources," will tell you how to find low initial deposit funds.

Dollar cost averaging is an effective, long-term investment strategy that just about anybody can participate in. It keeps you investing regardless of the market and takes away the issue of timing the market.

DRIPs AND DIPs

Despite your initial reaction, this section is not about your high school algebra and social studies teachers.

DRIPs and DIPs are ways to buy individual stocks without using a broker and without paying high fees and commissions. They allow you to use dollar cost averaging with individual stocks.

It should be noted that not all companies offer DRIPs and DIPs. Check Appendix B for sources of information about DRIPs and DIPs.

PROCEED WITH CAUTION

Even people with modest investment budgets can get started with investing. DRIPs and DIPs offer cost-effective ways to apply dollar cost averaging to the purchase of individual stocks. The only negative is that not all companies offer the plans. Shop with care, since fees and other costs vary.

HOW A DRIP WORKS

DRIP stands for Dividend Reinvestment Program; it originated as a way people could reinvest dividends in stocks. This is not difficult with mutual funds, since you can easily buy fractional shares. With stocks it is more difficult, since there is no way on the open market to buy fractional shares.

Companies set up DRIPs to allow people to reinvest dividends into an account that bought shares as enough money accumulated. The programs have been expanded to allow people to buy shares by investing on a regular monthly basis.

If there is one disadvantage to DRIPs, it is that they can be a hassle to set up. To open a DRIP, you generally must already own at least one share of the stock.

There are several ways you can acquire the needed one share. You can contact a broker to buy it for you. Some brokers advertise this service, others do not. It is important that the stock certificate be issued in your name and not in the "street name," which is how it normally would be issued. (The term "street name" means the stock is being held by a broker for a customer. This means that when the customer wants to sell, they don't need to endorse the certificates. If they hold the certificate in their name, it must be endorsed and transported to the new owner.)

Once you have the stock certificate, you can contact the company and they will send you the necessary paperwork to open a DRIP. Normally, a third party called a *transfer agent* will handle the actual paperwork. There may be fees associated with getting the program going and some companies require a minimum monthly deposit, although these can be as low as $10 a month.

There are also services that inventory stocks that offer DRIPs and will set you up for a fee. Appendix B lists a Web site where you can find these services. Not all of these services are the same, so check fees carefully. This is the easiest way to get started since they will walk you through all the paperwork.

Once the program is set up, your bank account will be debited for the amount you selected and the money will be invested in the DRIP account. This is a low-cost method for buying individual stocks without having to come up with a big initial deposit.

PROCEED WITH CAUTION

DIPs are also a great way to get a child started in investing. Check out the Web site listed in Appendix B, "Resources."

How a DIP Works

DIP stands for Direct Investment Plan. It allows you to buy individual stocks directly from the company without using a broker.

DIPs differ from DRIPs in that you do not need to own a share of stock to start one. You simply contact a company offering DIPs, and they will send you the necessary paperwork along with an explanation of how their system works.

Some DIPs require a large initial deposit, but many do not. Others may require a higher minimum monthly deposit. It pays to shop around. DIPs can also be used to set up an IRA. Appendix B lists a Web site where you can get more information.

Buy-and-Hold Strategy

Throughout this book, I have frequently extolled the virtues of a buy-and-hold strategy as a key to investment success. In this section, I am going to show you in more detail why this is true and how it is the cornerstone of a conservative investment program.

There is no other strategy that has consistently proven successful over the long term for the average investor. This strategy works on individual stocks as well as mutual funds.

JUST A MINUTE

Historically, the stock market has returned between 10 percent and 11 percent, but this average covers a long period of time. Staying in the market is the key to letting time work for you.

Before more detail is added to the strategy, let's look at its limitations:

- It will not guarantee you a profit.
- It will not prevent a loss.
- If you buy a rotten investment, it is unlikely it will get better with time.
- It is not an automatic pilot for your investments.

You might be wondering if it is such a good deal with those limitations. If you could take the risk completely out of investing, you wouldn't need any system. However, the real world of investing is that, even with a conservative strategy, there are elements of risk that no system can completely negate.

So much for the bad news. Now, let's look at some of the benefits of a buy-and-hold strategy:

- It takes market timing out of the investment decision.
- You will make more money being in the market than jumping in and out.
- It evens out market cycles.
- It will let a good investment get better or bounce back from a rough period.

Market Timing

You are probably getting tired of my long-running admonition against market timing, but it is one of the most frequent mistakes investors make—and they make it over and over.

We live in a culture that provides us with a vast array of tools to take control of our lives, including everything from handheld computers to cellular phones.

It is a natural tendency to want control of our environment. Unfortunately, the fastest and most appealing computer still can't help us time the market.

PROCEED WITH CAUTION

Taking control of your investments sometimes means turning them over to someone else (like a mutual fund manager) who has the time and expertise.

STAY IN THE MARKET

You will make more money staying in the market through downturns than you will by trying to guess when to get out or stay in.

A study by Value Line confirms this. It looked at numerous market downturns and what happened to the investors who withdrew their money and those who rode it out. The S&P 500 index was the portfolio model.

What the study found was that even if you bought at a peak just before a downturn and sold during the market low of 1990, you made a substantial recovery. This is an investor's nightmare: buying high and selling low.

Yet, in each case beginning with 1962, if you held onto your investment until 1990, you made at or above the stock market's historic return of around 10 percent per year. The only time you didn't make that return was the 1987–1990 period where there was not enough time to recover.

If you bought near the market high in:	Sold quickly near the market low in:	Your total return was:	But if you held longer and sold near the 1990 market low your total return would have been:	And your average annual return would have been:
1962	1962	−21.0%	+1,217.5%	+9.4%
1966	1966	−14.5%	+788.9%	+9.3%
1968	1970	−29.3%	+584.1%	+9.2%
1973	1974	−39.0%	+486.1%	+11.0%
1977	1978	− 9.7%	+443.1%	+13.1%
1981	1982	−13.9%	+233.0%	+13.0%
1984	1984	− 6.3%	+135.3%	+13.0%
1987	1987	−29.6%	+2.5%	+0.8%

Source: Value Line

The message is clear: Staying in the market makes more sense and dollars.

JUST A MINUTE

The only consistent factor about the stock market is that it goes up and it goes down. The long-term investor does not worry much about these cycles except to protect himself or herself when time is running out on an investment goal.

MARKET CYCLES

Thanks to the long-running bull market of the 1990s, there are a whole group of investors who have never known a down market, also known as a bear market. A bear market is simply a long-term decline in securities prices. Bear markets are often the result of high interest rates, which have a devastating effect on existing bonds and put a damper on new issues. Stocks decline because money is tight and consumers as well as businesses are reluctant to invest.

Those of us with longer memories find this unnerving. It suggests that these investors who have never known any direction but up are willing to bid up stock prices to unsupportable highs.

There is a lot of talk about bull markets forever, but the fundamental influences on the market haven't changed. By the time you read this book, the market may be higher than in late 1999 or it may be down. Either way, a buy-and-hold strategy that stays with quality investments will have a good chance of coming out okay.

GOOD INVESTMENTS BECOME BETTER

Good investments held over the long term usually become better investments, and those that stumble usually have a chance to recover. Keep in mind that good investments may suffer in a bear market or all by themselves due to the changing landscape of their markets.

IBM is another example I have used more than once in this book to illustrate a point. (Just for the record: I do not own or control any positions in IBM.) Once the icon of American management and technological success, IBM fell on hard times following the stock market crash in 1987.

Its personal computer business stumbled as low-cost competitors like Compaq and Dell soared. Bloated with managers, the company could not move quickly enough to keep pace with the radical changes in computing that were shaping a whole new industry profile in the early 1990s. In just a few short years, IBM laid off tens of thousands of workers and began reinventing itself.

It is not the IBM of old, by any means, but it has carved out a strong position in the e-commerce services and software market. Mainframe computers still account for a big chunk of its business, but that segment is not growing very fast.

Nevertheless, $10,000 invested in IBM in 1994 outperformed the computer industry and the S&P 500. The $90 billion company will never move as fast as some of the younger and smaller kids on the block, but when the dust clears my guess is that IBM will still be an important player in America's economy.

I doubt that many of the newbies that are so hot today could survive the kind of beating IBM has taken. I wouldn't bet my retirement on them.

JUST A MINUTE

Sticking with a quality investment, even when it is down, is often the best long-term strategy. However, buy and hold doesn't necessarily mean holding an investment forever. Your investment goals will change, and there may come a time to put an investment aside.

HOLDING PERIOD

The buy-and-hold strategy doesn't necessarily mean you hold a stock forever. I would suggest five years as a minimum, but a longer period would probably be better.

You may never want to let go of a good investment; as long as it is meeting your objectives, there is no reason to let go. However, even good investments are sometimes inconsistent with your financial goals.

For example, if you bought an aggressive growth fund for your retirement account when you were young, you may want to move into something more stable as the time approaches when you might need to cash out.

We have noted this already, but it is worth repeating. The closer you get to needing your money, the fewer chances you can take with market fluctuations. Shifting into a bond or bond fund, for example, to add stability might be the smart thing to do, even though you are not unhappy with your growth fund.

Buy and hold is not very exciting, nor is it very sexy, but it is the safest way to achieve your financial goals within the context of long-term investments.

INVESTMENT CLUBS

You may not be familiar with investment clubs, but they are an excellent way to become familiar with investing. Basically, an investment club is a group of people who agree to invest a set amount of money each month into the club. The club members collectively make investment decisions.

Club members research stocks and present their findings to the rest of the group. The club then decides what to invest in and what to sell out of their portfolio. Members participate in the profits of the club.

PROCEED WITH CAUTION

Investment clubs are a good way to take some of the emotional concerns out of investing. It is reassuring to discuss investing problems and opportunities with others.

Clubs are organized around a common set of rules and guidelines, so you're not reinventing the wheel every time a new one is started. There are hundreds of clubs all across the United States, and many folks find this a safe and entertaining way to invest.

Appendix B lists information on finding clubs in your area or starting your own.

What Can You Do?

The following is a list of five things you can do today:

1. Using the Web site listed in Appendix B, visit a couple of linked sites that specialize in DRIPs and note their fees and services. Even if you don't think you want to use DRIPs, you might consider setting one up for a special child in your life. You won't miss a few dollars every month, and the child will have a nice investment to start life as an adult.

2. If you consider yourself a conservative investor, start constructing a model portfolio based on any assets you may own and adding to them with appropriate investments for your level of risk tolerance. Don't worry about identifying individual stocks or bonds, but focus on what attributes you would like the asset to have (growth, income, and so on).

3. Review the chart in this Hour regarding buying at a market high and selling at a low. Were you surprised that investors could still make a profit? This illustrates the power of staying in the market. How would you feel if one year your portfolio dropped 20 percent or more? Would you be willing to stick it out, given the results of the chart?

4. How hard will it be for you to sell a profitable investment if it no longer fits your asset allocation model? Think about an exit strategy for

those elements of your portfolio that may no longer fit your asset allocation model.

5. Stock index funds are generally considered a conservative investment. Look through *The Wall Street Journal* for the index funds that track indexes other than the S&P 500. Pay particular attention to funds that track mid- or small-cap indexes.

WORKSHOP

Using the Internet or *The Wall Street Journal*, examine the latest prices for the stocks in the Dow Jones Industrial Average (the Web site is listed in Appendix B). Pay attention to the 52-week highs and lows for the stock. Would you have felt good about holding the stock during the lows?

How many of them are closer to the high than the low? What does the range suggest to you about stocks over the short term?

HOUR'S UP!

This Hour should have convinced you that there aren't too many good reasons not to start investing. If you are the cautious, conservative type, this Hour showed you how to get started with just a small investment. Check out your memory.

1. When is the best time to start investing?

   A. Now.

   B. Yesterday.

   C. Tomorrow.

2. Dollar cost averaging …

   A. Only works with large sums of money.

   B. Works best over the long term.

   C. Won't work on large-cap stocks.

3. You can open a mutual fund with …

   A. A couple of hundred dollars.

   B. No less than $1,000.

   C. Pokémon cards.

4. Automatic deduction is a great way to …

    A. Overdraw your checking account.

    B. Invest.

    C. Lose money.

5. A DIP is …

    A. Who you went to your senior prom with.

    B. A form of investing in options.

    C. A way to buy stock without using a broker.

6. Buy and hold means …

    A. Owning a car for a long time.

    B. Owning a house for a long time.

    C. Holding an investment for a long time.

7. Market timing …

    A. Is a way to make lots of money.

    B. Is not possible with any consistency.

    C. Always leads to profits.

8. Market cycles …

    A. Are never down.

    B. Are almost certain to occur again.

    C. Are never up.

9. A good holding period for an investment is …

    A. At least five years.

    B. Six months or less.

    C. Until Wednesday.

10. Investment clubs …

    A. Are a bad idea.

    B. Are a fun way to learn investing.

    C. May be illegal.

Quiz

HOUR 21
Active Investing

LESSON PLAN:

In this Hour, you will learn about ...

- Active investing defined.
- Disadvantages of active investing.
- Advantages of active investing.
- Disadvantages of online trading.
- Advantages of online trading.
- Tools of the active investor
- Buying on margin.
- Selling short.
- After-hours trading.

Active investing is not for everyone. It requires a greater commitment of time and energy to do successfully and may involve a higher degree of risk than conservative investing.

I define *active investing* as the greater participation of the investor in investing decisions. This pattern of investing may be marked by the use of actively managed mutual funds and investments in individual stocks and bonds.

On a risk scale, I would rank this pattern a moderate. Next hour, we are going to look at aggressive investing, which will definitely fall on the risky portion of the scale.

You may be wondering why I am even mentioning other forms of investment after so strongly advocating a buy-and-hold conservative strategy in the last hour. You might remember that I said a buy-and-hold conservative strategy was the best for the average investor. By that, I mean most people don't have the time, energy, or interest in spending several hours a week managing their investments.

PROCEED WITH CAUTION

Active investing is not the same as speculating, where traders jump in and out of the market in hopes of catching a quick profit.

However, there is a group of investors who really enjoy getting their hands dirty and working on their investments. They are willing to spend the time and energy it takes to follow the market more closely. If they approach investing with a thoughtful attitude and are more interested in information than intuition, their chances of success are high.

The real danger of taking an active role in investing is a lack of discipline to make a plan and stick with it. Too often, investment decisions are made on whims, rumors, tips, feelings—just about anything but solid information.

There is really no excuse for this. You have access to the greatest investment minds in the business for little or no cost. You have access to every shred of information available about your investments. To not use these is to shift from investing to gambling.

JUST A MINUTE

Active investing is a skill learned with time and practice and is founded on good research and analysis.

Active investors are not day traders or speculators. They may hold a position in an investment for several years. Their goal is not to churn their portfolio, but to continually fine-tune it, looking for a better-than-average return. As a group, they may have greater resources to work with than the average investor and a willingness to work harder.

Disadvantages of Active Investing

The following is a list of the disadvantages of active investing:

- It requires a lot of time and energy.
- It can be slightly more risky than average investing strategies.
- It can lead to addictive investing.
- It can run up big commissions and fees.
- It can create tax problems.

TIME AND ENERGY

You should plan to spend a couple hours per week on your investments if you want to actively manage your portfolio. This time will include keeping up-to-date on market activity, your investments, and general business and economic news.

The good news: There is plenty to work with in terms of news and information. I can't stress enough how helpful the Internet will be in doing your homework. You will be able to access news and information on your investments with amazing speed and ease.

For example, you can configure many of the news sites to collect information on industries or particular companies you are interested in following. Many sites will let you build your portfolio online and will update it during the day, and it's all free.

You can do the same thing using print media, but you have to do all the work of collecting prices. You will spend a lot more time and not have access to a fraction of the information and opinions available online.

SLIGHTLY MORE RISKY

The active investor is aiming higher than the conservative investor, which means he or she is willing to push the risk factor a little bit harder. The active investor may hold positions for shorter periods.

PROCEED WITH CAUTION

Active traders may tend to get overconfident and short cut established investment decision making. For some traders the only cure is the harsh slap in the face of a really bad investment. You do not have a special *gift* for picking stocks. Even the most seasoned investors will make mistakes. Learn from your mistakes.

Active investors are often not as diversified in their holdings as more conservative investors. This leaves them more vulnerable to market fluctuations. Focused investments can lead to big gains, but are also open to significant loses without close attention.

ADDICTIVE INVESTING

Addictive investing is when the investor's focus shifts from building a portfolio to the excitement of trading. These folks often begin investing with perfectly legitimate reasons, but get caught up in the whirl of the daily market. The same thing happens to some people who visit Las Vegas for the first time. The excitement gets the better of them.

The flashing numbers across a computer screen, the breathless reporting of every market tick by cable news reporters, and stories of instant wealth are powerful stimulants that some people find hard to resist.

BIG COMMISSIONS AND FEES

The more you trade, the larger fees and commissions you generate. It is easy to forget about seemingly small sums, but they will eat a big hole in your profits and make your losses even worse.

JUST A MINUTE

Online brokers offer the most inexpensive commissions (check out Gomez.com for the best rates), but you may not be comfortable working in an online environment. You do not have to use an online broker to be an active trader.

Choose a discount broker with your anticipated trading volume in mind. Some brokers will give even greater discounts for frequent traders.

TAX PROBLEMS

Unless you are trading inside a tax-deferred retirement account, you generate a taxable event every time you sell an investment for a profit.

Taxes on the sale of an asset held less than one year can be significant if you are in a high-income tax bracket. Whenever possible, hold assets for at least one year and one day to qualify for the long-term capital gains tax that right now is 20 percent. Also be aware that your state revenue department may want a piece of your profits if you live in a state with an income tax.

It is important to keep detailed records of your transactions. Don't rely solely on your broker to keep track of everything.

Know what you are getting into before you start a program of active investing. Be honest with yourself about your commitment to stick with such a program.

ADVANTAGES OF ACTIVE INVESTING

The following is a list of the advantages of active investing:

- It can generate market-beating returns.
- It involves you in your investments.
- It is fun.

PROCEED WITH CAUTION

There are many advantages to active investing. One of the main advantages is the knowledge that you are taking control of your financial affairs.

MARKET-BEATING RETURNS

Active investing can beat the market. There is certainly no guarantee, but it is not impossible by any stretch of the imagination.

Even if you are using actively managed mutual funds, it is possible to do better than the market. While many mutual funds did not beat the market in the mid-1990s, there was a reversal of that trend toward the end of the decade.

Fueled by huge advances in the technology stocks, many funds that focused on that sector or small- and mid-cap companies did very well. It must also be noted that many of these got clobbered when the market stumbled in early January of 2000.

Active investors, whether using mutual funds or buying individual stocks, can more sharply focus their investments. This focus, if correctly applied, will beat the market fairly consistently. The market, you remember, as measured by the S&P 500, is a broad cross section of mainly larger companies. If you take the technology sector out of the market, its overall returns in the recent past haven't been all that great.

JUST A MINUTE

The active investor is involved with his or her investments, not in love with them. Emotional attachments can cloud judgment.

This focus is not without its dangers as noted above, but prudent active investors should be able to protect themselves against severe and prolonged downturns.

INVOLVED IN YOUR INVESTMENTS

Active investing keeps you involved in your investments in a way that passively watching an index fund does not. Many people find they are actually more comfortable with a hands-on approach to investing.

This involvement brings them a sense of security in that they know what is going on with their investments at all times, rather than wondering what a stranger (a fund manager) is going to do with their money.

One of the basic tenets of investing is to know your investment. Some people find that they feel more comfortable with investing if they are intimately involved in the decision making.

IT IS FUN

As a rule, active investors really enjoy learning more about investing and various investment strategies. They enjoy digging up information and following the financial news.

Many of these folks are not motivated purely by money, but truly get a kick out of making a successful investment decision. If you think studying the financial markets and researching companies sounds about as exciting as scraping paint, consider using a more passive investment strategy.

However, if you enjoy finding new investment opportunities and researching potential new investments, active investing may be for you.

ONLINE TRADING

If it is your desire to become an active investor, I strongly suggest you consider online trading. You can be an active investor and use conventional discount brokers, contacting them by telephone, but you will not have access to the vast amount of information available on the Internet.

PROCEED WITH CAUTION

Online trading is the hottest thing in town. It can save you lots of money on commissions. Be aware that not all online brokers are equal. Check out services and fees before signing up.

Online trading has gotten some bad press in the past, and much of it deservedly so. However, I believe the benefits far outweigh the negatives for an active trader. Problems in the past have had to do with infrastructure of the operations that collapsed during periods of heavy trading.

Many of those problems have been fixed, but there is still the possibility of not being able to connect to your account. Some of these problems may not involve the online broker directly, but may be tied to other Internet problems or even a down telephone line.

PROCEED WITH CAUTION

The cheapest online broker may be just that. Be sure you are getting value for whatever you pay your broker.

DISADVANTAGES OF ONLINE TRADING

The following is a list of the disadvantages of online trading:

- Inability to connect to account during heavy trading
- Security breaches
- Overtrading

UNABLE TO CONNECT

I talked about these problems earlier in the book, but they bear repeating briefly here. During periods of heavy trading, it may not be possible to access your account. This can be very troubling if you are in a bad situation and want out.

Some online brokers offer backup contact by telephone, but that may be swamped also. When choosing an online broker, pay attention to their reliability of service. "Resources," Appendix B of this book, can direct you to a service that evaluates and ranks online brokers.

SECURITY BREACHES

Although there have been no major security breaches of online brokers that I am aware of, the potential is there. It is important that you do business with a broker insured by the SIPC for your protection.

The Internet is not foolproof, and there are plenty of fools out there to prove that. Choosing a reputable online broker will be your best protection.

OVERTRADING

This is one of the problems I presented earlier. The bells and whistles of online trading are very exciting, and it is possible to get caught up in the action.

Always trade with a plan. Avoid spur-of-the-moment trades and chasing hot tips. Information you get over the Internet should be considered with the same critical eye you judge any information. If it is too good to be true, it almost certainly isn't.

TIME SAVER

 Check out www.gomez.com for complete information on online brokers, including rankings by price, service, and so on.

ADVANTAGES OF ONLINE TRADING

The following is a list of the advantages of online trading:

- Inexpensive
- Greater sense of connection to the process
- Access to a wealth of information
- Quick execution and confirmation
- Learn for free

INEXPENSIVE

Online trading is the cheapest way to buy and sell stocks and bonds. Prices and services vary so it pays to shop, but you will find incredibly low commissions.

Low commissions translate into higher returns. However, as I noted in an earlier section of this book, be on the lookout for fees that may be charged for various services like fund transfers and so on.

Commissions charged by online brokers tend to follow the level of service they offer. Online brokers with extensive research areas on their site and comprehensive account statements may charge more than a bare-bones broker who doesn't offer as many extras.

CONNECTED TO THE PROCESS

Some online brokers offer a trading screen that makes you feel like you are right in the middle of the transaction. Depending on which broker you choose, you may see your portfolio updated online.

Information is not wisdom. Don't let the flood of information obscure your good common sense.

WEALTH OF INFORMATION

Online brokers, either on their site or through third parties, offer a wealth of information on stocks, bonds, and mutual funds. Everything from detailed research to investment suggestions is available.

Additionally, there are numerous independent sites not connected with a brokerage firm that analyze stocks and mutual funds. Professional investment analysts offer their take on market trends and try to spot future winners.

QUICK EXECUTION AND CONFIRMATION

Online brokers can often execute and confirm market orders in a few minutes or less. A note of caution that I have mentioned before: Make sure your broker is not giving you an e-mail form that looks like an order screen. These brokers may take much longer to execute your order.

LEARN FOR FREE

One of the great features of online brokers is that many of them offer a simulation area on their Web sites where you can practice submitting orders.

This lets you work with their interface in a nonthreatening environment. Once you've practiced and are comfortable with how the system works, you can go live and begin actual trading.

Other sites on the Internet offer trading games where you are given a sum of play money and invest it in the market using real market data. The games usually run a month or so and some offer prizes for the winner. The games are a lot of fun, but can create a false sense of expertise. Many online brokers offer areas on their sites to "practice" or you can look at games connected with information sites such as cnnfn.com.

It is one thing to invest $10,000 play dollars and quite another to lay down $10,000 of your real, hard-earned dollars. Don't let success in the games give you a false sense that you have a feel for investing.

PROCEED WITH CAUTION

Active investors may also be more aggressive than the average investor. As such, they are willing to take more risk when shooting for greater returns.

TOOLS OF THE ACTIVE TRADER

One of the things that separates an active trader from a more conservative trader is his or her choice of tools. Active traders take advantage of some of the more sophisticated (and risky) tools to help them beat the market.

These tools are not for the new investor to use on Day One. They are more suitable for the active investor who has been at it for a while and feels confident he or she is ready to move up a notch.

There are two main tools that active investors may choose to use. Certainly there are others, and we will look at some in the next hour. My decision to put these tools in this section as opposed to the next hour is based on the degree of risk involved; tools that are even more risky are in the next hour.

The main tools for active traders are

- Buying on margin
- Selling short

JUST A MINUTE

Buying on margin and shorting stocks up the risk factor, but also open the door to higher returns. There is nothing wrong with the prudent use of credit.

MARGIN

Buying on margin is a way to use leverage to extend your purchasing power. Leverage is simply using borrowed money.

When you open a margin account, your broker will lend you up to 50 percent of the purchase price of a stock. Not every stock is eligible for margin, so check with your broker.

What this means is if you have $10,000 to invest, with margin, you can buy $20,000 worth of stock. Your broker will charge you interest on the $10,000, usually at very reasonable rates (after all, they want your business). You, of course, have to repay the $10,000 when you sell, whether you make a profit or not. There is no real time limit for selling, but the interest on your loan keeps accumulating. For this reason, most margin buyers don't keep the loan for very long.

Margin works great when you buy a stock that rises. However, if the stock falls too far you may get a dreaded "margin call." A margin call occurs when the value of the account falls below 75 percent of the original value. To protect the loan, your broker will require you to add cash to the account to bring it up to the 75 percent level or make you sell the stock and repay the loan.

Like all uses of borrowed money, margin is not to be used indiscriminately. However, it is one of the main ways active investors can beat the market. Using margin, it is possible to double the return on your original investment.

PROCEED WITH CAUTION

Some investing tools are counterintuitive and seem at odds with common sense, but they work nonetheless. For example, as we'll see in the next hour, options traders can buy the right to sell and in the section below, traders can sell stock they don't own.

SELLING SHORT

Another tool used by active investors is *selling short,* which involves selling stock you don't own. (Is this a great country or what!)

As odd as it seems, this is perfectly legal and an accepted way of doing business in the market. You sell a stock short when you think its price is going to fall, unlike when you buy a stock with hopes that its price will rise.

Here's how it works: When you want to sell a stock short (or short the stock), your broker will "borrow" the stock from another client who owns it. (In these cases, the stock must be held in a "street name," which means it is held by the broker in trust for the client.) You sell the stock and pocket the proceeds. When the stock falls in value like you predicted, you buy it back at the lower price and replace the borrowed stock. The difference between what you sold it for and what you paid to buy it back is your profit.

Of course, if the stock rises, you are forced to buy it back for more than you sold it for and suffer a loss. There are other circumstances (such as if the owner wants it back) that might cause your broker to make you terminate a short sale before you were ready. When you buy back the stock to replace it, you are said to be "covering the short."

Selling short, like buying on margin, can extend your returns or turn around and bite you. Neither technique is for the brand new investor, but when used with full knowledge of the consequences they can be powerful tools for increasing your returns.

AFTER-HOURS TRADING

A fairly new tool on the horizon is after-hours trading. This is trading, as the name implies, after the close of the major stock markets. The trend reflects the increasing role of the electronic market in the trading economy.

JUST A MINUTE

After-hours trading is in the "fad" category now, but may move into the mainstream of investing very quickly.

As of Jan. 1, 2000, several brokers were experimenting with after-hour trading with limited success. On the surface, the advantage of trading when it was convenient for customers or acting on news after the market closed seems obvious.

However, the reality is that unless you are trading a widely held and actively traded stock, it may be hard to match buyers and sellers. When there is a small pool of buyers and sellers, a stock is said to be *thinly* traded. This means you may or may not get a good price for the trade.

One of the reasons we say the stock market is efficient is that it brings together large numbers of buyers and sellers. Prices reached in this market reflect the actual market value of a stock. When only a few buyers and sellers are in a market, it is not clear if a market value can be established.

The after-hours market will probably become a bigger part of the investment scene in the future and a place active investors will want to know about. Right now, it is probably best to keep a close eye on how it is developing rather than jumping right in.

What Can You Do?

The following is a list of five things you can do today:

1. Check out one or more of the sites listed in Appendix B under market simulation games. Get a feel for what online brokerage screens look like.

2. How much time are you willing to put in on your investments? There is no set amount of time, but it will require a couple of hours every week to two weeks. Can you schedule the time in advance and stick with it?

3. Do you have a compulsive personality? Do you have problems with gambling? If so, carefully consider the dangers of active investing, particularly online investing. What limits are you willing to set to guard against becoming overinvolved?

4. If you have not selected a broker or narrowed your choice down to a couple, do so now. Pay particular attention to fees as well as commissions. See the resource section for rankings of online brokers.

5. Make a checklist of everything you want to know about a stock, mutual fund, or bond before you will invest. This is one way of enforcing a disciplined approach to investing. If your partner is going to share investing responsibilities (a good idea), have him or her review the checklist for completeness before you make an investment. The following workshop will help you get started.

Workshop

Here are the beginnings of an investment checklist. Use it as a starting point for your own list.

Stock:

_____

Is this a growth, income, value, or blended stock?

_____

Which investment goal does this stock address?

_____

What do the analysts say about this stock?

_____

Does the stock pay a dividend?

_____

What is the P/E? What is the PEG?

_____

What percent have sales grown over last year?

_____

HOUR'S UP!

Active investors want to be involved in their investments. They enjoy getting their hands dirty and watching their investments. Check your knowledge of active investing with this short quiz.

1. Active investing can …

    A. Make you rich.

    B. Be fun and profitable.

    C. Cost almost nothing.

2. Active investing can …

    A. Run up big commissions and fees.

    B. Cause problems at work.

    C. Hurt your marriage.

3. Active investors need to be aware of …

    A. The danger of becoming antisocial.

    B. Losing their minds.

    C. Creating tax problems.

4. Active investors sometimes …

    A. Have market-beating returns.

    B. Forget to bathe.

    C. Lose sleep.

5. Online trading is …

    A. One step away from hell.

    B. An inexpensive way to trade.

    C. A passing fad.

6. Online traders may …

    A. Be prone to overtrading.

    B. Be unable to connect to their broker.

    C. Lose money due to security breaches.

    D. All of the above.

7. Online trading gives you …

    A. Access to tremendous amounts of information.

    B. Headaches.

    C. Slow executions.

8. Buying on margin is …

    A. Extremely dangerous.

    B. Against the law.

    C. A tool active investors use.

9. Selling short is …

    A. Against the law.

    B. A negative investment.

    C. An investment in a stock you think will go down.

10. After-hours trading is …

    A. Very expensive.

    B. Not a proven market yet.

    C. Dangerous for the uninformed.

Hour 22

Aggressive Investing

LESSON PLAN:

In this Hour you will learn about …

- Aggressive investors defined.
- Day trading.
- Options trading.
- Futures trading.
- Exotic deals.

Hold on to your hats, we're about to leave the rational world behind and move into the high-energy world of the aggressive investor. These folks live on the edge. They are the financial equivalent of skydivers.

Many financial professionals suggest that these folks are not investors but gamblers and speculators. Admittedly, the line between gambling and aggressive investing may be somewhat obscured at times.

I personally do not practice aggressive investing. I believe that many people who are aggressive investors should be properly classified as gamblers.

Why, you might ask, do I include it in this book if I don't believe in it? For two reasons:

- You are grown-ups and capable of making up your own minds.
- I want to give you a realistic picture of what is involved. There are a lot of people and companies selling dreams of instant riches in the stock market. Almost all of them are frauds at worst or irresponsible at best.

Active trading is not for the faint of heart. Master the basics before you try to fly.

So, with that, I define *aggressive investors* as people who engage in one or more of the following activities as their main investing activity:

- Day trading
- Options trading
- Futures trading
- Exotic deals

DAY TRADING

Day trading is a form of trading that seeks to exploit small movements in stocks for profit. A day trader may hold a position in a stock for just a few seconds or minutes.

Day traders risk large sums of money, hoping for small profits they can take quickly before exiting the market.

They have become very popular in the last couple of years, but day traders have been around for a long time. It is hard to find a news or business publication these days that doesn't have an article about day trading. The article will often profile a former cab driver who now makes $20,000 a month by day trading.

Unfortunately, these stories, if they are at all real, are the exception and not the rule. One study estimates that over 80 percent of all day traders lose money. Still, the lure is almost magical for some people. They will spend their days hunched over a computer watching the market for signals that a stock is going to move.

The few people who engage in day trading have systems based on technical signals that guide their actions. Unfortunately, most of the people involved in day trading are graduates of get-rich-quick seminars offered by brokers who cater to day traders.

Day trading took on a new dimension when online brokers became a common presence on the market. Many day traders work directly from their homes, although they usually purchase additional trading services that most of us don't need.

One of the "must-have" services is live access to the market. In most cases, stock quotes you see on the Internet are delayed 15–20 minutes, depending on the exchange. This delay was originally built into the quote system to give exchange brokers time to prepare for sudden market moves based on breaking news.

There are various levels of service you can buy. Some offer access to live market data and can cost from $300 a month to over $1,000 a month. Many of the more sophisticated systems allow customers to access their network through a direct connection, as opposed to an Internet-based system.

Other brokers catering to day traders offer terminals in their offices. For a fee, you can access their systems and services. Another advantage is associating with other day traders. This human connection is missing for the day traders who work out of their homes.

The success of a day trader is directly related to his or her ability to manage money. It usually takes at least $30,000 to get started in day trading, and more is better. Some of the brokers who cater to day traders will provide margin accounts to expand the trader's ability to take a position.

The basic strategy is to spot stocks that are giving signals that a movement is imminent. A day trader may buy 1,000 shares of a company, hoping to catch a one-quarter or one-half point upward movement. They will grab this small profit and move on to the next trade, which may in fact be the same stock.

It is not uncommon for a day trader to make 100 trades during one market session. Since most day traders don't hold positions overnight, this translates into 50 "round-trips," or 50 buy orders and 50 sell orders.

JUST A MINUTE

Successful day traders always have a plan and stick with it. Day traders who chase "sure things" aren't day traders for very long.

Thoughtful day traders will target an entry and exit point in a stock's price and stick with their plan. Where amateurs run afoul is trying to day trade on intuition and guessing when to get in and when to get out.

Some of the hucksters running day-trading seminars make it look almost impossible to lose money day trading. All of the signals seem so clear. All of the stocks to watch seem to be waving a flag for your attention.

The truth is that proving a system will work using historical stock market data is simple. Without much effort, I could devise a system that picked stocks based on how many times professional baseball players scratch themselves while waiting to bat.

When you have an activity so rich in numbers as the stock market or baseball, you can draw all sorts of conclusions and "prove" them with statistics. Common sense tells you that whether the American League or the National League wins the World Series has nothing whatsoever to do with the direction the stock market is going to move.

Yet, all sorts of stock market schemes, day trading and otherwise, have about as much scientific basis as this example.

JUST A MINUTE

Day traders are a hard-working group. Despite some media impressions that they are high rollers who only work a few hours a day, successful day traders work very hard for profits.

Even with a legitimate shot at day trading, the odds are stacked against you. A couple of the barriers you have to overcome are practical in nature: commissions and taxes.

Even though the brokers that cater to day traders charge very low commissions, they are still a factor pulling down your return. For example, if the friend we talked about above made 50 round-trip trades a day, his commissions alone could be $400 or more each day. That obviously means he would need a $400 profit per day just to break even.

Unfortunately, it is not that simple. The other big cost is taxes on your profits. Because you are holding for less than a year, any gains are subject to regular income tax, plus self-employment taxes, by the federal, state, and local governments. This could easily reach 30 percent of your gross.

Now, to break even just on trading costs you would need a profit of about $571 per day to pay your taxes and commissions. Of course, these expenses don't include the overhead of your communications costs, whatever system you use, and so on.

It might be daunting to many of us to know that every morning when we begin our work, we need to make $750—$1,000 in gross profits just to break even.

However, day traders will tell you they can make that much on one trade. Of course, they can also lose that much. There is no doubt that a small number of day traders do make substantial money, but the odds are against you duplicating their success.

PROCEED WITH CAUTION

Thoughtful day traders watch for technical "signals" that a stock is getting ready to move. Many follow complex charts that track a stock's price. They look for signals that when a stock's price hits a specific mark, it will tend to move in a certain way.

Another hurdle for those day traders working out of their homes is the isolation from other humans. You will find that these folks spend a lot of time in online chat rooms looking for some kind of human connection and support.

Like many activities that experts make "look easy," day trading is an intensive and time-consuming way to make money. One of the reasons amateurs lose their shirts is they enter day trading with the notion that they can spend a few hours each day and make a fortune.

Nothing could be further from the truth. Day trading is a complicated, intensive activity requiring lots of homework and sharp analytical skills.

Should you day trade? It's my book, so you get my opinion: No. If you feel like you must, be sure you are not using your retirement or college fund. Don't take a second mortgage on your house, and be prepared to lose your whole stake in a relatively short period.

OPTIONS TRADING

I have included options trading in this aggressive investing section, even though there are some legitimate uses for options under certain conditions.

PROCEED WITH CAUTION

There are a number of get-rich-quick schemes that use complex options trades. Like most hit-the-jackpot plans, be very careful of bloated claims and unaudited histories.

First, let's review and expand on our previous understanding of options. An option is a derivative; that is, its worth is tied to another financial instrument. An option gives you the right, but not the obligation, to buy or sell a specific security at a specific price within a defined time period.

A *call* option gives you the right to buy the security and a *put* option gives you the right to sell the security. For example, if you believe that stock XYZ is going to rise in the next couple of months you can do one of two things:

First, you can buy the stock outright and hold it, hoping the gain will materialize. Secondly, you could buy a call option that gives you the right to buy the stock at a certain price during the next few months.

Here's how the numbers might look: XYZ is currently selling for $50 per share. You believe, based on your research, that it is due to climb sharply in the near future. You can buy 100 shares for $5,000 and hope the price does rise, or you can buy a call option that gives you the right to buy 100 shares at $60 per share in a defined time period and pay a premium of $200 for the option.

If the price of ABC stock does begin to rise within the option's life, the value of the option will increase also. If the stock price rises above $60 per share, you may make a substantial profit on your option by selling. However, if the price remains under $60 per share, your option will decline in value and could expire worthless.

JUST A MINUTE

A successful options trade can reap a nice reward. A failed options trade will often lose the whole investment.

Here is the key point with options: you can lose 100 percent of your investment. Had you bought the stock outright and it declined from $50 to $40 per share, you could have sold it and recovered a substantial part of your investment.

Put options work the same way as calls except you are thinking the stock is going to decline in price. If it does within the life of your put option, you may sell it for a profit.

WHAT IS TO LIKE ABOUT OPTIONS?

In a word, leverage. For a small amount of money you can control a larger asset. If the underlying stock moves in either direction, the option can increase or decline in value.

Here's how it might work: Our XYZ stock is selling at $50 per share. If you buy 100 shares, you have invested $5,000. A call option to buy the stock at $60 per share costs $2 per share. If you invest the $5,000 in options instead of buying the stock outright, you can control 2,500 shares of stock.

If the price of XYZ does go up to $60 per share, your 100 shares you bought are now worth $6,000. However, if you had purchased the call options, they may have increased to $12 per share, making your gross profit 2,500 × $12, or $30,000. Deduct the cost of the options and you have a profit of $25,000!

Note: These numbers are for illustration only and do not necessarily reflect actual market conditions. A number of other factors may influence the price of the option.

Of course, we know that not all plans go well. What happens if the stock declines? If we own the stock outright, we might hold on, thinking that over the long term it will bounce back, or we can sell and recover part of our investment.

Options don't have quite that many options, as it were. Options, unlike the underlying stock, have expiration dates. If you do not exercise the option or sell it, the option expires on a certain date and you lose everything.

PROCEED WITH CAUTION

Options are the kind of investment you need to keep a close watch on, since they have a limited life.

Fortunately, options are highly liquid if there is any time remaining on them and it is possible to sell the options at a loss and recover some of your investment. However, the options market is not as liquid as the stock market, especially when there is only a short amount of time before they expire, so you may not get a good price or find a buyer at all.

There are all sorts of sophisticated trading strategies for options that are too complicated to explore here. There are also a number of get-rich-quick schemes floating around that use bizarre options strategies to make "fortunes."

In addition to options on stocks, there are options on virtually all the major stock market indexes such as the S&P 500 and the Dow.

JUST A MINUTE

Options can be used in a legitimate trading situation to protect a profit in a stock for a short period of time. For example, if you owned 100 shares of XYZ and had a profit of $10 per share, but were concerned the price might drop, you could purchase a put option on XYZ. If the price did drop, you would have a profit in the put option to offset or reduce any loss in the XYZ stock.

WHAT IS A LEGITIMATE USE OF OPTIONS?

If you own a stock that is not giving you much in the way of a return, you might consider writing options on the stock. This puts you on the other side of the options transaction. Someone will pay you a premium for an option to buy or sell your stock at a certain price within a certain time frame.

You receive the premium, less broker's fees. If the option expires, as most of them do, you still own the stock, but have used it to generate extra income. If the option is exercised, you will be paid the option price for the stock.

Your broker can make the arrangements, but be sure you understand that it is possible to have the stock taken (but paid for) if you sell options on it.

If you are interested in learning more about options, Appendix B, "Resources," will point you towards some more information.

SHOULD YOU INVEST IN OPTIONS?

Like any investment, you should never invest in anything you don't understand, and options can be fairly complicated despite my simplistic example above. Any investment where you stand to lose everything has got to be approached with extreme caution.

JUST A MINUTE

Futures trading began as a way for agricultural producers and users to lock in profits and/or costs. They have expanded to include a wide variety of goods and financial instruments.

FUTURES TRADING

If you think options trading is hair-raising, wait until you encounter futures trading. This is where only the very brave or very foolish dare to tread. If options trading is a fast sports car, futures trading is a rocket ship that is potentially out of control.

A *futures contract* is like an option in some ways. For example, it is also a derivative taking its value from an underlying source.

The one critical difference between an option and a futures contract is that an option is the *right* to buy or sell the underlying security. A futures contract is an *obligation* to buy or sell the underlying commodity.

The owner of an option is not obligated to do anything. He or she can let the option expire without doing anything. Owners of futures contracts, on the other hand, are obligated to fulfill the terms of the contract. In reality, very few contracts are ever held to maturity—most are negated by an offsetting order.

JUST A MINUTE

The huge amount of leverage used in futures contracts makes them highly volatile.

You are probably familiar with the underlying commodities of many futures contracts. They are things like live cattle, orange juice, lumber, pork bellies, and more recently, financial contracts involving currencies, stock indexes, and interest rates. Commodities are traded on several exchanges. You can find a list in Appendix B.

Futures contracts employ a huge amount of leverage. You are required to make a margin deposit to control a contract, but the margin may be just 10 percent or less of the underlying contract. With this type of leverage, small movements can create big gains or big losses in a very short period of time.

For example, you could control a contract for $35,000 worth of a commodity selling at $350 per unit for a margin of $3,500 or less. If the price of the contract goes up 10 dollars, your contract increases $1,000 to $36,000. If you were to close out your position at this point you would have a profit of $1,000 (less commissions). Of course, it goes the other way, too. If the price were to drop to $340 per unit, your contract would decline in value by $1,000 and you may be required to deposit this amount in your margin account.

Position	Margin	Value per Unit	Contract
Buy 10	$3,500	$350	$35,000
Sell 10		$360	$36,000
Profit			$1,000

It is helpful to remember that the margin is not a down payment. It does not leave your brokerage account, unless you default on the contract. You make money by taking an opposite position, called "offsetting." For example, to close out a buy contract you enter a sell contract. The difference, as shown in the table above, is your profit (or loss if the price goes against you).

The bottom line is that you cannot only lose your initial margin, but a whole lot more. Because of trading rules, it is possible to watch your losses mount and not be able to get out of the contract.

One estimate suggests that up to 90 percent of futures traders lose money. There is an old saying in the futures industry: "If you want to make a small fortune in the futures market, start with a large one."

PROCEED WITH CAUTION

Futures trading is not a do-it-yourself project. If you are going to have any chance, work with an experienced broker and still plan to lose money.

Futures play an important role in our economy by creating a market where producers of commodities and users of commodities can protect themselves against price fluctuations. Speculators in the futures market also play a role. They provide the liquidity by taking risks that others want to avoid.

Don't feel like it is your civic duty to trade in the futures market. There are plenty of very knowledgeable people who work very hard at making a living trading futures.

The bottom line: No. I don't think I need to say any more, do I?

JUST A MINUTE

Go to just about any good-sized motel during the week and you will likely run into a seminar for a can't-miss scheme to make money. Guess what? Most of them miss.

EXOTIC DEALS

Some people seem to think they have to have an edge or shortcut to get ahead. These folks are prime candidates for every flaky scheme that comes down the road. I had a friend years ago who had "sucker" stamped on his forehead.

Every snake-oil salesman who came to town got him involved in some weird scheme to make money. He was a very intelligent and well-educated person, but something drove him to find shortcuts. He could have been very successful at any career he wanted, but instead he spent his time and money on one deal after another.

Many of these deals are what is known as multilevel marketing or networking companies. Some of these, such as Amway, are quite legitimate, while others are barely disguised pyramid schemes built to make a few people at the top rich.

I went to one of these pitches with my friend. The organization sold personal security systems, which were alarms you could activate if someone tried to assault or rob you. We were told about the proprietary technology and the exclusivity of the products. Everyone was encouraged to buy a $75 starter kit.

PROCEED WITH CAUTION

Be very careful if a person offers to sell you a $20 bill for $1.

Like most of these programs, there was money to be made in selling the products, but the real money was in signing up other people to sell for you. About a week after the presentation, I was in a sporting goods store and, guess what, there was a whole shelf of the identical products we had been told were exclusive.

Be very careful of these get-rich-quick-and-only-work-30-minutes-a-day schemes. They may come over the Internet or through a magazine, or worst of all, from your unsuspecting neighbor.

Several years ago, I became aware of a group that was involved in buying and selling foreign currencies. The idea was that you bought yen if you thought it was going to rise relative to the U.S. dollar or sold yen if you thought it was going to weaken.

Like most speculative investments, these were heavily leveraged. The company offered the opportunity to practice using real data before you opened an account. I did this and was quite successful in the practice, although I really knew nothing about international monetary policy.

It seemed too easy, which raised a red flag. I passed on opening an account despite pressure to do so. Some months later I read that the company had been closed down because they were manipulating the currency prices that traders saw on their screens.

PROCEED WITH CAUTION

 There are too many legitimate business opportunities to waste your time on flaky deals.

All of these schemes have at least one thing in common: The promoters try to convince you that only a fool would pass up this opportunity. One of their common tricks is, in the middle of their pitch to a room full of people, to suddenly hold up a $20 bill and offer it for sale for $1.

Almost always, the room becomes real quiet until someone in the audience or one of their shills stands up and takes the deal. The point the promoter makes is that we are so conditioned to disbelieve a good deal that we won't even buy a $20 bill for a dollar.

I would counter by noting that in the real world, no one sells $20 bills for $1 unless they are phony.

WHAT CAN YOU DO?

The following is a list of five things you can do today:

1. Visit some of the day-trading sites listed in the resource section, Appendix B. What are their requirements for opening an account? How much money do they require to open an account?

2. Scan the options listings in *The Wall Street Journal* and notice what stock options are traded. Can you detect the relationship between the time remaining and the option price? (If the price is listed as $2, that means you can buy a call or put option for $2 per share.)

3. Using options on market indexes is a way to hedge against a loss on an index mutual fund. Can you see how that might be advantageous if you were planning to get out of an index fund with a profit in a short period of time?

4. Visit the options-trading site listed in Appendix B. Try your hand at the simulations. Options are probably the safest of the aggressive strategies, but not by much. Could you stand to lose your whole investment?

5. Looking back at the three investing styles—conservative, active, and aggressive—which ones seem to fit your style and temperament?

WORKSHOP

What part of the aggressive investing activities of options and futures trading sounds interesting to you? To see how one might work, pick a volatile stock (almost any of the Internet stock will do) and follow its options for several days. How much change do the option prices experience? Were you able to pick which way they were going the next day?

HOUR'S UP!

Aggressive investing sounds exciting, sexy, and the easy road to riches. Traders who successfully take this route will share with you that there is nothing easy about it. See how well you have grasped the concepts behind this fast-moving train.

1. Aggressive investing …

    A. Is characterized by high-risk investments.

    B. Is easy money.

    C. A good place to start investing.

2. Day trading is …

    A. A good way to spend the morning.

    B. A risky way to spend the morning.

    C. A profitable way to spend the morning.

3. Day traders look …

    A. For technical signals a stock is getting ready to move.

    B. For tips on the Internet about hot stocks.

    C. For any excuse to buy a stock.

4. Day trading is …

    A. Not for beginners.

    B. The modern pot of gold.

    C. A quick way to double your stake.

5. Trading options …

    A. Always makes money.

    B. Never makes money.

    C. Is not for beginners.

6. Options are …

    A. An obligation to buy or sell a stock.

    B. The right to buy or sell a stock.

    C. Neither of the above.

7. Trading futures …

    A. Is easy money.

    B. Makes perfect sense for every investor.

    C. May lose more money than you invested.

8. Futures trading …

    A. Is something you can learn in your spare time.

    B. Requires professional help.

    C. Is worth trying to see if you like it.

9. Exotic deals …

    A. Are great if you get in now.

    B. Are easy money.

    C. Are usually a waste of time at best and a scam at worst.

10. The road to financial success …

    A. Is quicker if you take a short cut.

    B. Is usually short and sweet.

    C. Is simple and straightforward, but long.

Quiz

Hour 23
Retirement Planning

CHAPTER SUMMARY

LESSON PLAN:

In this Hour you will learn about ...

- How much to defer into your 401(k).
- Which funds to pick.
- What fees to expect.
- Traditional vs. Roth IRA.
- Retirement planning— long term.
- Retirement planning— short term.
- Retirement expenses.
- Retirement income.

One hundred years from now a historian will note, while slowly shaking her head from side to side and making clucking noises with her tongue, that the culture of late 20th-century America was built on immediate gratification.

Having what we want is not good enough, we want it *now*. In this culture of the Internet, microwave ovens, and overnight delivery, retirement planning seems very old-fashioned and out of place.

However, millions of Americans, to their credit, spend a lot of time and money preparing for retirement. As noted elsewhere, retirement is the single biggest financial goal most of us will need to fund. How we go about planning and funding our retirement will have a direct impact on how we live out the last 20 percent of our years.

We have already had a brief overview of some of the retirement plans available to us and had indirect discussions about the types of investments to house in those plans. In this Hour, I want to look in more detail at two of the most popular plans, the 401(k) and the Roth IRA, and talk specifically about planning for retirement.

THE 401(K) PLAN

A *401(k) plan* is an employer-sponsored, qualified retirement account under IRS statutes. These plans allow an employee to contribute to the account with pretax dollars, usually through salary deduction. In some cases, employers may match part of the employee's contribution.

PROCEED WITH CAUTION

As more and more companies shift to defined contribution plans like the 401(k), it puts more responsibility on individuals to choose the correct investment mix for their plan.

Money contributed by the employee is deducted before taxes, thus lowering current taxes, and the contribution and earnings are not subject to income tax until withdrawn. Premature withdrawals may trigger a tax liability that includes a 10 percent penalty.

The maximum that can be deferred is $10,000 per year. Many plans also have a percentage cap of 15–20 percent of the employee's salary. Whichever cap is hit first is the prevailing one. For example, if you make $100,000 per year and your employer capped the plan at 15 percent, you would hit the $10,000 limit before you would reach the 15 percent cap.

Most plans offer three to five mutual funds for you to select from for your account. Unlike IRAs, you must choose from a list of funds your employer selects. Usually there will be a range of funds to pick from such as income, growth, balanced, and perhaps a bond fund.

Another consideration is that many employers require you to be employed for a certain period of time before you can receive any matching contributions from your employer. This is called *vesting* and the rules vary from company to company.

For example, your employer may phase in your vesting over a three- or four-year period beginning after one or two years of employment. Employers hope attractive 401(k) plans will help attract and retain valuable employees, so they build in incentives to stay on the job. However, all employees must be treated the same under the plans.

How Much to Defer?

If your employer matches your contribution up to a certain percentage, that part is easy. You double your money before it is even invested. You won't find a better deal than that. Beyond the matching amount, the question becomes: Can you do better someplace else?

The only way to answer that is to look at the performance of the funds in the 401(k). Don't assume that just because they are in your retirement plan, that they are the best available. However, you will be hard-pressed to do better, considering any investment outside your 401(k) is going to be taxed (unless you invest in a low-paying tax-free fund or an IRA).

JUST A MINUTE

Defer as much as you are comfortable with into your retirement plan.

Of course, trying to beat your 401(k) funds presumes you will take an active role in investing for your retirement. This takes discipline, because it is way too easy to find other uses for cash in our checking accounts, despite the fact that it is already earmarked for investing.

The beauty of the salary-deduction plan is that you never see the money and never miss it. You order your life around your take-home pay and don't have to make adjustments for its absence.

A good rule of thumb is to defer as much as you can past any percentage matched by your employer. Unless you are a successful active or aggressive investor, it is unlikely that you will beat your 401(k) account. Your 401(k) doesn't have to be and probably shouldn't be your only retirement savings vehicle, but it doesn't make much sense to start something else until you are doing all you can in the tax-deferred environment.

Under certain income conditions (see Hour 5, "Existing Benefits Review") you can have an IRA and receive a tax deduction in addition to your 401(k). This may make sense if the funds available in your 401(k) were not so great. You could fund your 401(k) to meet the matching funds from your employer, and then put the rest in an IRA you control.

Even if you don't meet the income conditions to take a tax deduction, you can still invest in an IRA with after-tax dollars.

Which Fund?

Choosing the right fund is always a challenge. Generally, you want to be as aggressive as you are comfortable with if you are 10 years or more away from retirement. This is the safest place you can be aggressive because all your earnings are tax-deferred.

PROCEED WITH CAUTION

If your employer doesn't offer a wide choice of investments for your 401(k), lobby for expanded choices. Offer some suggestions.

If the funds in your 401(k) are not doing well, petition your employer to switch to better-performing funds.

Many financial professionals believe that if your plan offers a stock index fund (like an S&P 500 fund), that is all you need to know; you should put all of your contribution there and forget about it.

This strategy certainly has historical evidence to suggest a good index fund will beat an actively managed fund over time. Rather than put your retirement account on autopilot, keep an eye on how all the funds are performing. In the late 1990s, many actively managed funds beat the S&P 500 index, so don't assume that is a given. Most plans let you switch the allocation within reasonable limits.

If you are within 10 years of retirement, you may want to consider some of the asset allocation strategies we discussed earlier; you want to avoid getting caught in a down market just when you need to begin living off your retirement nest egg.

Fees

Remember our time spent on mutual funds and the fees they charge? Well, all those same warnings apply to the fees in your 401(k). Just because it is in your retirement account doesn't mean you can forget about fees.

JUST A MINUTE

Fees are the leeches on your retirement plan. Keep them as low as possible. If your employer selects mutual funds with high fees for the 401(k) plan, see if they will reconsider.

In addition to the normal mutual fund fees, there will be fees for administering the 401(k) plan itself. Basically, the more complicated and feature-laden your plan is, the higher the administrative fees will be.

Some employers will pay the fees themselves (bless their hearts), but an increasing number of plans are turning to the participants to pay the fees. If this is the case, ask for a clear breakdown of the fees to see how much of your retirement is going to a mutual fund company.

You may not have any choice, but you can petition your employer to change funds if you feel the fees are extraordinarily high. It never hurts to raise a concern.

IRAs—Traditional and Roth

The Roth IRA is the newest and unquestionably the most complicated of all IRAs, yet its benefits make it worth the hassle.

PROCEED WITH CAUTION

For many people, a company-sponsored retirement plan is not a reality. These folks must look to IRAs and other plans for their retirement planning.

As a brief review, here are the different types of IRAs, including the Roth IRA. We will look at the Roth IRA in more detail after the chart.

Type	Contribution Limits	Comments
Individual Retirement Account	$2,000 may be deducted	Accounts can include mutual funds, stocks, bonds, CDs, and so on.
Individual Retirement Annuity	$2,000 may be deducted	Special annuity.
Simplified Employee Pension (SEP-IRA)	$30,000 or 15 percent of annual compensation	Offered by employer. Employee owns IRA and has control of it.
Savings Incentive Match Plan for Employees IRA (SIMPLE-IRA)	Employees may contribute up to $6,000 and receive some level of matching funds from employer. Combined total cannot exceed $12,000.	Offered by employer. Employee owns IRA and has control of it.

continues

continued

Type	Contribution Limits	Comments
Spousal IRA	Up to $2,000 may be deducted.	Taxpayer may set up IRA for nonworking spouse in addition to theirs.
Employer and Employee Association Trust Account		A group IRA often set up by unions and other employee groups.
Inherited IRA		IRA inherited by non-spousal beneficiary. Consult tax expert regarding distributions and taxes.
Education IRA (EIRA)	$500 (In addition to $2,000 of regular IRA)	IRA for under 18-year-old child. Earnings and contributions may be withdrawn tax-free if used for higher education costs.
Roth IRA	Contributions are not deductible	Deposits and earnings may be withdrawn tax-free.
Rollover (Conduit) IRA		IRA set up to absorb contributions and earnings from another qualified plan.

JUST A MINUTE

It is possible to switch from a traditional IRA to a Roth IRA, but there are conditions that must be met. Consult a tax professional before deciding.

The Roth IRA has only been around a few years and has probably generated more questions than all the other IRAs combined. While like a traditional IRA in many ways, the Roth IRA has some distinct and unique characteristics. Let's compare the two:

Traditional IRA	Roth IRA
$2,000 tax-deductible	$2,000 non–tax-deductible
Deposits and earnings are tax-deferred	Deposits are taxable, but earnings and deposits can be withdrawn tax-free within guidelines.
Can only fund one traditional IRA, except for spousal and education IRAs	Can fund a SEP, SIMPLE, and/or educational IRAs at the same time.
Not available to persons in qualified company retirement plans unless they meet income requirements	Available to participants in company retirement plans.
No income limitations	$95,000 for single taxpayer and $150,000 for joint filers of adjusted gross income is the top limit for full $2,000 contribution. Above that and it becomes problematic. Best to check with your tax adviser.

Basically, the Roth IRA is a good deal for most people, and especially for folks already covered by an employer-sponsored retirement plan. You don't get an immediate tax benefit, but your contributions and earnings grow in a tax-free environment.

Investments that make sense in a Roth IRA are basically the same as in a traditional IRA. However, since qualified distributions are not taxed at any rate, they make great vehicles for high income-generating funds, bonds, stocks, and so on.

The exact Roth IRA details in your particular situation may not fit the recommendations here. It is always a good idea to seek qualified tax help when dealing with matters of concern to the IRS. The resource section lists places to go for more information.

RETIREMENT PLANNING—LONG TERM

It is all well and good to get your retirement accounts in order and funded to the maximum, but how do you know how much you are going to need to retire?

Forty years ago when today's retirees were young workers just beginning their careers, they had no idea that milk was going to cost $2.35 a gallon or that a hamburger and fries with a drink could run $4–$5. They never would have guessed that a mid-priced automobile would cost $25,000. How could they plan for these prices?

The same problem faces today's workers. How are you to plan for future expenses and how much money will you need to enjoy the lifestyle you want?

If inflation, which is the general increase in the cost of goods, is 2.5 percent (about the historic average), what costs a dollar today will cost $2.69 in 40 years. That would put the price of a gallon of milk at around $6.32. Yikes!

Well, it is not quite that bad. In the first place, it is going to take 40 years to get to those levels. Hopefully, your income will at least stay even with inflation and your investments beat it rather handily.

For simplicity's sake, we can ignore inflation and assume that your income and investments will at worst match inflation, and probably do a lot better. Let's work a simple problem to get a general idea of what you should be shooting for in a retirement nest egg using today's dollars.

First, you need to set a goal of what kind of annual income you want in today's dollars. For argument's sake, we'll say that figure is $50,000.

As a rule of thumb, count on needing 70–80 percent of that number. You won't need as much income if you aren't working.

Okay, using the 80 percent, we are now at $40,000. For this example, we will assume you are not going to get anything from Social Security (who knows what 2040 will be like with all the baby boomers lined up for their checks).

What we want to shoot for is a nest egg that will generate $40,000 a year. Because we will be concerned with the stability of that annual income, the nest egg will be invested in lower interest but more stable investments. Let's assume we can earn 5 percent on our retirement nest egg.

Doing the math tells us that our retirement nest egg should be $800,000 rounded up (40,000/5 percent = 800,000).

Therefore, we now have a goal—$800,000—of how much we need to save in the next 40 years. Whoa! That's $20,000 a year.

JUST A MINUTE

The more time you let your investments grow, the more you will have to enjoy retirement.

Don't panic. Remember we have time and the miracle of compounding on our side. If we can earn about 10 percent on our investments, we will be close to the historic average growth of the stock market.

Would you believe that all we have to do is save $1,650 a year earning 10 percent in investments to reach our $800,000 goal?

Of course, this is an overly simple example, but what it does point out is that if you start early, the sacrifice is much smaller. For example, say our future retiree waited until age 35 to begin investing for retirement.

Now to reach the same $800,000 nest egg at retirement, our slacker has to come up with over $4,400 a year.

If you have 25–40 years before you retire, there is probably only one thing you need to do and that is to put as much money as you can into your retirement account. The worst that can happen is you get ready to retire and find you have too much money. (Give me a call if this happens.)

RETIREMENT PLANNING—SHORT TERM

If your retirement is 25 or fewer years away, you should begin thinking more concretely about what life will be like and, more importantly, what it will cost during your retirement.

PROCEED WITH CAUTION

If you haven't started retirement planning and investing by age 40, it is time to get serious.

There is a worksheet at the end of this Hour (see the "Workshop" section) that will get you started thinking about your expenses during retirement. Also, Appendix B, "Resources," lists other places you can look for information.

The most effective way to plan for your retirement is to use one of the many retirement calculators available on the Internet. These handy tools let you play around with a number of scenarios and can factor in taxes and inflation to give you a real world picture of what retirement will be like.

There are two basic forms of calculators: expense planning and investment planning. Both of these calculators make doing the math very simple. The retirement calculator listed in the resource section is free, so if you want to go to your local library, you can get access to it.

Here are a couple of calculators from The Motley Fool. The first looks at what your savings will be worth when you retire. The second looks at expenses of retirement.

What Will Your Savings Be Worth?

Amount You Have Invested	$25,000
Rate You Can Earn	10 percent
Additional Deposits (monthly, quarterly, yearly)	$300
Years Invested	25
Your Federal Tax Rate	30 percent
Your State Tax Rate	8 percent
Inflation Rate	3 percent

In 25 years, your investment
will be worth:

$326,889 if you pay taxes on
the interest earned

$668,918 if your investment
is tax-deferred or tax-exempt

What Will Your Expenses Be?

Costs That May Be Decreased at Retirement

Monthly Amounts	Current	Estimated
Housing	$1,700	$1,200
Life Insurance	$50	$40
Transportation	$200	$100
Clothing	$250	$100
Debt Payments	$400	$100
Education	$350	$0
Other	$300	$200

Costs That May Be Increased at Retirement

Monthly Amounts	Current	Estimated
Medical	$80	$200
Food	$400	$200
Recreation	$60	$150
Property Liability Insurance	$20	$30
Years Until You Retire		25
Annual Inflation		3 percent

Monthly Living Expenses

	Not Adjusted for Inflation	Adjusted for Inflation
Current	$3,810	$3,810
At Retirement	$2,320	$4,907

Based on these numbers, your retirement nest egg would be $668,900 and
your monthly living expenses would be $4,900, or $58,800 annually. Will
that be enough?

A quick answer is to find out what you would have to earn on $668,900 to generate $58,800 per year.

$58,800/$668,9000 = 8.79 percent

Yikes! That's a pretty aggressive return for your retirement nest egg and we haven't figured in taxes, which don't retire when you do. I know, we also haven't figured in Social Security. I am sure there will be a Social Security in 25 years, but I am not so sure what it will be paying. We are about to enter a period where baby boomers are going to be retiring in huge numbers. I don't have much confidence that our elected leaders have the foresight to plan adequately for this. My conservative suggestion is to plan to fund your own retirement, and if you get anything from Social Security, so much the better.

PROCEED WITH CAUTION

 Predicting future expenses is hard, but we can be fairly certain they will be higher than today.

It's clear from this example that our friend from the illustrations in the previous sections needs to make some adjustments in her plans to meet her projected needs. Since future expenses are not something we can predict with great accuracy, it makes sense for her to figure out a way to sock more money in her retirement account.

The point of these examples is not to show you the "right" answers, but to get you thinking about the future and what you can do today that will help your retirement be a time of rest and relaxation rather than deprivation.

RETIREMENT MANAGEMENT

Managing our retirement nest egg will be one of our biggest financial challenges. Not only is it probably the largest sum of money we have ever handled, for the most part, that's all there is. Spend all of it before you check out and you face an uncertain future.

There are a few key decisions along the way that will help or hurt our chances that our money will last as long as we do. The very first decision is how to tap into our nest egg when it is time to retire.

If you are in a defined benefit plan, your employer has promised a certain benefit for your retirement, often based on a formula using length of service and some period of salary, like your last three years. However, when it comes time to retire you will probably be faced with a confusing array of choices about how you want to receive the money.

JUST A MINUTE

The moment they hand you the gold watch is too late to begin thinking about managing your retirement nest egg.

The choices usually involve a series of possible annuities or a lump sum distribution. The decision you make is irrevocable, so you need to get it right the first time. You may not have many (or any) choices about the distribution. Several years before retirement check with your human resources department or whatever unit handles pensions. See if they offer pre-retirement planning services. Some companies do this in-house, but many contract with outside consultants to assist you in planning.

If you take a lump sum payout, you can, in most cases, roll it over into a traditional IRA (not a Roth IRA). You don't have to roll all of it into the IRA, but that portion that you keep out of the IRA may be taxed as current income, so give some thought to how much you want to hold out of the IRA.

Unfortunately, it is not that simple. This one-time event in your life is worth spending some money on a professional advisor. The tax laws here are fairly complicated (so, what else is new?) and change with surprising regularity.

You also need to take into account any other sources of retirement income and how reliable they might be. A good fee-based financial advisor would be worth the money for the peace of mind that you are doing the right thing.

If you have been in a defined contribution plan—a 401(k), for instance—you will want to roll your nest egg into an IRA to keep it protected from taxes until you begin taking money out. You can't goof up on this one. Make a mistake and you may face a tax bill on the whole amount, unless everything is in a Roth IRA.

Because the decision will impact the rest of your life, don't wait until the last minute to come to some conclusions. Many companies will offer preretirement planning services that may help you evaluate the options.

This may be one time you are better off paying a professional to help you work through the possibilities. You will buy yourself a big chunk of peace of mind if you contract with a financial planner to help you get all of your retirement ducks in order.

Do yourself a big favor and work with a fee-only financial planner. They have nothing to gain in recommending a course of action, so you can feel more comfortable with their objectivity.

Appendix B has information on contacting fee-only financial planners.

WHAT CAN YOU DO?

The following is a list of five things you can do today:

1. If you qualify, consider opening a Roth IRA. Tax-free money when you retire is going to be hard to beat. Since it is tax-exempt as opposed to tax-deferred, you can be as aggressive as you want or pile on income-producing stocks or mutual funds.

2. Do you have a will? If not, make an appointment with an attorney to get one made as soon as possible. This is especially important if you have dependent children.

3. Go to the retirement calculator listed in the resource section and see how your expenses and projected income compare. This calculator will let you play "what if" scenarios.

4. If retirement is in the near future (five years or less), consider contacting a fee-only financial planner. They can help you position yourself for retirement and suggest ways to deal with your pension or 401(k) distributions.

5. If you are not covered under an employer-sponsored retirement plan, check out the resource section on SEP-IRAs. You may be eligible for significant contributions.

WORKSHOP

Here is the start of a list of possible expenses after your retirement. Feel free to add to it to cover your own situation. Keep track of the amount of each expense.

Expense	Amount		Expense	Amount
Housing	_____		Prescriptions	_____
Utilities	_____		Travel	_____
Maintenance	_____		Food	_____
Taxes	_____		Recreation	_____
Medical	_____		Insurance	_____

HOUR'S UP!

You may still be years away from retirement, but some planning now will make retirement something to look forward to, rather than dreading flipping burgers to supplement your Social Security. How much did you absorb?

1. The 401(k) is …
   A. Designed to save you taxes.
   B. Designed to help you fund retirement.
   C. What happens when you don't save.

2. You should defer in your 401(k) …
   A. Every penny you can, but at least enough to meet the matching level if your employer offers that.
   B. 2 percent.
   C. Your age minus 25.

3. 401(k) fees can …
   A. Be inconsequential.
   B. Work to your benefit.
   C. Diminish your return.

4. Traditional IRAs …
   A. Allow deductions of up to $5,000.
   B. Are available to anyone.
   C. Allow only $2,000 in deductions.

5. Roth IRAs …
   A. Are available only to people named Roth.
   B. Provide tax-free distributions within certain guidelines.
   C. Cannot be used by employed people.

Quiz

6. Roth IRAs …

   A. Are more complicated than traditional IRAs.

   B. Often cause problems with the IRS.

   C. May not be used for retirement.

7. Long-term retirement planning …

   A. Is beyond the grasp of most people.

   B. Is hard to pin down when costs may be so far in the future.

   C. Is easy.

8. You will need …

   A. More money than you think in retirement.

   B. Less money for medical care in retirement.

   C. More money for gambling in retirement.

9. Short-term retirement is …

   A. Not worth worrying about.

   B. An immediate concern that needs your attention.

   C. An inexpensive problem.

10. Your savings will be …

   A. Worth nothing upon retirement.

   B. Worth less than you think.

   C. Worth more than you think.

HOUR 24
Putting It All Together

CHAPTER SUMMARY

LESSON PLAN:

In this Hour you will learn about ...

- Preparation.
- Setting goals.
- Controlling debt.
- Existing benefits.
- Appropriate tools.
- Buying quality.
- Understanding risk.
- Investment styles.
- Tracking your progress.
- Constant review.
- Asset allocation.
- Have fun.
- Giving back.

Whew! Did you think this was never going to end? There were times when I thought it wouldn't.

Congratulations on making it through. We have covered a tremendous amount of information in a relatively small amount of time. Investing is not a hard subject, but there is a lot to it.

You may have concluded that some of what we have covered really doesn't apply to you, and that's fine. The process of discovering what is and is not important is the essence of understanding a subject.

PROCEED WITH CAUTION

Investing isn't about becoming rich, at least not for me. It is about taking control of your financial future to provide for yourself and your family.

I hope you will want to keep going with your education in investing, because you will find it a rewarding and entertaining effort—not to mention that investing is a work in progress with new twists and turns appearing almost daily.

If you have made it this far and decide that investing is really not your cup of tea and you want to put your 401(k) contribution in an index fund and forget it, good for you. You made that decision based on what you learned and not because you guessed it was the right thing to do.

In this final Hour, I am going to try to tie the concepts together in a big-picture overview. We have been somewhat immersed in the details of investing, and now is a good time to step back and see where we are.

For my purposes, I am going to divide the whole pie into four pieces and show you how everything you learned fits into the first three. The fourth piece is the "why" we invest, as opposed to the "how."

PIECE NO. 1—PREPARATION

There is an old military saying that describes the way some folks approach investing: "Ready, fire, aim!" How much energy you put into preparation may have more impact on your chances for success than just about any other activity.

There are tons of clichés about planning that make the point. One of my favorites is, "No one plans to fail, they fail to plan." Sanctimonious, isn't it? Life insurance salespeople are especially fond of this one.

PROCEED WITH CAUTION

 A plan will help you reach your goals. It doesn't need to be extensive, but it should be written down and reviewed regularly.

Annoying as it is, there is a rather large grain of truth there. Without a financial plan it will be hard to put together any kind of investing program that makes sense. If you don't know where you are going, how will you know when you get there? (This one is also favored by the life insurance industry.)

SETTING GOALS

We covered goal setting in the first Hour, but I want to revisit the subject now that you have a broad overview of the investing process. I hope one of the messages that you noticed repeated time and again throughout the book was to start early.

When you did the goal-setting exercise in the front of the book, you might have felt like you were guessing in terms of what was possible. Now that we are at the end of the book, you will have noticed that it is probably wise to shoot for a 10–11 percent return on a stock portfolio.

This is the historic return of the stock market and, of course, may not apply to individual stocks. You might wonder why this figure is so low when the stock market is so hot. As this book is being written, the Dow is up about 26 percent for the past 12 months. By the time you read this book several months later, who knows? The market may be rocking on as hot as ever, or a big interest rate hike or some other factor may cool it way down.

JUST A MINUTE

Plans based on a super-heated market continuing forever will probably fall short. History doesn't give us much hope that the good times will go on unchecked.

Stocks have traditionally returned in the 10–11 percent range over a long period of time. In short time frames the market has soared and fallen rather dramatically.

A good index fund will probably get you this type of return. On the other hand, if you can stand the risk and fluctuations, well-chosen individual stocks will probably do better, as will some actively managed mutual funds.

Don't base your goals on clobbering the market year in and year out. The odds of that happening are very slim. It is better to be conservative and pleasantly surprised than aggressive and sadly mistaken.

Goals need to be specific: "I want to retire in 26 years with an income in today's dollars of $45,000." "I want $18,000 in the college fund in 12 years." "I need $5,000 for a down payment on a new car in three years." They need to be written down and, if you have a partner in life, agreed upon by all involved.

Goals are not laws, but they should not change without a good reason. Life happens. The college fund goal sounded good until you found out that you were having twins. Be flexible when you have to accommodate new circumstances.

DEBT

High-interest debt is a severed financial artery. It needs to be attended immediately. You cannot expect to get anywhere with investing if you are gushing 18 percent interest to a credit card.

JUST A MINUTE

If you can't control high-interest debt, seek professional help. Suffocating under high-interest debt will kill your investment plans.

Pardon the graphic description, but I want to be very clear about how important it is to eliminate high-interest debt. Does this mean you should never borrow money? Of course not; but you need to be very disciplined about credit and how it is used. Except in an emergency, you should never charge a big-ticket item on a credit card without a plan to pay it off as soon as possible, but no longer than four months.

In Hour 2, I discussed some strategies for getting rid of your debt. If you find yourself overwhelmed, there are some places to go for help. Appendix B, "Resources," lists some services that will help you get out from under this high-interest burden.

EXISTING BENEFITS

Before you charge off on an investing crusade, be sure you understand what you already have available to you. In particular, pay attention to any retirement plans offered by your employer.

PROCEED WITH CAUTION

 Not taking advantage of your existing benefits doesn't make any sense. Like my grandfather used to say, "If it ain't broke, don't fix it."

If your employer matches your contributions up to a certain percent in a retirement plan and you are not taking advantage of it, shame on you. Free money is impossible to beat, and it doesn't make any sense not to take advantage of it.

Even if your employer doesn't match any of your contribution, be sure you understand what the plan is all about and what your options are. If it is a defined contribution plan, make sure you are participating to the maximum level you can. Here is another reminder why this is a good idea:

$5,000 as income	=	$3,333 take home after tax
$5,000 put in 401(k)	=	$6,666 benefits ($5,000 in 401(k) plus $1,666 not paid in current taxes)

You may have all or most of the tools you need already in hand, but if you don't completely understand them or take advantage of them, they won't do you much good.

If you are self-employed or work for a small company that doesn't have a retirement plan, look into the various options open to you.

The SEP-IRA is a powerful tool for the self-employed and folks working for small companies. It allows you to build a retirement fund quickly. For two-income families, where all or part of the self-employed persons' income is not needed for day to day living expenses, you can sock away up to $30,000 a year in a SEP-IRA. If you work for a small company, see if they will convert you to a contract consultant (you get a 1099 instead of a W-2 at the end of the year for taxes). Be careful of this tactic because you will lose benefits, including health insurance, and you will have to pay self-employment tax, which is a big bite.

Retirement funding is the single biggest financial challenge we face—know your tools and use them.

APPROPRIATE TOOLS

Matching your investment goals with the proper tools is the heart of investment success. Our discussions on a variety of investment products raised some of the key strengths and weaknesses of each. Those who want to take a more passive role have one set of tools, while folks interested in a more active role have another set.

Use the correct investment tool for the job. Don't try to make it into something it is not.

LONG-RANGE GOALS

Long-range goals need to match with products that do best over the long term. Your best returns are probably in the long-term stock and stock mutual fund areas. The use of income instruments such as bonds, income stocks and mutual funds, and cash work best for shorter-term goals and in environments where current income is not a severe tax problem.

Here is a review of the main features of the four main investment instruments:

- Mutual funds offer professional management, ease of administration, diversification, and low fees, if you choose correctly. They are certainly recommended for people who do not want an active role in investing. You must be cautious of high fees and excessive turnover of assets, which raises expenses and creates tax problems.

- Individual stocks offer greater focus in their particular industries or sectors, but they are subject to large fluctuations and ups and downs. A lack of diversity creates a higher order of risk, but also raises the upside potential. They require more supervision than mutual funds.

- Bonds have been lukewarm in the past few years, despite the fact that there is more money in the bond market overall than in the stock market. Bonds historically produce lower returns than stocks, but they may provide more stability for retirement accounts.

- Cash accounts are normally used to park money for a very short period of time, often in anticipation of an upcoming expense. Cash has not been a great investment in recent years.

In all of your investments, look to keep expenses low, whether it is through using a discount broker or buying mutual funds with low expense ratios—the less money you pay in fees, the more you have to invest.

PROCEED WITH CAUTION

 There is no substitute for quality. It is better to buy 10 shares of a quality stock than 100 shares of junk.

MID-RANGE GOALS

Mid-range goals (5 to 15 years out) are long enough to consider both mutual funds and individual stocks, although five years is just barely long enough to qualify as a sufficient holding period. For goals on the shorter end of this range, high-quality bonds become an option for a known expense goal.

Mid-range goals command more attention to exit strategies as you approach your goal's deadline.

- Mutual funds are a viable vehicle for mid-range goals, but are problematic for the shorter time periods. Consider shifting to a less aggressive fund or fixed income instrument as you approach the deadline.

- Individual stocks may be too volatile for goals on the short end of the mid-range. Like mutual funds, you need to pay attention to your exit strategy as you get closer to the deadline. Since individual stocks are more likely than mutual funds to move quickly, be on guard and prepared to sell quickly if needed.

- Bonds may be a good choice for the shorter mid-range goals. As you will remember, bonds are more risky the longer it is until their maturity. If you have a fixed-cost expense coming up and have the money for it, a high-quality bond with a maturity to match your time frame makes sense. However, trading bonds to reach your goal is not for beginners.

- Cash accounts offer the safest way to meet your goal, but for goals more than seven years out you will be better off with a mutual fund or stock.

SHORT-RANGE GOALS

Short-range goals (fewer than five years) are risky turf for mutual funds or individual stocks. In this short time period, bonds and cash accounts may be your safest and surest bets.

Short-range goals are the hardest to achieve in some ways because there is little time to let compounding work for you. Plan to put a major portion of the needed dollars into what ever vehicle you choose.

- Mutual funds are more risky the fewer years you hold them, as a general rule. However, an index fund will probably do okay in the short run as long as the market stays healthy. Still, they are not your best option.

- Individual stocks held for less than five years are very unpredictable in many cases. As you approach your goal, what happens if the stock takes a nose dive?

- Bonds start looking much more attractive as a way to lock in the needed dollars for a future, known expense. Match the maturity with the expense and you won't have to worry about rising interest rates sucking the value out of your bond.

- Cash accounts for short-term goals are a way to be sure you will have the money when you need it. Once you have your goal, back up and figure out how much you will have to put away every month. For just a couple of years, you won't gain much from compounding.

PIECE NO. 2—BUYING QUALITY

Buying quality is the cheapest way to invest. A quality investment is one that you can stick with for the appropriate length of time to achieve your goal. Taking the time to find the quality stock, mutual fund, or bond will be worth it in the long run.

Once you become comfortable with the numbers that tell you about quality, finding good buys becomes easier. The process will be a lot easier if you use the services available on the Internet.

Free software will let you screen thousands of choices to find those stocks or mutual funds that match your particular needs. If you would feel better with a professional opinion, there are numerous places on the Internet where you can pick the best minds in the business.

You do not have to find the perfect investment to be successful. If your goals need a large-cap growth mutual fund, there are dozens of good ones to choose from. Avoid jumping after hot stocks. There are also dozens of quality stocks that will meet any need or goal you have.

RISK

Risk and the associated potential reward are part of investing. You need to find your own, not someone else's, comfort level with risk. Once you have established where your risk tolerance is, make sure you are receiving the appropriate reward. There is nothing more frustrating than taking a significant risk in an investment, only to receive a mediocre reward.

Buying quality investments minimizes risk because they are more predictable than high-flying speculative stocks. A quality buy can be a buy with significant risks. The key is the anticipated reward and the potential that the investment will actually reward the risk.

PICK AN INVESTMENT STYLE

Based on your risk tolerance and goals, you will come to a conclusion about your investing style: conservative, active, or aggressive. It makes sense for someone just starting out in investing to begin at the conservative level.

JUST A MINUTE

A stock index fund is an excellent, low-risk way to get started in investing.

Remember my encouragement to begin early. I would suggest you start off with a stock index mutual fund. This is not a hard investment to make, and Appendix B will tell you how to find quality index funds. More than likely, you are going to pick an index fund that is part of a larger family of funds. As you gain confidence, you may want to move money into another mutual fund or transfer money from the index fund to another type of fund.

If you lean toward a more active investment style, you still might want to get started with a stock index fund. The point is to get going, now. You will not go wrong starting off with a stock index fund.

Tracking Your Progress

Once you have specific goals and the tools to achieve them, come up with a way you can understand to track your progress. Some people find that charts are very helpful in seeing where they are in the process.

To reach your goal of $18,000 in the college fund in 12 years, you are going to need to invest $850 per year and earn 10 percent interest.

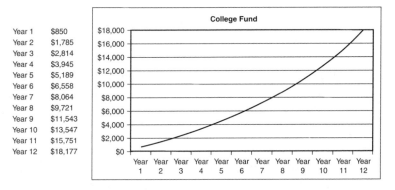

Year 1	$850
Year 2	$1,785
Year 3	$2,814
Year 4	$3,945
Year 5	$5,189
Year 6	$6,558
Year 7	$8,064
Year 8	$9,721
Year 9	$11,543
Year 10	$13,547
Year 11	$15,751
Year 12	$18,177

Here is what your account should look like each year. This assumes that you pay the tax on the gains out of another account.

If you aren't earning 10 percent, you need to know that along the way and increase the yearly contribution to make up for the shortfall.

Keeping score can be a fun activity, but don't get caught up in the daily ups and downs of the market. Following on a weekly or monthly basis is often enough for mutual funds. Individual stocks may require more attention if they tend to be volatile.

Piece No. 3—Constant Review

Someone once said the only constant in life is *change*. Nothing could be truer when it comes to investing. Even the passive investor who is planning to let professional mutual fund managers do all the hard work should be aware of this caveat: Even plans that are working will need to change as the circumstances of our lives change.

This relates back to our very first steps of setting goals, but goes beyond simply keeping score. A young person with no family will seldom stay that way. Marriage, children, houses, education, and other life milestones all require rethinking our goals and how we are going to reach them.

Not all the changes in our lives are positive, unfortunately. Jobs are lost, health suffers, and families separate. All of these influences may also force a reconsideration of our goals and priorities.

The way we address changing circumstances, planned or otherwise, is known as asset allocation. It acknowledges that our needs will change with age and different circumstances.

PROCEED WITH CAUTION

 Don't be afraid to adjust your portfolio's balance, but avoid micro-tweaking, which will just run up expenses with limited benefit.

Asset allocation shifts resources when appropriate and may call for getting out of one investment in favor of another more appropriate for the circumstances. The closer you are to retirement, the more frequently you should check your asset allocation.

The last years leading up to retirement are pivotal in positioning yourself for a successful and fulfilling retirement. Go to sleep here and you may find yourself asking, "Do you want fries with that burger?"

PIECE NO. 4—HAVE FUN

My unscientific—but I believe accurate—assessment of human behavior is that people will do something they enjoy with more energy and gusto than something they don't enjoy.

Find a way to manage your investments that is fun and rewarding. Some people find more confidence and fun in working in groups. If this is you, join or form an investment club.

The Internet is a great place to chat with people about investing, as long as you are careful about following advice from someone you don't know. If you are lucky, you and your partner may find this a rewarding way to spend time together.

Some people take up investing as a hobby and spend free time reading and studying books and magazines. Whatever you can do to make it fun will keep you involved for the long haul.

If you find there is nothing about investing that you could remotely call fun and you would rather have a root canal than read a stock market table in the newspaper, find a way to keep investing that causes the least amount of pain. You will probably end up with a portfolio of mutual funds, but there is nothing wrong with that. The important thing is that you will have a portfolio of investments.

GIVING BACK

Finally, I would encourage you to find a way to give something back to your community. Despite what we would like to think, no one truly makes it on their own.

We are each part of a larger community and have a responsibility to be more than a taker. If you are more comfortable making monetary donations, there are innumerable good causes out there that you can support.

However, my own experience tells me that monetary support alone is not the whole answer. The community needs you and your experience and your maturity and your creativity. Whether it is through a religious organization or some civic group, the community will benefit from your presence and you will benefit by becoming more than the sum of your investments.

Your family will also benefit by your presence at home—physically, emotionally, and mentally. Working hard to achieve success will be of little comfort to your family if they never see you. It is unlikely your children will stand over your grave and say, "I sure am glad Dad/Mom worked themselves to death so I could go to summer camp."

Best wishes, and happy investing.

What Can You Do?

The following is a list of five things you can do today:

1. Are you ready to begin investing? If you still feel a little nervous, there are plenty of resources in the back of this book to help you get going.

2. Get out your financial goals for one last pass. You now have a good idea of what your strategy will be and how risk-tolerant you are. Start putting some names of stocks, mutual funds, etc. under the appropriate goal. Begin your evaluation process.

3. If your partner hasn't been a part of this education, be sure to discuss your thoughts and concerns about investing with him or her so you both are on the same page.

4. Tracking your progress will give you a sense of accomplishment and keep you on track. Develop a system you are comfortable with and will follow. Share it with the family if that is appropriate.

5. Have some fun!

Workshop

Your assignment is to make dinner reservations at your favorite place and enjoy a great meal with someone special.

Hour's Up!

Actually, the whole book is up. Congratulations on getting through it. Here is a quiz that addresses the main points I hope you learned about investing.

1. The best time to begin investing …
   A. Was yesterday.
   B. Is today.
   C. Is tomorrow.

2. High-interest debt is …
   A. Okay.
   B. The financial equivalent of a severed artery.
   C. Better than not getting what you want now.

3. The miracle of compounding …

    A. Only happens once a year.

    B. Requires large sums of money.

    C. Is the most powerful wealth builder known.

4. Loaded mutual funds will …

    A. Always have trouble beating a comparable no-load fund.

    B. Always make money.

    C. Seldom lose money.

5. Mutual fund expenses …

    A. Are often too high.

    B. Can destroy your return.

    C. Make it difficult to beat index funds.

    D. All of the above.

6. You should use a discount broker …

    A. If you want to keep expenses low.

    B. If you only buy cheap stocks.

    C. If you believe the market is going down.

7. A good stock index fund …

    A. Will never make money

    B. Is a good, safe first investment.

    C. Lacks any growth potential.

8. Individual stocks …

    A. Are not worth the effort.

    B. May provide superior returns.

    C. Can't beat bonds.

9. Retirement planning …

    A. Should begin with your first job.

    B. Is the biggest investing goal we will face.

    C. Is easier if you start early.

    D. All of the above.

10. Investing and life will …

    A. Work better if you have fun.

    B. Work better if you have fun.

    C. Work better if you have fun.

Quiz

APPENDIX A
20-Minute Recap

HOUR 1

This chapter will introduce you to investing and jettison some of the myths and mysteries. Traditional and non-traditional investments are discussed and the groundwork is laid for the rest of the book.

HOUR 2

Hour 2 is spent getting you and your finances ready for an investment program. Your first job is to get rid of high-interest credit card debt. You'll get some concrete tips and suggestions for not only getting rid of your debt, but also for finding money in your existing budget for investing. This is an extremely important step, and we will include a discussion of emergency cash reserves and life insurance.

HOUR 3

In Hour 3, you will be reassured about the math required for investing. We will introduce you to the most powerful wealth builder available to the average investor: compounding. We will go over basic investment terms so that we are all speaking the same language. The various stock markets will be explored and you will learn the differences between them. Finally, you will get an update on some of the major market indicators such as the Dow Jones Industrial Average and the S&P 500 and understand why they are important and what they tell you.

Hour 4

In this Hour, we will look at the basic investment instruments—stocks, mutual funds, and bonds. This basic overview will provide a solid foundation as we get deeper into the subjects covered later in the book. We will also cover cash instruments such as CDs and money market accounts. Annuities, real estate limited partnerships, REITs, and precious metals will be reviewed. The pluses and minuses of these investments, along with fees and other expenses, will be explored.

Hour 5

You don't want to overlook investing opportunities you may already have at your disposal. Employee stock options, dividend reinvestment programs, and retirement plans can all be used for your benefit. We will spend a good part of the chapter reviewing various retirement plans and funding mechanisms such as 401(k) plans and IRAs. Examples of why starting early on a retirement plan is so important will open your eyes to some possibilities.

Hour 6

In Hour 6, we look at the language of investing: numbers. Even the mathematically challenged will find this Hour easy to get through. We will explain some of the basic numbers you will need. In addition, you will get a hands-on guide to how to read and interpret those pages of numbers in the newspaper that report prices for stocks and mutual funds. We will also go over some numbers that are peculiar to mutual funds. Annual reports and prospectuses will be examined.

Hour 7

Investing is about making informed decisions, not taking guesses or following "hot" tips. In this Hour, we will look at all the sources of news and information available to investors. The scams and schemes aimed at investors are numerous, but we will give you some tools for evaluating what you hear and read about investing and investments. Finally, we will go over reliable sources of information, including newspapers, magazines, and Web sites; you can be confident that our sources will not try to sell you the latest get-rich-quick scheme.

Hour 8

Even though the stock brokerage business has changed dramatically in the last 25 years, you still need a broker to buy and sell securities on the open market. This Hour will be devoted to an evaluation of the strengths and weaknesses of the different types of brokers. We will look at cost, service, and execution. Discount and online brokers get special attention because these are the fastest-growing types of services. We'll show you a Web site that evaluates online brokers based on several criteria and ranks them best to worse.

HOUR 9

Hour 9 begins a three-part examination of mutual funds. In this Hour, we look at ways they are classified by fees and management style. Expenses are examined in detail and you can see how important they are to the success of the fund. You will know what to expect in terms of expense ratios. This knowledge will help you make informed decisions. Fund management is examined with an eye toward how it affects the fund's performance. We conclude the Hour with a look at two unusual hybrid mutual funds.

HOUR 10

Hour 10 continues the mutual fund discussion with a look at the four broad categories of funds. Stock and bond mutual funds are the two most popular types with long-term investors. Each one is broken down into subcategories based on what the funds hold. Money market funds, which are a popular holding place for the short term, and specialized funds that invest in real estate and foreign economies are also discussed.

HOUR 11

We conclude our detailed look at mutual funds with an examination of the different investment objectives that drive funds. We use these objectives to help us match funds that meet our personal investment objectives. There are thousands of mutual funds on the market. Without some system to understand their objectives, it would be an impossible task to find the right ones for us.

HOUR 12

In Hour 12, we begin a two-part look at stocks. Stocks don't lend themselves to easy, black-and-white classifications, yet you will see that there are definite categories. Stocks, unlike mutual funds, don't start out to fill an investment objective. Companies are focused on making money, and as they grow and mature, how they are perceived by the market may change their classification. It is important to understand the difference between a stock that is acting like a growth stock and another stock that is acting like a value stock.

Hour 13

The second part of the stock discussion focuses on the importance of size in your decision-making process. Size *does* matter with stocks, and we give you some tools for identifying a stock by size and what the expectations are for such a stock. Stocks of similar size in the same industry are expected to behave in a certain manner. Deviation from these norms sends signals to the market. We conclude the Hour with a look at initial public offerings, or IPOs, and how they have become the lottery of Wall Street.

Hour 14

Bonds, with all their variations, are the subject of this Hour. We look at U.S. Treasury Bonds, U.S. government agency bonds, municipal bonds, and corporate bonds. Figuring what a bond is worth takes more work than valuing stocks or mutual funds. In addition, we cover the three main risks associated with bonds and the two major rating services that tell you how risky a particular issue is. Junk bonds, convertible bonds, and subordinated bonds are also discussed.

Hour 15

In Hour 15, we examine various investment strategies, including growth, income, and balanced. We discuss how you might use one or more of these strategies to meet different financial goals. How you relate your personal investment strategies to your life circumstances and goals is the heart of investing. Previous discussions of investment products will make more sense in the context of meeting your personal goals.

Hour 16

Risk is part of investing. Return is what you hope to achieve given an acceptable level of risk. We will explore this relationship in detail. High-, medium-, and low-risk investments are discussed in terms of what you can realistically expect in the way of returns. Some financial goals may require more risk than others, while it may be foolhardy to take much—if any—risk to meet other goals. Managing risk is an important component of investing.

Hour 17

In this Hour, we look at how you might go about picking a mutual fund to buy. We examine how to match your objectives to those of an appropriate mutual fund. Several age groups are discussed in order to show you how you need to adjust your investments as you grow older. Changes in life circumstances means you will leave some objectives behind and pick up or add emphasis to others. The tax consequences of these decisions are raised. Since you will need, and should have, a copy of the mutual fund prospectus, we will spend some time interpreting it.

Hour 18

Hour 18 is devoted to examining the process we use to select an individual stock. The difference between owning mutual funds and individual stocks is examined. We cover researching individual stocks and look at various sources of information, including the annual report and other reports required by regulatory agencies. Finally, we look at how you go about evaluating the business behind the stock.

Hour 19

Many financial professionals feel that how you allocate your assets based on your age and investment objectives may be as important as which particular stock, mutual fund, or bond you buy. This Hour, titled "Asset Allocation," will help you understand how your investments need to match not only your objectives, but also your stage in life.

Hour 20

Hour 20 is the first of three Hours looking at different investing styles. This Hour focuses on the conservative/low-cost investing style. The concept of dollar-cost averaging is discussed, along with other proven investment strategies including DIPs and DRIPs. The buy-and-hold strategy is explained in connection with market timing. Finally, we look at the very popular investment club concept and how you might benefit from this type of group effort.

Hour 21

The second investment style we look at is the active investor. The active investor wants to get his or her hands dirty while working on investments. We examine online trading and look at the advantages and disadvantages. A couple of tools used by active traders, margin trading and selling short, are explained along with their associated risks. After-hours trading is also examined.

Hour 22

The third part of this series looks at the aggressive investor. These folks are out there on the edge using high-risk techniques and products. We will explore options, futures, and exotic deals. We will also spend considerable time looking at the phenomenon of day trading and whether these investors make or lose money in a fast-moving market.

HOUR 23

In this Hour, we spend our time looking at retirement products such as 401(k) plans, IRAs, and Roth IRAs. We will examine the differences between regular IRAs and Roth IRAs. We will also look at some models for calculating how much you will need in order to retire and what your expenses are likely to be during retirement.

HOUR 24

Hour 24 wraps everything up and places it in a broader context. Here is where we step back and consider what we have covered. We review the major points and concepts and conclude the Hour with some philosophical thoughts on how investing might be considered in the context of your whole life.

APPENDIX B
Resources

WEB SITES

- **Balance Sheet** www.zdnet.com/zdtv/ moneymachine/personalfinance/: This site has an interactive balance sheet that you can use to get your personal finances in shape.

- **Best Credit Cards** www.bankrate.com/brm/ccard.asp: This site lists the best credit cards for all types of users. They are ranked by interest rate, annual fees, and so on.

- **DIPs and DRIPs** www.buckinvestor.com/drips/planlist.html: A complete list of companies that participate in Direct Investment Plans and Dividend Reinvestment Plans.

DAY TRADING

- **Day Trading Site** www.daytrading.about.com: A whole site devoted to day trading.

- **Tips of Day Traders** www.daypicks.com: One of many services that offer stock recommendations.

DEBT COUNSELING

- **Credit/Debt Site** www.credit.about.com: A whole site devoted to credit and debt issues.

- **Consolidated Credit Counseling Services** www.debtfree.org: Non-profit site helps with money management problems in families.

- **Consumer Credit & Budget Counseling** www.cc%2Dbc.com: This non-profit group helps you get out of debt and manage your personal finances.
- **Debt Counselors of America** www.dca.org: Another non-profit agency that works to get you out of debt and back on your financial feet.

FINANCIAL PLANNING PROFESSIONALS

- **Financial Planning Web Site** www.financialplan.about.com: A whole Web site devoted to financial planning from About.com.
- **Chartered Financial Consultants** www.amercoll.edu: Background information about the designation "Chartered Financial Consultant" and other financial planning designations.
- **Certified Financial Planners** www.cfp%2Dboard.org/index.html: Information on choosing a financial planner (CFP) Certified Financial Planner Board of Standards.
- **Finding a Financial Planner** www.planningpaysoff.org: Search the database of the International Association for Financial Planning to find a Financial Planning professional near you.

FINANCIAL PLANNING SOFTWARE

- **Managing Your Money** www.zdnet.com/pcmag/features/finance: A review of Managing Your Money personal finance software.
- **MS Money** www.computershopper.zdnet.com: Reviews of Microsoft Money, Managing Your Money Plus, Quicken Deluxe, and Kiplinger's Simply Money.
- **Quicken** www.intuit.com: Order Quicken Deluxe, Quicken Home and Business, Quicken Suite, Quicken Personal Financial Planner, Turbo Tax, and other Quicken products.

FUTURES EXCHANGES

- **Chicago Board of Trade** www.cbot.com: Here you will find Treasury Bond futures, Dow Jones Industrial Average futures, and the agricultural complex. 141 West Jackson Boulevard, Chicago, Illinois 60604-2994, phone (312) 435-3500.

- **Chicago Mercantile Exchange** www.cme.com: Futures and options products are traded on the CME, divided into financial products such as currencies and agricultural commodities such as cattle. 30 South Wacker Drive, Chicago, Illinois 60606, phone 312-930-1000.
- **New York Mercantile Exchange** www.nymex.com: Physical commodities are traded at Nymex: gold, silver, platinum, crude oil, natural gas, and more. One North End Avenue, World Financial Center, New York, NY 10282-1101, phone (212) 299-2000.

OPTIONS EXCHANGES

- **Chicago Board Options Exchange** www.cboe.com: The CBOE is more than just an options exchange, it has plenty of free educational material and software as well. 400 S. LaSalle Street, Chicago, IL 60605.
- **NASDAQ** www.nasdaq.com: The NASDAQ is a good resource for equity and index options as well as stocks. 33 Whitehall Street, New York, NY 10004, phone (212) 858-4000.
- **Pacific Stock Exchange** www.pacificex.com: The PSE has good coverage of technology stock options. 301 Pine Street, San Francisco, CA 94104, phone (415) 393-4000.

MARKET INDICATORS

- **Dow Jones Industrial Average** dowjones.wsj.com: The oldest and best known of all market indicators, the Dow consists of 30 stocks representing the leading companies in their industries.
- **NASDAQ** www.nasdaq.com: The NASDAQ is home to many of the high-flying, high-tech companies on the market today.
- **New York Stock Exchange Composite Index** www.nyse.com: This index covers all the stocks traded on the New York Stock Exchange.
- **Russell 2000 Index** www.russell.com: The Russell 2000 is a key indicator for how the nation's small companies are doing.
- **Standard and Poor's 500** www.standardpoor.com: The S&P 500 is the most widely used benchmark for the market by investment professionals.

RETIREMENT PLANNING CALCULATORS

- **Retirement Planning Site** www.retireplan.about.com: A complete site devoted to retirement planning.

- **Before/After Retirement Investing** www.interest.com: This calculator helps you figure the future value of money before and after retirement.

- **Can You Afford to Retire?** www.firstar.com/persfin/: FirstStar bank's calculator includes inputs for a 2nd income in the household.

- **Retirement Spending** www.moneycentral.msn.com/articles/retire: MSN.com shows how much you can spend after you retire.

- **Expenses After Retirement** www.principal.com/: The Principal Financial Group discusses this difficult topic.

RISK TOLERANCE

- **Risk Tolerance and Investment Decisions** www.better-investing.org: An article discussing risk tolerance and how yours should impact your investment decisions.

- **Risk Tolerance** www.seninvest.com/article2.htm: This may be more technical than you want, but it raises some interesting points.

- **Risk Tolerance Quiz** www.cigna.com/retirement: A short risk tolerance quiz will help you sleep better at night with your investment decisions.

- **Another Risk Tolerance Quiz** www.scudder-u.working4u.com: Another look at risk tolerance and the role it plays in investing.

ROTH IRA

- **SmartMoney** www.university.smartmoney.com: Online magazine from Wall St. Journal has complete Roth IRA information.

- **Motley Fool** www.fool.com/retirement.htm: The Internet wits have sound advice for IRA shoppers.

- **Family Money** www.familymoney.com: Good site with lots of information about IRAs.

SEP-IRA INFORMATION

- **SEP-IRAs** www.dainrauscher.com: Find out how much you can contribute to a SEP, SIMPLE IRA, or Keogh plan from Dainrauscher.com.

- **Retirement Planning Made Easy** www.newyorklife.com**:** New York Life details the benefits of using a SEP-IRA.
- **Calculating SEP Contributions** www.bankrate.com: Bankrate.com helps you calculate your eligible SEP-IRA contribution.
- **IRS Publication 590** www.irs.ustreas.gov/basic/forms%255Fpubs/ pubs/p590toc.htm: IRS's guide on setting up and maintaining a SEP plan.

STOCK EXCHANGES

- **American Stock Exchange** www.amex.com
- **Chicago Board of Trade** www.cbot.com
- **Chicago Board Options Exchange** www.cboe.com
- **Chicago Mercantile Exchange** www.cme.com
- **Kansas City Board of Trade** www.kcbt.com
- **NASDAQ** www.nasdaq.com
- **New York Cotton Exchange** www.nyce.com
- **New York Mercantile Exchange** www.nymex.com
- **New York Stock Exchange** www.nyse.com
- **Philadelphia Stock Exchange** www.phlx.com

STOCK SCREENING

- **Microsoft** moneycentral.msn.com/investor/finder/welcome.asp: Comprehensive and easy to customize.
- **Marketguide's StockQuest** www.marketguide.com/mgi/stockquest/ sq-about.html: A powerful screening tool, but it takes a while to get used to.
- **Morningstar.com** screen.morningstar.com/stocksearch/ stockinterim.html: The stock and fund selectors are easy to use and don't overwhelm you.

STOCK TRADING GAMES

- **Market Simulation** www.smartstocks.com: Play the market without risking any money.

- **Multiple Games** www.game.etrade.com: E*Trade, the online broker, offers several different games.
- **Play the Game** www.stocktrak.com: Offers prizes for best performance in monthly games.

PUBLICATIONS

The Intelligent Investor: A Book of Practical Counsel
by Benjamin Graham

The Only Investment Guide You'll Ever Need
by Andrew Tobias

The Complete Idiot's Guide to Making Money With Mutual Funds
by Alan Lavine and Gail Liberman

Beating the Street
by Peter Lynch

The Complete Idiot's Guide to Managing Your Money
by Robert Heady and Christy Heady

Motley Fool's You Have More Than You Think: The Foolish Guide to Investing What You Have
by David and Tom Gardener

Technical Analysis of Stock Trends
by Robert D. Edwards and John Magee

FINANCIAL STATEMENTS

How to Read a Financial Report: Wringing Vital Signs out of the Numbers
by John A. Tracy

Financial Statement Analysis: The Investor's Self Study Guide to Interpreting and Analyzing
by Charles J. Woelfel

OPTIONS

Trading for a Living: Psychology, Trading Tactics, Money Management
by Alexander Elder

Option Delta
by Richard Marcinko

Getting Started in Options
by Michael C. Thomsett

Trade Options Online
by George A. Fontanills

UNDERSTANDING TAX BRACKETS

Tax Rates	Married Filing Jointly	Singles
15%	Less than $43,050	Less than $25,750
28%	$43,050–$104,050	$25,750–$62,450
31%	$104,050–$158,550	$62,450–$130,250
36%	$158,550–$283,150	$130,250–$283,150
39.6%	More than $283,150	More than $283,150

Using the preceding table you can figure your "marginal" tax rate, which is the tax you pay on your last dollar of income. Here's how it works: If you are married and your taxable income was $50,000, you would pay 15 percent on the first $43,050 and 28 percent on the last $6,950. Your marginal tax rate would be 28 percent.

OPENING AND USING A MUTUAL FUND ACCOUNT

Opening a mutual fund account is a simple matter of filling out a few forms and sending in an opening deposit.

You may contact the mutual fund company by telephone or over the Internet. Some funds will let you download forms and a prospectus, while other funds will send you everything in the mail.

The mutual fund company will want to know which funds you are interested in and whether or not the account is for an IRA. IRA accounts often have a lower initial deposit requirement. If you want to roll over another IRA or some other qualified retirement funds, the mutual fund company can help you do that.

Normally, a company will wait until your personal check has cleared before they will open your account. For faster activation, ask about wiring funds directly from your bank to the mutual fund company.

If you wish to have a specific amount withdrawn from your account for deposit, the fund will help you set that up.

Buying and Selling Mutual Fund Shares

Mutual funds are revalued every day after the market has closed and the net asset value is adjusted up or down. You will usually buy into or sell out of a fund in round dollar amounts, except when selling out of the fund completely.

Purchases are made three basic ways:

- You mail the fund a check for an initial or additional investment.
- You wire the fund for an initial or additional investment.
- You transfer money out of one fund and into another fund within the same family. Mutual funds will often let you move your money around within the family for little or no fee. Most funds also offer a money market fund that pays interest on uninvested cash.

Sales or redemptions are made two basic ways:

- You call the fund or contact them over the Internet (if they offer that feature) and say you want to redeem $X worth of (fund name). If you want out of the fund altogether, you indicate that to the representative. The fund will mail you a check or wire you the funds. There may be additional charges for expedited handling.
- You can contact the fund and have them sweep a specific dollar amount or the full amount out of that fund and into another.

Opening and Using a Discount Brokerage Account

Opening a discount brokerage account is a simple, straightforward process. The brokers are eager for your business and will be glad to help with any questions.

You can contact the brokerage firm by telephone or over the Internet. If you use the telephone, request a new account package and it will be mailed to you. Some online brokers will let you download the forms.

The brokerage will want to know what type of account (cash or margin) you want to open, what type of trades other than stocks and mutual funds (options, futures, and so on) you plan, and if this is an IRA account.

They will also want to know whether the account is to be set up in your name only or your and your partner's, and who is authorized to trade on this account. There may be other questions particular to that brokerage.

You will be sent the appropriate forms and disclosure statements. Once you have filled out the forms, you will return them along with a check for your initial deposit. Most brokerages will require the check to clear before they will activate your account. If you want to trade more quickly, ask about wiring money from your bank account to the brokerage.

You will be given an account number and password for an online account. If you are trading by telephone, you may be asked for personal information to verify that you are the account holder before the brokerage will process certain transactions.

The best advice for selecting a broker is to stick with a name you know. Better yet are recommendations from people you trust. Use a ranking service like the ones listed in the next section for online brokers.

Working with Your Broker

It is natural to want to avoid looking foolish. This reluctance often holds people back from getting involved with a discount broker.

Put your mind at ease. The discount brokers want your business so badly that they will be glad to help you over the rough spots; if you go with an online broker, there is a good chance you will never talk to a human.

If You Deal by Telephone

The telephone experience with a discount broker is likely to be short and to the point, although never at the expense of courtesy. You may talk to a different broker every time you call, which is okay since they all have access to your account information.

The representative you speak to will want your account number and perhaps some additional identifying information. Once that is out of the way, the broker will ask for your order. This is not a time for chitchat, but clear and precise communication.

The brokerage may even give you a sample "script" to use when placing an order. If so, follow these suggestions. However, if you are on your own, here is what you might say:

"I would like to buy (or sell) 100 shares of IBM at market."

I would always have the stock's symbol handy, but order using the full name of the company. Remember, there are a lot of companies with similar names, so it is important to be precise.

The broker will read your order back to you for confirmation. She may include the symbol just to double-check that you are both talking about the same stock. She will ask you to confirm that you do indeed want to buy IBM. She may also quote the current price. This does not mean that is the price you will get, but it is another bit of information that confirms the order.

After the broker has determined you have enough money in your account, she will attempt to fill your order. Depending on the market and the broker-age policy, you may get a confirmation of your order in that same conversa-tion. Otherwise, they will probably call you back with the information.

IF YOU USE AN ONLINE BROKER

If you use an online broker, you will receive instructions about your account number and password when you open your account.

Once you access your brokerage's Web site, you will be directed to an order entry screen. Since they are all different, I can only tell you what common elements to look for on the screen. Many online brokers have simulated trad-ing areas that will let you enter trades and get accustomed to their system. This is a great way to practice without risk.

The process will be basically the same in terms of specifying the type of order, the stock, and the price. You may be asked to use the stock's symbol to place your order, so have it handy. You may get a quick confirmation, or some systems may e-mail you the confirmation later.

There are two basic flavors of personal computers: Apple and Windows-based. The truth is that Apple is the superior machine with superior software. However, its marketing department couldn't sell a cure for cancer, and if you want a lesson in how to give away a whole industry, read the history of Apple.

Your second choice is a Windows-based system, which takes up about 95 percent of the market. Folks like Dell, Compaq, IBM, and Hewlett Packard populate it.

You can buy a desktop computer or a laptop. Either one will do the job, but you will pay more for a laptop. Here is the minimum configuration I suggest for a machine that will help you with your investing:

Specifications	Desktop	Laptop
Celeron or Pentium II Processor	400 MHz	400 MHz
Memory	64 meg.	64 meg.
Hard Drive	6 gig	6 gig
CD-ROM	24 X	24 X
Modem	56K	56K
Monitor	17"	Active Matrix
Expect to Pay	$1,000–$1,200	$1,500–$2,000

This is your basic workhorse system. If you plan to use it for gathering information off the Internet and for word processing, most systems that fall within these specifications will meet your needs. I would suggest staying with a major brand if you are not a technical person.

Most of these systems are easy to set up and the software is already installed, including your Web browser and a word-processing program and other office software.

A salesperson may try to sell you a more expensive system, claiming you must have a Pentium III or faster processor, a huge hard drive, and other accessories. If you plan to do extensive multimedia applications or complex database functions, educate yourself on the system you need. However, to gather investing information and process it, the system I described above will handle everything you need.

The only real accessory you need is a printer, and often one will be included in a "bundle" on sale at a store or online. If not, your two choices are an inkjet printer and a laser printer.

The inkjet can print in color, but if you get carried away with printing every pretty page you see, the cost of replacing cartridges will soon get out of hand. Plan to spend around $200. I prefer Hewlett Packard printers, but there are other good models on the market.

A laser printer will only print black and white, unless you have at least $3,000 for a color laser. The laser printer's output is much sharper and clearer than the inkjet's. If you are going to print business documents, I would go with the laser. Plan on spending $400 or so on a name-brand laser.

You will need access to the Internet through a local or national Internet service provider (ISP). Avoid the free computer offers from ISPs who want you to commit to a three-year contract for Internet access (you will have to put up with annoying ads all over your screen). Expect to pay about $20 per month for dial-up service.

Dow Stocks

Here is a list of the stocks that make up the Dow Jones Industrial Average as of January 2000:

Alcoa Inc.	International Business Machines Corp.
American Express Co.	International Paper Co.
AT&T Corp.	J.P. Morgan & Co.
Boeing Co.	Johnson & Johnson
Caterpillar Inc.	McDonald's Corp.
Citibank	Merck & Co.
Citigroup Inc.	Microsoft Corp.
Coca-Cola Co.	Minnesota Mining & Manufacturing Co.
DuPont Co.	Philip Morris Companies
Eastman Kodak Co.	Procter & Gamble Co.
Exxon Mobil Corp.	SBC Communications Inc.
General Electric Co.	United Technologies Corp.
General Motors Corp.	Wal-Mart Stores Inc.
Hewlett-Packard Co.	Walt Disney Co.
Home Depot Inc.	
Intel Corp.	

Glossary

12b-1 Distribution Fees   12b-1 distribution fees are charged to shareholders by the mutual fund company to provide for advertising and marketing as well as distribution costs, which include handling all the paperwork.

401(k) Plan   A 401(k) plan is a qualified defined contribution plan offered by employers. It allows employees to have a certain percentage of their salary deducted and invested in the plan. The deduction is pretax, so current income tax is reduced. The plan has a number of mutual funds (usually five to seven) that the employee can designate for his or her contribution to be deposited. In some cases, the employer may match a portion of the employee's contribution. The deposits and earnings are tax-deferred until withdrawn in retirement.

403(b) Plan   Similar to the 401(k) plan, the 403(b) is offered to religious, educational, and other nonprofit groups. This plan is also known as a tax-deferred annuity plan since the investments must be annuities.

active investing   Frequent trading and significant personal commitment to investments characterize active investing.

active investment strategy   An active investment strategy places primary decision-making with the investor. Such an investor prefers actively managed mutual funds to index funds and individual stocks to mutual funds.

actively managed mutual funds   Actively managed mutual funds meet their investment objectives by actively buying and selling securities. These funds may have high expense ratios and create tax liabilities, which are passed on to the investor.

administrative fees   Administrative fees are charged by the mutual fund company to maintain and administer the fund.

after-hours trading   After-hours trading is a fairly new way to trade stocks and securities after the major markets have closed. Some brokers are facilitating this activity.

agency bonds   Agency bonds are issued by other governmental agencies for reasons such as financing student loans, highway construction, residential mortgages, and so on.

annual report   An annual report is a required document that all publicly traded companies, including mutual funds, have to produce. It presents the financial results for the past fiscal year, which are audited by an accredited accounting firm.

annuity   An annuity is a periodic payment of equal amounts over a period in time. Annuity also refers to a contract with a life insurance company guaranteeing a certain payout over a period of time. It may contain a death benefit that would pay a survivor in the case of death.

asset allocation   Asset allocation is the process of distributing your investment assets in a manner that is consistent with your investment goals. This allocation will change as your life circumstances change.

back-end load fund   A back-end load mutual fund is one that charges a sales fee when you sell your shares.

balance sheet   A balance sheet is an accounting for a company's assets, liabilities, equity, and net worth at a certain point in time; it's part of the annual report.

balanced investment strategy   A balanced strategy looks for a blend of income and growth, hoping for the best of both.

balanced mutual funds   Balanced mutual funds attempt to marry income and growth by investing in companies that pay dividends, but are growing.

bear market   A bear market is one in which there are significant and long-term declines in market value as shown by falling market indicators.

blue chip stocks   Blue chip stocks refer to the most prestigious and solid companies on the market. It is thought the term comes from the fact that blue chips in poker are the most expensive ones.

bond mutual funds   Bond mutual funds invest in bonds and may target long or short maturities and different issuers. Triple tax-exempt bond funds are sold in specific states where residents may enjoy federal, state, and local tax-free income from the bond fund.

bonds   Bonds are debt instruments. They represent an obligation on the part of the issuer to repay the debt. Governments and private corporations may issue bonds.

book value   Book value is the stockholder's equity after all liabilities have been paid.

bull market   A bull market is one characterized by significant and long-term growth in value in the stock market, as shown by rising market indicators.

buy-and-hold investment strategy   A buy-and-hold investment strategy suggests that buying and holding quality investments for long terms will yield profits.

buy and sell   The unusual twist from an investment perspective is that it is possible to buy an instrument that gives you the right to sell, and sell an instrument that gives you the right to buy.

call option   A call option gives the owner the right, but not the obligation, to buy a stock at a certain price within a specified time frame.

callable bonds   Some bonds have a call clause that allows the issuer to pay them off before maturity.

capital gain   A capital gain is the profit from the sale of an asset. They are realized when you sell a stock or bond for a profit and when a mutual fund does the same. Capital gains are passed on to mutual fund shareholders. Any asset sold for a profit and held less than one year is subject to ordinary income tax by the owner. This is known as a short-term capital gain. An asset held for more than one year and sold for a profit is a long-term capital gain, and the tax is 20 percent.

capital preservation strategy   A capital preservation strategy values preservation of capital above return. It's an ultra-conservative strategy often used to pass a large "corpus" or body of a trust to the next generation.

cash equivalents   Cash equivalents are financial instruments that represent a deposit of cash. They include certificates of deposits, money market accounts, and savings accounts. They are characterized by their high liquidity.

cash management accounts   Cash management accounts are often offered by brokerage services to high-end investors as a way to manage assets.

certificates of deposit   Banks issue certificates of deposit which have a maturity ranging, for the most part, from six months to five years and pay a fixed interest rate. There can be penalties for withdrawing the money early.

certified financial planner   A certified financial planner is a professional who has extensive training in financial planning. Many certified financial planners charge a fee only for their services, while others may take a commission off products they recommend you buy.

closed-end mutual fund   A closed-end mutual fund is a hybrid type of investment that offers shares for sale only once. After that there are no new shares sold. The remaining shares are traded like stocks and can be bought and sold on the open market.

commissions   Commissions are fees brokers charge to buy or sell securities for you.

common stock   Common stock is the primary unit of ownership in a corporation. Holders of common stock are owners of the corporation with certain rights, including voting on major issues concerning the corporation. These shareholders, as they are known, have liability limited to the value of stock they own.

compounding   Compounding is the mathematical means by which interest is earned on the principal during one period, and then the next period interest is earned on the resulting principal plus interest in the first period. Another way to say this is interest-earning interest.

convertible bonds   Convertible bonds carry a feature that allows the bond to be converted to common stock instead of being paid off with cash.

corporate bonds Corporations issue bonds to finance a number of different projects, including the acquisition of other companies. Issuing bonds is often cheaper than commercial loans and better than issuing new stock. One or both of the major services (Moody's and Standard & Poor's) rate corporate bonds.

coupon rate The coupon rate (or simply coupon) is the interest rate that the bond pays.

day trader A day trader is someone who engages in aggressive trading using an Internet connection to a broker or a terminal in the broker's office. Day traders may make dozens of trades each day with the hope of making numerous small profits.

defined benefit plan The defined benefit plan states what the ultimate benefit will be in advance; typical company pension plans fall into this category. The benefit is often determined by an employee's years of service and an average of the last three years' salary.

defined contribution plan Defined contribution plans are plans where the contribution is specified, but not the benefit. These plans focus on what goes into the plan and who contributes what. How much the plans will pay on retirement is dependent on the return earned by the plan.

depression Depression is a long-term (multiple-year) decline in the national standard of living.

direct investment plans DIPs are a way to buy stock directly from a company without using a broker.

discount brokers Discount brokers facilitate the buying and selling of securities, but don't make product recommendations. They are, for the most part, order takers. Discount brokers charge commissions that are considerably less than full-service brokers. Online brokers are, for the most part, discount brokers.

diversification Diversification is the calculated spreading of your investments over a number of different asset classes. This cushions your portfolio if one part is down, since different asset classes (stocks, bonds, cash) seldom move in the same direction. In mutual funds, you achieve diversification by the fund owning 50 stocks instead of a few.

dividend reinvestment plans DRIPs allow stock and mutual fund owners to reinvest dividends back into the investment program. You can also set up a DRIP and make periodic payments as a way of buying stock without going through a broker.

dividend yield The dividend yield of a stock is calculated by dividing the current price per share into the annual dividend per share. The resulting percentage tells how cheap or expensive a dividend is relative to the stock price.

dividends Dividends are portions of a company's profits that are paid to its owners, the stockholders. Dividends are usually paid quarterly. Not all companies pay dividends; the board of directors makes that decision. Companies that don't pay dividends reinvest the profits back into the company to finance additional growth; stock in this type of company is often referred to as growth stock. Companies that pay regular dividends are sometimes known as income stocks.

dogs of the Dow A passive investment strategy built upon buying high-yielding stocks of the Dow Jones Industrial Average.

dollar cost averaging Dollar cost averaging is an investing technique that makes regular deposits in an investment account regardless of market conditions.

Dow Jones Industrial Average Also known as the Dow, this index is the best known and most widely quoted in the popular press. The Dow consists of 30 companies considered leaders in their industries. Together they account for a significant amount of the value in the market. Although not as reflective of the whole market as other indexes, the Dow is watched earnestly.

earnings-based evaluation Earnings-based evaluation of a stock looks at the relationship between earnings and stock price, the price/earnings ratio (or P/E), and the P/E and growth ratio (PEG).

e-commerce E-commerce refers to the buying and selling of goods and services over the Internet.

economic indicators Economic indicators are key measurements of the economy's health, such as unemployment, wages, and prices.

economic risk Economic risk is the danger that the economy could turn against your investment. An example would be a real estate company during a period of high interest rates.

economics The production, distribution, and consumption of goods and services, as well as other factors such as taxes, inflation, and labor, that affect the financial state of a society.

Educational IRA An EIRA is set up for a child under 18; contributions may be withdrawn tax-free to pay for higher-education costs.

Employee Stock Ownership Plan Also known as ESOPs, these plans use company stock to fund part of the employee's retirement. ESOPs may be combined with other plans such as the 401(k).

equity Equity is what remains after all liabilities have been paid.

equity-based evaluation A method of relating a company's equity to the stock price that uses price-to-book ratios and return on equity to find this relationship.

execution Execution refers to the actual consummation of a buy or sell order. A good execution is a quick exchange at the target price.

expense ratio The expense ratio for a mutual fund is the total of all fees charged to shareholders by the mutual fund.

Federal Reserve Board The Federal Reserve Board, also known as the Fed, controls the nation's interest rates by setting the key rates charged to banks. Alan Greenspan has headed the Board for many years. "When Alan Greenspan sneezes, the market gets a cold," is the saying on Wall Street. A change in interest rates will have a dramatic effect on the markets if it is not anticipated. Raising and lowering interest rates is analogous to turning up or down the heat while cooking.

fill   Fill is an order to execute a buy or sell order for securities. A good fill would be at the price sought in the shortest amount of time.

fiscal year   A fiscal year is the bookkeeping year for a company. It may or may not correspond with the calendar year.

focused portfolios   Focused portfolios are another name for stock unit investment trusts. A specific group of stocks is bought, held for a certain length, and then liquidated.

full-service brokers   Full-service brokers offer comprehensive services to persons wishing to invest, including recommendations on specific products and proprietary research.

fundamental analysis   Fundamental analysis is a method for evaluating a stock on the basis of observing key ratios and understanding the underlying business.

futures   Futures are contracts that obligate the owner to deliver a specific commodity or financial instrument by a certain date. Futures facilitate a more stable market for the producers and consumers of commodities. In addition to agricultural products such as cattle, orange juice, and lumber, futures are also sold on a number of financial instruments.

growth investment strategy   A growth strategy identifies companies with significant growth potential; the investor is willing to ride out frequent market fluctuations.

growth mutual funds   Growth mutual funds seek investments in stock of companies with potential for rapid and sustained growth.

growth stock   A growth stock is defined as a stock that usually pays no dividends, but puts profits back into the company to finance new growth. Investors buy growth stock for its potential price appreciation as the company grows.

income investment strategy   An income strategy identifies sources of immediate income, whether through stocks or bonds.

income mutual funds   Income mutual funds invest in stocks and bonds that provide high levels of current income.

income statement   An income statement is a financial document listing the income and expenses of a company that reveals how much was made or lost; it is part of the annual report.

income stock   An income stock is characterized by the current income it produces in the form of dividends. Utilities are often classified as income stocks for the strong dividends they pay.

index   An index is a way to measure financial activity. An index has an arbitrary beginning value, and as the underlying issues change the index either rises or falls.

index mutual fund   An index mutual fund will seek to mimic a specific key market index like the S&P 500. Index funds are known for very low expense ratios since they do little buying or selling unless the underlying index changes.

Individual Retirement Accounts   These accounts are available to people not covered by an employer's retirement plan. They allow a person to deduct a $2,000 per year contribution to the IRA. Earnings must stay in the account until age $59\frac{1}{2}$, when withdrawals may begin without penalty.

inflation   Inflation is too much money chasing too few goods. The result is a sharp rise in prices without any extra value added, making money worth less. Inflation leads to rising interest rates and a cooling of the economy. If the economy slows down too quickly and too far, it may slip into a recession or even a depression.

initial public offering   The first time a company issues stock for sale to the public is known as the initial public offering, or IPO. The company is said to be "going public" when this happens. The offering is highly regulated and often surrounded by a lot of media attention. Hot technology stocks often see immediate price increases of 300 percent or more.

international mutual funds
International mutual funds make it possible for you to participate in the economic systems of foreign countries. These funds buy stocks and bonds in foreign economies.

Internet   A vast network of computers that allows anyone with access to connect to this network and have available tremendous amounts of information. See Appendix B, "Resources," for a description of an adequate computer system to find and analyze investment information.

Internet access   This is the portal through which you access the Internet. Local or national companies called Internet service providers (ISPs) offer this access to the vast majority of users.

Internet service provider   A local or national company that gives you access to the Internet, usually through your existing telephone line. The going rate is about $20 per month.

investing   Investing is using your money to make money, while minimizing risk. It is proactive.

investment clubs   Investment clubs are groups of people who get together to learn about investing and collectively make investments.

investment goals   You invest money in order to meet financial goals that you have set for yourself.

junk bond   Junk bonds, also known as zero coupons, do not pay periodic interest, but are bought at a deep discount from the face value. When redeemed at maturity for face value, the interest is realized in the difference between the discounted purchase price and the face value.

Keogh plan   Keogh plans are for self-employed people, partnerships, and unincorporated businesses and may be defined benefit or defined contribution plans.

large-cap stock   A large-cap stock would be any company with a market capitalization of $8 billion or more.

limit order   A limit order instructs your broker to buy a stock when the price drops to the level you set.

limit order to sell   A limit order to sell instructs your broker to sell a stock when the stock climbs to a predetermined level.

liquidity   Liquidity refers to the characteristic of a financial instrument to be converted to cash. A mutual fund is considered highly liquid, while an apartment building would be highly illiquid.

loaded fund   A loaded mutual fund is one that charges a sales fee or commission which is paid to the broker who sold the shares. The load may be up-front or deferred.

long and short   Somewhat the equivalent of buy and sell with an investing twist. If you enter an order to "go long 100 shares of IBM," it means you want to buy IBM. Likewise, to "short IBM" is to sell the stock. "Long" also describes your position in a stock. For example, your brokerage statement might show you were "long 100 IBM," which means you own 100 shares of IBM. Your account could also show you were "short 100 IBM," which means you sold 100 shares of IBM. (See "short selling.")

management fee   The management fee, also called the investment advisory fee, is charged by the mutual fund company and is used to pay the fund's manager, who is responsible for making sure the fund meets its objectives.

margin   Margin is a way to finance your stock purchases. Your broker will lend you up to 50 percent of the purchase price. For example, if you had $5,000 to invest, you could buy $10,000 worth of stock. You pay interest on the loan and repay it when you sell the stock. If the price of the stock falls below 75 percent of the original price, your broker will require you to deposit more money into your account or sell the stock to pay back the loan.

market capitalization   Market capitalization or market cap is a way of measuring the size of a company and is calculated by multiplying the current stock price by the number of outstanding shares. A stock trading at $55 with 10,000,000 outstanding shares would have a market cap of $550 million.

market cycles   Market cycles are periods of up markets and down markets that have been historically documented.

market indicators   This is a collective name for a number of indexes and other measurements of market activity.

market order   A market order to buy or sell placed with your broker requests the best price at that moment. Market orders are filled the fastest.

market timing   Market timing is the attempt to determine when market lows and highs are going to occur. This strategy almost always fails over the long run.

market value risk   Market value risk is the danger your investment will fall out of favor with the market or may simply be ignored.

the markets   This phrase is used to generally mean the collective stock exchanges.

mid-cap stock   A mid-cap stock would be any company with a market capitalization of $1–$8 billion.

money market accounts   Money market accounts are special savings accounts usually offered by financial institutions that pay a higher interest rate than regular savings, but require a higher minimum balance. They are not the same as money market mutual funds.

money market funds Money market funds are mutual funds that invest in very short-term cash instruments. These funds are often used within a family of mutual funds to park uninvested cash.

money market mutual funds Money market mutual funds invest in short-term money market instruments. You can often withdraw money on short notice without penalty. Some offer check-writing privileges.

Moody's Investors Services Moody's analyzes and rates investments, including bonds, along with Standard and Poor's.

multiple Multiple is another term for price/earnings ratio.

municipal bonds Municipal bonds, also known as munis, are issued by state and local governments to finance a variety of projects such as road construction, new schools, and so on. They are repaid out of tax revenue. When bought by residents within the jurisdiction, these bonds are free from federal, state, and local income tax. Moody's and/or Standard and Poor's rate these bonds. Their rating will affect the interest they must pay to attract investors.

mutual funds Mutual funds represent a group of individuals who have pooled their money and hired a professional management company to invest this money. Each mutual fund has specific goals and objectives that drive its buy and sell decisions. Mutual funds may invest in stocks, bonds, or both.

NASDAQ The NASDAQ (National Association of Securities Dealers Automated Quotations), also known as the over-the-counter market, is the new kid on the block. Trades are executed over an electronic network of brokers. Many on the companies listed here are fairly young, and this is the home of many of today's high tech stars.

The NASDAQ Composite Index The NASDAQ Composite Index covers the NASDAQ market of over 5,000 stocks.

National Association of Securities Dealers This self-regulatory body of securities brokers is supervised by the SEC. The NASD licenses and examines brokers and handles consumer complaints.

Net Asset Value The NAV is the mutual fund equivalent of a share price. This is the price you pay when you buy into a mutual fund. Unlike stocks, mutual funds have no problems with fractional shares. However much you deposit is divided by the NAV to arrive at your number of shares. The NAV is calculated by subtracting the liabilities from the holdings of a mutual fund, then dividing by the outstanding shares.

New York Stock Exchange The oldest and most prestigious of all stock exchanges, the NYSE is home to most of the blue chip companies.

The New York Stock Exchange Index This index covers all the stocks on the NYSE, making it a broad measurement of larger companies.

no-load fund A no-load mutual fund is one that charges no sales fees or commissions, either up-front or deferred.

online brokers Online brokers allow investors to buy and sell securities over the Internet without ever talking to a human.

Online brokers offer the least expensive commissions.

options Options give the owner the right, but not the obligation, to purchase or sell a specific number of shares of a stock at a specific price. Options are bought and sold on the open market.

par value Par value refers to the original issue of a bond at full price.

passive fund A passive fund is one in which there are no investment decisions. An index fund would be a passive fund.

passive investment strategy A passive investment strategy puts most of the work into a professional's hands or adopts strategies that are more mechanical than analytical. Dogs of the Dow is a passive investment strategy.

penny stocks Penny stocks are a special category of low-priced (usually $1 or less) stocks often issued by highly speculative companies. They are the focus of numerous stock scams and manipulations.

portfolio A portfolio is the collection of all your investing assets.

position Position describes your current holdings. If you owned 100 shares of IBM, your position would be "long 100 IBM."

precious metals mutual funds Precious metals mutual funds invest in stocks and bonds of the mining and trading companies of precious metals (gold, silver, and so on).

preferred stock As the name implies, preferred stock is a different class of stock with additional rights not granted to common stock owners. Among these rights is first call on dividends.

price/earnings growth ratio (PEG) The price/earnings growth ratio (PEG) is used to look into the future relationship of earnings and growth. It is calculated by dividing forward earnings estimates into the price/earnings ratio.

price/earnings ratio The price/earnings ratio (P/E) is a way to show how a company's earnings relate to the stock price. The P/E is calculated by dividing the current price of the stock by the annual earnings per share. The higher the P/E, the more earnings growth investors are expecting.

price-to-book ratio Taking the current stock price and dividing it by book value per share calculates the price-to-book ratio. This relationship shows the value of the equity as it relates to the stock price.

profit-sharing plan These plans pass a portion of the company's profits to the employee's retirement account and are often used in connection with 401(k) plans. The employer makes all the contributions, but is not obligated to pay out a portion of the profits.

prospectus A prospectus is a legal document that potential shareholders of mutual funds and initial public offerings of stocks must have before they can invest. It lists complete financial details of the fund, as well as the associated risks.

put option A put option gives the owner the right, but not the obligation, to sell a stock at a certain price within a specified time frame.

qualified retirement plans Qualified retirement plans are authorized by the Internal Revenue Service and must adhere to certain rules and regulations. Participants in the plans, often sponsored by an employer, are allowed to accumulate money in their accounts on a tax-deferred basis.

ratio A ratio is simply a comparison of the relationship between financial items. For example, price/earnings ratio shows the relationship between a company's earnings and its stock price.

real estate investment trusts REITs are similar to mutual funds in that they are traded as securities, making them more liquid than other forms of real estate investments.

real estate limited partnerships A real estate limited partnership pools investors' money and buys income-producing properties.

recession Recession is marked by declining standards of living and rising prices. Officially, a recession is marked by a decline in the nation's gross national product for two consecutive quarters.

return Return is another term for "yield" and is an investment's profit expressed most often as a percentage.

return on equity Return on equity is a way to look at how earnings are related to stockholder equity. Annual earnings are divided by the stockholder's equity.

risk Risk measures the possibility that an investment will not earn the anticipated return.

risk tolerance Risk tolerance is a way to judge how much risk you are willing to take to achieve an investment goal. The higher your risk tolerance, the more risk you are willing to take on.

Roth IRA The Roth IRA differs from a regular IRA in several ways, chief among which is the fact that contributions are not tax-deductible; however, withdrawals are tax-free. There are income restrictions and withdrawal schedules.

round lot A round lot is the standard transaction unit in stocks and is 100 shares. Any order not divisible by 100 is considered an odd lot and may trigger a fee from your broker.

Russell 2000 Index The Frank Russell Company, now a part of Northwestern Mutual, developed this index of 2,000 smaller companies. Russell also has numerous other indexes that measure other market segments.

The S&P 500 The S&P 500 is an index developed by Standard and Poor's that measures the health of the market's larger companies. Because it is a broad measure (500 companies), many consider it more reflective of the market's condition than the Dow index. It is the benchmark used by most financial professionals to represent "the market." When a mutual fund boasts that it beat the market, it is most often the S&P 500 index it is referencing.

sales-based evaluation Sales-based evaluations look at how sales and price relate. This measurement works well for companies with no earnings. It uses the sales-price ratio.

sales-price ratio Taking the stock's market capitalization plus any long-term debt and dividing that by sales for the preceding 12 months calculates the sales-price ratio.

saving Saving is the passive use of your money where safety is more important than return.

Savings Incentive Match Plan for Employees IRA SIMPLE-IRA is a qualified retirement plan offered by small companies. Under the plan, a company establishes an IRA for each employee and may contribute to it along with the employee.

sector mutual funds Sector mutual funds invest in various sectors of the economy such as technology or healthcare.

Securities and Exchange Commission The SEC is the chief regulatory body over the stock markets and companies that are publicly traded.

Securities Investor Protection Corporation Securities Investor Protection Corporation is a private government-sponsored agency that provides insurance to protect your assets at a brokerage firm in the event the brokerage fails. Coverage is up to $500,000 per account. The insurance does not protect against trading losses.

short selling Short selling is selling a stock you do not own in anticipation that the price is going to fall. Your broker will "borrow" the stock from another client. You sell the stock and put the money in your account. If you are correct, you buy back the stock at the lower price and pocket the profit. The original owner then gets the stock back. This is all perfectly legal.

Simplified Employee Plan The SEP-IRA is designed for self-employed people, partnerships, or unincorporated businesses.

The employer sets up an IRA for each employee, but the employee owns and controls it. The employer may or may not make contributions.

small-cap stock A small-cap stock would be any company with a market capitalization of $1 billion or less.

socially responsible mutual funds Socially responsible mutual funds invest in carefully screened companies that meet certain social or ethical standards; they are also known as "green funds" or "planet-friendly" funds.

spousal IRA A spousal IRA is set up by a working taxpayer for a nonworking spouse.

Standard and Poor's Standard and Poor's is an investment research service that provides a number of market indexes, including the S&P 500. It also provides a rating service for bonds.

statement of cash flow The statement of cash flow is part of the annual report and describes the source of a company's cash and how that has changed from the previous year.

stock certificate A stock certificate is an ornate certificate issued by the company. Once common, most certificates these days are electronic records. Brokers may charge you a fee if you want an actual paper certificate.

stock mutual funds Stock mutual funds invest exclusively or primarily in stocks. The stocks may be broad-based or in one sector. They may include foreign as well as domestic stocks.

stock options   Stock options are often offered as incentives to employees. They grant the owner the right to buy the stock at a certain price. These options are usually not transferable or sold on the open market.

stockbroker   A stockbroker, also known simply as a broker, is a person licensed and authorized to buy and sell securities. He or she is required to pass examinations and meet certain standards of conduct set by the National Association of Securities Dealers (NASD).

stop-loss order   A stop-loss order tells your broker to sell if the price falls to a certain level. This order will prevent further losses.

subordinated bonds   Subordinated bonds are secondary issues after a primary bond issue. They are paid back only after the primary issue is paid off.

tax-deferred   Tax-deferred refers to investment vehicles that allow principal and interest to grow without paying taxes on the earnings until some time in the future. Qualified retirement accounts allow tax-deferred growth.

tax-free mutual funds   Tax-free mutual funds invest in bonds that provide tax-free income.

technical analysis   Technical analysis focuses on the supply and demand for a stock and tries to predict future moves in the price.

The 10-K   The 10-K is a report required by the Securities and Exchange Commission containing all the information in the annual report, plus some additional information, such as income from divisions or subsidiaries that may appear only in consolidated form in the Annual Report.

The 10-Q   The 10-Q is a quarterly version of the 10-K and includes management discussions of recent business activity.

trade   Trade refers to the buying or selling of stocks, bonds, mutual funds, and other financial instruments. Depending on the usage, it can mean a single transaction, or refer to the total market ("trading was heavy").

transaction fees   Transaction fees can be charged for just about any service provided by a financial institution, including mutual funds.

Treasury Bill   U.S. Treasury-issued bonds with maturities from 90 days to one year, or T-Bills, are sold at a discount off the face value.

Treasury Note   A Treasury note is a U.S. Treasury-issued bond with maturities from 2 to 10 years.

Treasury Strips   Treasury Strips are U.S. Treasury issues with no periodic interest and are sold at discount off face value. The interest is realized when the bond is redeemed for the full face value.

turnover   Turnover in the mutual fund industry refers to what percentage of a fund's holdings are bought and sold each year. The higher the turnover, the higher the expense ratio and tax liabilities.

U.S. Treasury Bonds   U.S. Treasury Bonds are considered the safest investment available because they are backed by the full faith and credit of the U.S. government.

They range in maturity from under one year to more than 10 years. U.S. Treasury Bonds are free from state and local income tax, but not federal tax.

unit investment trusts A unit investment trust is another hybrid fund that buys a fixed portfolio of stock or bonds and never sells or buys any more. They are sold by brokers and traded on the open market.

value mutual funds Value mutual funds look for companies the market is undervaluing for some reason with the hope that their fortunes will return and the stock will experience significant growth.

value stock A value stock is one that is underpriced by the market for whatever reason. Often a stock's only sin is not being a part of the current hot sector.

volatile A stock is said to be volatile if it has wide swings in price each day.

warrants Warrants give the holder the right, but not the obligation, to purchase a specific number of shares of a stock at a specified price. Warrants are often issued along with new stock as an incentive to investors.

wealth builder Wealth builders are concepts founded in fact and reason that provide for the accumulation of wealth. Compounding of interest is the best known and most powerful of all wealth-building concepts.

yield Yield is another term for "return" and is expressed as a percentage. For example, yield is the percentage returned to stockholders in the form of dividends.

yield-based evaluation The yield-based evaluation is a model used to value a stock. It is based on the dividend yield calculation.

zero coupon bonds Zero coupons bonds pay no periodic interest, but are sold at a discount to face value. Interest earned is the difference between the purchase price and the redeemed face value.

APPENDIX D

Answers to Quiz Questions

HOUR 1

1. A
2. B
3. B
4. C
5. D
6. C
7. A
8. B
9. D
10. C

HOUR 2

1. A
2. D
3. B
4. C
5. A
6. A
7. B
8. B
9. A
10. B

HOUR 3

1. D
2. B
3. A
4. D
5. C
6. B
7. C
8. A
9. C
10. B

HOUR 4

1. C
2. B
3. D
4. D
5. A
6. A
7. D
8. A
9. A
10. C

Hour 5

1. C
2. A
3. B
4. A
5. B
6. B
7. A
8. A
9. B
10. C

Hour 6

1. B
2. D
3. C
4. C
5. A
6. B
7. B
8. C
9. C
10. B

Hour 7

1. C
2. C
3. A
4. D
5. A
6. B
7. C
8. A
9. C
10. D

Hour 8

1. A
2. B
3. B
4. A
5. C
6. B
7. B
8. C
9. C
10. A

Hour 9

1. B
2. A
3. A
4. C
5. A
6. B
7. B
8. C
9. A
10. C

Hour 10

1. A
2. B
3. C
4. B
5. C
6. B
7. B
8. B
9. A
10. C

Hour 11

1. A
2. C
3. B
4. D
5. C
6. A
7. B
8. A
9. A
10. D

Hour 12

1. C
2. D
3. C
4. B
5. A
6. B
7. B
8. C
9. C
10. B

Hour 13

1. B
2. C
3. B
4. B
5. A
6. B
7. B
8. C
9. B
10. C

Hour 14

1. C
2. C
3. A
4. A
5. B
6. B
7. B
8. C
9. A
10. D

Hour 15

1. A
2. B
3. A
4. C
5. C
6. A
7. A
8. C
9. B
10. A

Hour 16

1. A
2. A
3. C
4. B
5. C
6. B
7. B
8. A
9. C
10. A

HOUR 17

1. D
2. B
3. A
4. C
5. C
6. B
7. B
8. B
9. A
10. C

HOUR 18

1. B
2. C
3. D
4. B
5. C
6. B
7. A
8. C
9. B
10. B

HOUR 19

1. C
2. B
3. A
4. B
5. C
6. A
7. C
8. A
9. B
10. C

HOUR 20

1. B
2. B
3. A
4. B
5. C
6. C
7. B
8. B
9. A
10. B

Hour 21

1. B
2. A
3. C
4. A
5. B
6. D
7. A
8. C
9. C
10. B

Hour 22

1. A
2. B
3. A
4. A
5. C
6. B
7. C
8. B
9. C
10. C

Hour 23

1. B
2. A
3. C
4. C
5. B
6. A
7. B
8. A
9. A
10. B

Hour 24

1. A
2. B
3. C
4. A
5. D
6. A
7. B
8. B
9. D
10. C

Index